you woman sky with palms broad enough to hold egypt

I cannot say upon which luminous evening
I shall go out beyond the stars,

Heav
The v

# Word and Witness

*100 Years of North Carolina Poetry*

Down here the mule leans in the traces,
The plow swims through the loam,
And men at dusk turn quiet faces
To chimney smoke and home.

I do not know the power of my black hand.

we flower in talk, we slake
our thirsts in a brandy of heated speech

*Edited by*
### Sally Buckner

*Afterword by*
### Fred Chappell

In the slow                              comes through
In circlets a                            fallen leaf
Like a tribe

I will sing in the rising
of wind, the warming
of sun
                                Hope is a bird's wing
                                Broken by a stone.

*Developed Under the Auspices of*
*The North Carolina Poetry Society*

# CAROLINA ACADEMIC PRESS

# Word and Witness

## 100 Years of North Carolina Poetry

This dazzling array of poems preserves in precise and imaginative language many of the crucial perceptions, dreams, experiences, and concerns of North Carolinians during this exceptional century. The quietest personal moments, the noisiest public conflicts, the most profound social issues — all are treated in these 252 poems representing 137 poets whose work spans the century. *Word and Witness* demonstrates the development of poetry — remarkable in both quantity and quality — occurring through these tumultuous decades, as well as the extraordinary versatility of the poets who have, during significant years, called North Carolina home.

*Word and Witness* is organized chronologically, with each section prefaced by an introduction explaining the literary scene during those years and the factors — social, economic, and historic — which influenced the poetry of that era. Fred Chappell, North Carolina Poet Laureate and winner of the national Bollingen Prize for poetry, has furnished the Afterword. Partially funded by a grant from the North Carolina Arts Council, the book includes brief biographies, a selected bibliography, and lists of poets who have won significant state awards.

The compilation of *Word and Witness* was conceived and sponsored by the North Carolina Poetry Society, the oldest and largest organization devoted to poetry in this state. Like *North Carolina's 400 Years: Signs Along the Way*, one of the four other anthologies created by NCPS since its inception in 1932, this collection is designed as a gift to the state, commemorating North Carolina's rich literary heritage. It also testifies to the breadth and depth of the state's exceptional community of writers.

*1999   336 pp*
*ISBN 0-89089-686-0   jacketed hardcover   $28.00*
*ISBN 0-89089-687-9   paper   $17.95*

# Word
# and
# Witness

*This anthology was conceived and sponsored by the North Carolina Poetry Society, celebrating a century of poetic achievement in this state.*

Editor:    Sally Buckner

Editorial Board:    Marsha Warren, Project Director
Shelby Stephenson
Stephen Smith
MariJo Moore
Lenard Moore
Susan Meyers
Rebecca McClanahan
Cecil Cahoon

Consultants:    Kathryn Stripling Byer
Fred Chappell
Mark Smith-Soto

Cover Design:    Tim Colton

Illustrations:    Talmadge Moose
Evalynn Halsey
Thomas Whisnant

The North Carolina Poetry Society expresses appreciation to
the North Carolina Arts Council and Peace College
for grants which helped make this anthology possible.

**Poems in *Word and Witness* represent each era of this remarkable century as well as North Carolina's geographic, ethnic, and cultural diversity. Authors include:**

John Charles McNeill • Olive Tilford Dargan • Helen Bevington
Charles Edward Eaton • Randall Jarrell • Thad Stem, Jr.
Jonathan Williams • Eleanor Ross Taylor • A. R. Ammons
Guy Owen • Robert Morgan • Betty Adcock • Gerald Barrax
Stephen Smith • James Applewhite • Fred Chappell • Sam Ragan
Heather Ross Miller • Shelby Stephenson • Kathryn Stripling Byer
Reynolds Price • Ronald Bayes • Ann Deagon • Michael McFee
Nancy Simpson • Rebecca McClanahan • Peter Makuck
Chuck Sullivan • Jaki Shelton Green • Alan Shapiro • James Seay
Michael Chitwood • Gibbons Ruark • Lenard Moore • Ruth Moose
Earl S. Braggs • Deborah Pope • MariJo Moore • Cathy Smith Bowers

## and many more!

CAROLINA
ACADEMIC
PRESS

700 KENT STREET
DURHAM, NORTH CAROLINA 27701
(800) 489-7486
FAX (919) 493-5668

WW99

**See Our Web Site: www.cap-press.com**

# Word and Witness

*100 Years of
North Carolina
Poetry*

*Edited by*
Sally Buckner

*Afterword by*
Fred Chappell

CAROLINA ACADEMIC PRESS

Durham, North Carolina

ISBN 0-89089-687-9
LCCN 99-65880

CAROLINA ACADEMIC PRESS
700 Kent Street
Durham, NC  27701
Telephone (919) 489-7486
Fax (919) 493-5668
www.cap-press.com

Printed in the United States of America

## Dedication

To all North Carolina poets
throughout the century
who through their dedication to their art
have broadened our horizons,
enriched our perceptions,
illuminated our lives.

# Contents

# Acknowledgments

## Appreciation

No effort as immense as the compilation of this anthology is accomplished by one or two persons or even a small committee. We, the North Carolina Poetry Society, acknowledge our profound gratitude to the following:

Robert Anthony and Alice Cotten, The North Carolina Collection,
    University of North Carolina at Chapel Hill
The North Carolina Writers' Network
The North Carolina Writers Conference
The North Carolina Arts Council—especially Debbie McGill
Quail Ridge Books, Raleigh, NC
Peace College
Carolina Wren Press
Wake County Public Libraries Reference Service
James Clark, Humanities Extension, North Carolina State University
Kimberly Drake
Mary Kratt
Anne Logan
Sally Logan
Ruth Moose
Carolyn Sakowski
Mary Snotherly
And, of course, our editor, editorial board, and consultants.

We also acknowledge our debt to those historians and anthologists whose works have provided valuable historical, biographical, and literary information: Richard Walser, Guy Owen, Mary Williams, Michael McFee, Stephen Smith, and William Powell,

*Editor's Note*:
    This anthology is unusual in that from the first it has been a cooperative project. My own efforts have been heartened and eased by the whole-

hearted support of the North Carolina Poetry Society as well as by the aid of the Editorial Board that since July, 1996, has provided invaluable guidance and specific information. I especially express appreciation for the extraordinary contributions of the following: Marsha Warren, Susan Meyers, Fred Chappell, Lenard Moore, Shelby Stephenson, and Kathryn Stripling Byer. Without their advice and assistance, my own work would have been much more difficult and not nearly so fruitful.

Finally, I owe deepest gratitude to my husband, Bob, whose unfailing encouragement and patience have undergirded my efforts and lifted my spirits throughout the long, exciting, and complex process of assembling this literary treasurehouse.

## Permissions

Anthony Abbott. "Evening Light," from *The Girl in the Yellow Raincoat,* © 1989 by Anthony Abbott. Reprinted by permission of the author.

Betty Adcock. "Prophecy," from *The Difficult Wheel,* © 1995 by Betty Adcock. "The Clouded Leopards of Cambodia and Vietnam" and "Box-Camera Snapshot," from *Nettles,* © 1983 by Betty Adcock. Reprinted by permission of the author and Louisiana State University Press.

Annette Allen. "This River," from *Country of Light,* © 1996 by Annette Allen. Reprinted by permission of the author.

A. R. Ammons. "The Yucca Moth," from *Collected Poems* 1951–1971, © 1972 by A. R. Ammons. Reprinted by permission of W. W. Norton & Company, Inc. "Apologetics," "Giving up Word with Words," "Zero and Then Some," from *Lake Effect Country,* © 1983 by A.R. Ammons. Reprinted by permission of W. W. Norton & Company, Inc.

Shirley Anders. "The Words," © Shirley Anders. Printed by permission of Judy Longley, literary executor.

Maya Angelou. "A Good Woman Feeling Bad," from *Shaker, Why Don't You Sing?* © 1983 by Maya Angelou. Reprinted by permission of Random House, Inc.

James Applewhite. "A Forge of Words," from *Statues of the Grass,* © 1975 by James Applewhite. Reprinted by permission of University of Georgia Press. "The Morning After" and "A Leaf of Tobacco," from *Ode to the Chinaberry Tree and Other Poems,* © 1986 by James Applewhite; and "Storm in the Briar Patch," from *A History of the River,* © 1993 by James Applewhite. Reprinted by permission of the author and Louisiana State University Press.

Stewart Atkins. "Lynching," from *The Halting Gods,* © 1952 by Stewart Atkins. Reprinted by permission of Claire Atkins Pittman.

Margaret Baddour. "What Color Is the Sun?" from *Easy Magic,* © 1991 by Margaret Baddour. Reprinted by permission of the author.

Gerald Barrax. "Strangers Like Us: Pittsburgh, Raleigh, 1945–1985," "Whose Children Are These?" and "Something I Know About Her," from *A Person Sitting in*

*Darkness: New and Selected Poems*, © 1999 by Gerald Barrax. Reprinted by permission of the author and Louisiana State University Press.

Joseph Bathanti. "Sneedsborough," from *Anson County*, © 1989 by Joseph Bathanti. Reprinted by permission of the author.

Ronald Bayes. "Makura-Kotoba," from *A Beast in View: Selected Shorter Poems, 1970–80*, © 1985 by Ronald Bayes. "But to Tell the Truth," from *The Casketmaker*, © 1975 by Ronald Bayes. "General John Meditates on Being Lonely," from *Guises: A Chainsong for the Muses*, © 1992 by Ronald Bayes. Reprinted by permission of the author.

Jeffery Beam. "Snake in Autumn," from *Carolina Quarterly*, Winter, 1998, © *Carolina Quarterly*, 1998. Reprinted by permission of the author.

Helen Bevington. "The Oceans of Dr. Johnson," "January Jasmine," and "Postcard from Here," from *When Found, Make a Verse Of*, © Helen Bevington, 1961. Reprinted by permission of the author.

Denise Blue. "Apocalypse," from *Asheville Poetry Review*, Spring, 1999, © *Asheville Poetry Review*, 1999. Reprinted by permission of the author.

Cathy Smith Bowers. "Learning How to Pray," from *Traveling in Time of Danger*, © Cathy Smith Bowers, 1990. Reprinted by permission of the author.

James Boyd. "Song for the Silent" and "Long Distance, 1944," from *Eighteen Poems*, © The Atlantic Monthly Company and Harper and Brothers, 1943; Charles Scribner's Sons, and *This Week*, 1944; Friends of Weymouth, 1994. Reprinted by permission of James Boyd, Jr.

Earl Braggs. "I'll be calling you up tonight" from *Turning Dances*, © 1991 by Steven D. Peck. Reprinted by permission of the author. "The Sunday Facts of a Partly Cherished Life," from *Hat Dancer Blue*, © Earl S. Braggs, 1993. Reprinted by permission of the author.

Grey Brown. "Bear," from *Staying In*, © Grey Brown, 1992. Reprinted by permission of the author.

Linda Brown. "I Want to Make the Drums Talk Again," from *A Living Culture in Durham*, © Carolina Wren Press, 1987. Reprinted by permission of the author

Sally Buckner. "Embroidery," from *Potato Eyes*, #17/18, © Potato Eyes Foundation, 1998. Reprinted by permission of the author.

Kathryn Stripling Byer. "Mountain Time," from *Black Shawl*, © 1998 by Kathryn Stripling Byer. Reprinted by permission of the author and Louisiana State University Press. "The Backwoods," from *The Girl in the Midst of the Harvest*, © 1986 by Kathryn Stripling Byer. Reprinted by permission of the author and Texas Tech Press. "Diamonds," from *Wildwood Flower*, © 1992 Kathryn Stripling Byer. Reprinted with permission of the author and Louisiana State University Press.

Mary Belle Campbell. "Pine Lake at Twilight," from *On the Summit: A Poetic Quest*, © 1988 by Mary Belle Campbell. Reprinted by permission of the author.

Marion Cannon. "Grammar," from *Collected Poems*, © 1980 by Marion Cannon. Reprinted by permission of Charleen Swansea.

Fred Chappell. "The Story," "Fast Ball," "A Prayer for the Mountains," "Grace Before Meat," and "The Stories," from *Spring Garden*, © 1995 by Fred Chappell. "Earthsleep," from *Midquest,* © 1985 by Fred Chappell. Reprinted by permission of the author and Louisiana State University Press.

Richard Chess. "Two and One," from *Tekiah,* © 1994 by Richard Chess. Reprinted by permission of the author and University of Georgia Press.

Michael Chitwood. "Weave Room," "Big House," and "I'll Fly Away," from *Salt Works,* © 1992 by Michael Chitwood. Reprinted by permission of the author.

L. Teresa Church. "Tending and Turning," "Cafe Au Lait," and "Dancing for Old Folks," from *Hand-Me-Down Calicos,* © 1998 by L. Teresa Church. Reprinted by permission of the author.

Ann Deagon. "Hitting the Old Mark," and "Augury," from *Poetics South,* © 1974 by Ann Deagon. Reprinted by permission of the author.

Debra Kang Dean. "Immigrants," from *News of Home,* © 1998 by Debra Kang Dean. Reprinted by permission of the author and BOA Editions, Ltd.

Grace DiSanto. "The Eye Is Single," from *The Eye Is Single,* © 1981 by Grace DiSanto. Reprinted by permission of Roxanne DiSanto.

Stuart Dischell. "Magic Fathers" and "Fool's Gold," from *Good Hope Road,* © by Stuart Dischell, 1993. Reprinted by permission of the author.

Harriet Doar. "Cats at Twilight" and "Around the Block," from *The Restless Water,* © 1983 by Harriet Doar. Reprinted by permission of James F. Doar.

Hilda Downer. "Shadows That Steep in Dreams of the New Ground," from *Weymouth,* © 1987 St. Andrews Press. Reprinted by permission of the author.

Charles Edward Eaton. "The Bright Plain" and "Witness for the Defense," from *New and Selected Poems, 1942–1987,* © 1987 by Associated University Presses, Inc. Reprinted by permission of the author.

Keith Flynn. "The James River Express," from *The Book of Monsters: Poems,* © 1994 by Keith Flynn. Reprinted by permission of the author.

Charles Fort. "Prose Poem for Claire Aubin Fort " and "For Martin Luther King," from *The Town Clock Burning,* © 1985, 1991 by Charles Fort. Reprinted by permission of the author.

Becky Gould Gibson. "Putting Up Damson Preserves," from *Holding Ground,* © 1996 by Becky Gould Gibson. Reprinted by permission of the author.

Grace Gibson. "Myth: To the Fourth Generation," from *Drakes Branch,* © 1982 by Grace Gibson. Reprinted by permission of the author.

Marie Gilbert. "On Watching Challenger," from *Connexions,* © 1994 by Marie Gilbert. Reprinted by permission of the author.

Evalyn Gill. "Blue Ridge Parkway," from *North Carolina's 400 Years: Signs Along the Way,* © 1986 by The North Carolina Poetry Society. Reprinted by permission of the author.

Judy Goldman. "Between Losses," from *Wanting to Know the End,* © 1993 by Judy Goldman. Reprinted by permission of the author.

Jaki Shelton Green. "things break down ," "the griot's song," and "praise song," from *Conjure Blues,* © 1996 by Jaki Shelton Green. Reprinted by permission of the author.

Paul Green. "Men of America" and "Stopping in Albert Behind the Germans," from *Paul Green's War Songs*, © 1993 by Paul Green Foundation. Reprinted by permission of the Paul Green Foundation.

Lucinda Grey. "Letter to No Address," from *Letter to No Address*, © 1987 by Lucinda Grey. Reprinted by permission of the author.

Robert Waters Grey. "Topsail Beach/Columbus Day," from *Saving the Dead*, © 1992 by Robert Waters Grey. Reprinted by permission of the author.

Kathryn Bright Gurkin. "Meditation," from *Stainless Steel Soprano*, © 1990 by Kathryn Bright Gurkin. Reprinted by permission of the author.

R. S. Gwynn. "Body Bags," from *Texas Poets in Concert: A Quartet*, © 1990 by University of Texas Press. Reprinted by permission of the author.

Frank Borden Hanes. "Inner Ear" and "Old Arrowhead Thoughts of a Late War," from *The Seeds of Ares*, © 1977 by Frank Borden Hanes. Reprinted by permission of the author.

William Harmon. "Redounding" from *One Long Poem*, © 1982 by William Harmon. Reprinted by permission of the author and Louisiana State University Press. "Memory in February," from *Quicksilver*, 1960. Reprinted by permission of the author.

Tom Hawkins. "The Yankee King," from *The Sandhills/St. Andrews Review*, 1997. Reprinted by permission of the author. "Hospital Ship: Cua Viet," from *Jam Today*, No. 7, 1979. Reprinted by permission of the author.

David Hopes, "Driving Home," from *Cardinal*, © 1986 by Jacar Press. Reprinted by permission of the author.

Gladys Owings Hughes. "Survival," from *A Cell, A Door*, © 1989 by Gladys Owings Hughes. Reprinted by permission of the author.

Randall Jarrell. "The Player Piano," "The Mockingbird," and "The Death of the Ball Turret Gunner," from *Randall Jarrell: The Complete Poems*, © 1969 by Mrs. Randall Jarrell. Reprinted by permission of Mary von S. Jarrell.

Lance Jeffers. "When I Know the Power of My Black Hand," and "On Listening to the Spirituals," from *When I Know the Power of My Black Hand*, © 1974 by Lance Jeffers. Reprinted by permission of Trellie Jeffers.

Paul Jones. "Against Morning," from *A Living Culture in Durham*, © 1986 by Carolina Wren Press, 1986. Reprinted by permission of the author.

Debra Kaufman. "Dialogue Concerning a Blue Convertible," from *Still Life Burning*, © 1986 by Debra Kaufman. Reprinted by permission of the author.

Deborah Kinsland. "Ahaluna," from *Asheville Poetry Review*, 1999. © *Asheville Poetry Review*, 1999. Reprinted by permission of the author.

Stephen Knauth. "The Runner," from *The Pine Figures*, © 1986 by Stephen Knauth. Reprinted by permission of the author.

Mary Kratt. "Of Mother and Father," from *Spirit Going Barefoot*, © 1982 by Mary Kratt. "A Memory Not Quite Abandoned," from *On the Steep Side*, © 1993 by Mary Kratt. Reprinted by permission of the author.

Steven Lautermilch. "The Canticle of the Skeleton," from *The Little Hours*, © 1986, 1990 by Steven Lautermilch. Reprinted by permission of the author.

Sarah Lindsay. "US," from *Primate Behavior*, © 1997 by Sarah Lindsay. Reprinted by permission of the author.

Amon Liner. "Things That Are True of Blue," from *Rose, A Color of Darkness*, © 1981 by Amon Liner. Reprinted by permission of Carolina Wren Press.

Lou Lipsitz. "Word," from *Seeking the Hook*, © 1998 by Lou Lipsitz. Reprinted by permission of the author.

Robert Long. "Piece by Piece," from *The Power to Die*, © 1987 by Robert Hill Long. Reprinted by permission of the author.

Susan Ludvigson. "Some Notes on Courage" and "The Night We Sang," from *The Swimmer*, © 1984 by Susan Ludvigson. Reprinted by permission of the author and Louisiana State University Press.

Norman Macleod. "The Bitterroots," "The Spanish Loyalist," "Stride on the Desert," and "In Memory: Northern Navajo," from *The Distance: New and Selected Poems, 1928–1977*, supplementary issue of *Pembroke Magazine*, © 1977 by *Pembroke Magazine*. Reprinted by permission of *Pembroke Magazine*.

Al Maginnes. "Father-Son Basketball, 1970," from *Outside a Tattoo Booth*, © 1991 by Al Maginnes. Reprinted by permission of the author.

Peter Makuck. "After" and "Dogwood Again," from *Against Distance*, © 1997 by Peter Makuck. Reprinted by permission of the author and BOA Editions, Ltd.

Rebecca McClanahan. "X," from *The Intersection of X and Y*, © 1996 by Rebecca Mc-Clanahan. Reprinted by permission of the author and Copper Beech Press. "Teaching a Nephew to Type," from *Poetry*, March, 1997, © The Modern Poetry Association, 1997. Reprinted by permission of the editor of *Poetry*.

Harold G. McCurdy. "Goldfinches," from *And Then the Sky Turned Blue*, © 1982 by Harold G. McCurdy. Reprinted by permission of the author. "Lizard," from *The Chastening of Narcissus*, © 1970 by Harold G. McCurdy. Reprinted by permission of the author.

Agnes McDonald. "Text," from *Quickest Door, Smallest Room*, © 1992 by Agnes McDonald. Reprinted by permission of the author.

Michael McFee. "Shooting Baskets at Dusk" and "Cold Quilt," from *Vanishing Acts*, © 1989 by Michael McFee. Reprinted by permission of the author and Gnomon Press. "Phantoum," from *Prairie Schooner*, Spring, 1998, © University of Nebraska Press. Reprinted by permission of the author and University of Nebraska Press.

Susan Meyers, "My Father Never Talked of Love," from *Lessons in Leaving*, © 1998 by Susan Meyers. Reprinted by permission of the author.

Heather Ross Miller. "Breadstuff," from *Hard Evidence*, © 1990 by Heather Ross Miller. "Loss of Memory" and "Seventh Grades," *from Friends and Assassins*, © 1993 by Heather Ross Miller. Reprinted by permission of the author.

Jim Wayne Miller. "Brier Losing Touch with His Traditions" and "Restoring an Old Farmhouse," from *The Brier Poems*, © 1997. Reprinted by permission of Gnomon Press.

Shirley Moody. "A Whole Different Spin on the Ball" and "Women on the Pamlico," from *Charmers*, © 1990 by Shirley Moody. Reprinted by permission of the author.

Lenard Moore. "The Song Poem," from *Spirit and Flame: An Anthology of Contemporary African American Poetry*, © 1997 by Syracuse University Press; "Raleigh Jazz Festival," from *Raleigh: A Guide to North Carolina's Capital*, © 1992 by Raleigh Fine Arts Society. "Pathway: From Son to Father," from *Forever Home*, © 1992 by Lenard Moore. Reprinted by permission of the author. Haiku selections from *Desert Storm*, © 1993 by Lenard Moore. Reprinted by permission of the author.

MariJo Moore. "Solidarity in the Night" and "Ahlawe Usv' Tsigesvgi," from *Spirit Voices of Bones*, © 1997 by MariJo Moore. "Invisible Tongues," from *Returning to the Homeland*, © 1994 by MariJo Moore. Reprinted by permission of the author.

Ruth Moose. "Dowry," from *Making the Bed*, © 1995 by Ruth Moose. "That Sunday," from *Smith Grove*, © 1998 by Ruth Moose. Reprinted by permission of the author. "When the Water Wore My Face," printed by permission of the author.

Robert Morgan. "Audubon's Flute," "Vietnam War Memorial," and "The Gift of Tongues," from *Green River: New and Selected Poems*, © 1991 by Robert Morgan, Wesleyan University Press, by permission of the author and University Press of New England. "Mountain Bride," from *Groundwork*, © 1979 by Robert Morgan. Reprinted by permission of the author and Gnomon Press.

Pauli Murray. "Trade a king," "America was a new dream," and "Hope is a crushed stalk," from *Dark Testament and Other Poems*, © Pauli Murray, 1970. Reprinted by permission of Charlotte Sheedy Literary Agency, Inc.

Paul Baker Newman. "Skimmers" and "Wreath," from *The Ladder of Love*, © 1970 by Paul Baker Newman. Reprinted by permission of the author.

Sallie Nixon. "Seasons Such as These," © Sallie Nixon. Reprinted by permission of the author. "Blue Hosanna," from *Spiraling*, © 1990 by Sallie Nixon. Reprinted by permission of the author.

Charles Olson. "Maximus, to Himself," from *Maximus Poems*, © 1960 by Charles Olson. Reprinted by permission of Jargon/Corinth Books, Jonathan Williams, publisher, the Jargon Society.

Guy Owen. "Deserted Farm" and "When We Dropped the Bomb," from *The White Stallion and Other Poems*, © 1969 by Guy Owen. "For James," from *Contemporary Poetry of North Carolina*, © 1977 by Guy Owen and Mary C. Williams. "An Image of Lichen," from *Kentucky Poetry Review*, Fall, 1980. Reprinted by permission of Dorothy Owen.

James Larkin Pearson. "Fifty Acres," "Homer in a Garden," and "God," from *Fifty Acres*, © 1933 by James Larkin Pearson. Reprinted by permission of Dr. Fay Byrd, James Larkin Pearson Library, for Agnes Fox.

Gail Peck. "Heaven," from *Drop Zone*, © 1994 by Gail Peck. Reprinted by permission of the author and Texas River Press.

Keith Petersen. "How Long Did It Take?" from *Pembroke Magazine*, 1996. Reprinted by permission of the author.

Bruce Piephoff. "Honky Tonk Stradivarius," from *Honky Tonk Stradivarius: Songs and Poems*, © 1994 by Bruce Piephoff. Reprinted by permission of the author.

Diana Pinckney. "Lot's Wife Looks Back," from *White Linen*, © 1998 by Diana Pinckney. Reprinted by permission of the author.

Keith Petersen. "How Long Did It Take?" from *Pembroke Magazine*, 1996. Reprinted by permission of the author.

Deborah Pope. "The Secret," and "Another Valentine," from *Fanatic Heart*, © 1992 by Deborah Pope. Reprinted by permission of the author and Louisiana State University Press.

Dannye Romine Powell. "Let's Say We Haven't Seen Each Other Since Ninth Grade" from *At Every Wedding Someone Stays Home*, © 1994 by Dannye Romine Powell. Reprinted by permission of the author.

Barbara Presnell. "Clarissa and the Second Coming," from *Snake Dreams*, © 1994 by Barbara Presnell. Reprinted by permission of the author.

Reynolds Price. "A Heron, A Deer—A Single Day" and "First Christmas," from *Collected Poems*, © 1997 by Reynolds Price. Reprinted by permission of the author.

Margaret Rabb. "Dogwood Alarm," from *Figments of the Firmament*, © 1998 by Margaret Rabb. Reprinted by permission of the author.

Sam Ragan. "October Statement," "That Summer," "The Girl in the Green Bathing Suit," "Seasons," and "The Marked and Unmarked," from *The Collected Poems of Sam Ragan*, © Sam Ragan, 1990. Reprinted by permission of Talmadge Ragan.

Becke Roughton. "Passage," from *The Arts Journal*, September, 1986. Reprinted by permission of the author.

Gibbons Ruark. "Singing Hymns Late at Night for My Father," from *Passing Through Customs: New and Selected Poems*, © 1999 by Gibbons Ruark. Reprinted by permission of the author and Louisiana State University Press. "Nightmare Inspection Tour for American Generals," from *Reeds*, © 1978 by Gibbons Ruark. Reprinted by permission of the author and Texas Tech Press.

Rebecca Rust. "Haiku" from *The Outside of Haiku*, © 1984 by Rebecca Rust. "Carolina's Boat People," from *North Carolina's Four Hundred Years: Signs Along the Way*, © 1986 by North Carolina Poetry Society. Reprinted by permission of the author.

Carl Sandburg. "New Weather" from *Honey and Salt*, © 1958 by Carl Sandburg and renewed 1986 by Margaret Sandburg, Helga Sandburg Crile and Janet Sandburg, reprinted by permission of Harcourt Brace & Company. "Love is a Deep and a Dark and a Lonely" from *Honey and Salt*, © 1960 by Carl Sandburg and renewed 1988 by Margaret Sandburg, Helga Sandburg Crile and Janet Sandburg, reprinted by permission of Harcourt Brace & Company. "Personalia" from *Honey and Salt*, © 1961 by Carl Sandburg and renewed 1989 by Margaret Sandburg, Helga Sandburg Crile and Janet Sandburg, reprinted by permission of Harcourt Brace & Company.

Roger Sauls. "First Instruction in Prayer," from *Asheville Poetry Review*, Fall, 1994. Reprinted by permission of the author.

James Seay. "Cisternal Anecdote" from *Open Field, Understory: New & Selected Poems*, © 1997 by James Seay. Reprinted by permission of Louisiana State University Press. "The Weather Wizard's Cloud Book," from *The Light as They Found It*, © 1990 by James Seay. "Valentine with Hyphens, for CLS-S" from *Carolina Quarterly*, Winter, 1998. Reprinted by permission of the author.

Mab Segrest. "Winter's Secrets" from *Living in a House I Do Not Own*, © 1982 by Mag Segrest. "Grandfather's Mandolin," from *Lyricist*, Spring, 1978. Reprinted by permission of the author.

Elizabeth Sewell. "How, for love, no poem will do," from *Acquist*, © 1984 by Elizabeth Sewell. Reprinted by permission of the author.

Alan Shapiro. "Mud Dancing—Woodstock, 1969," and "Turn," from *Covenant*, © 1991 by Alan Shapiro. Reprinted by permission of the author.

Marty Silverthorne. "Barrel of Prayer," from *Pot Liquor Promises*, © 1997 by Marty Silverthorne. Reprinted by permission of the author.

Nancy Simpson. "Night Student," from *Night Student*, © 1985 by Nancy Simpson. Reprinted by permission of the author.

Mark Smith-Soto. "Lying Out" and "Bubble," from *Edge of Our World*, © 1990 by Trans Verse Press. Reprinted by permission of the author.

R. T. Smith. "Second Waking" and "Vet," from *Cardinal Heart*, © 1991 by R. T. Smith. Reprinted by permission of the author.

Stephen Smith. "How the River Took Daughtry McLamb," from *The Complete Bushnell Hamp Poems*, © 1991 by Stephen Smith. "The 1950s" and "Whatever There Was to Say," from *Most of What We Take Is Given*, © 1991 by Stephen Smith. Reprinted by permission of the author.

Mary Snotherly. "Birthright: To Catch the Light," from *I Have Walked*, © N.C. Poverty Project, 1989. Reprinted by permission of the author.

Thad Stem. "Boy on the Back of a Wagon," from *The Jackknife Horse*, © 1954 by Thad Stem, Jr. Reprinted by permission of Marguerite Stem. "Blotting Paper" and "Uptight," from *Journey Proud*, © 1970 by Thad Stem, Jr. Reprinted by permission of Marguerite Stem.

Shelby Stephenson. "When January Is Cold" and "When in the Sun I Dream," from *Middle Creek Poems*, © 1979 by Shelby Stephenson. Reprinted by permission of the author. "Tobacco Days," from *Finch's Mash*, © 1990 by Shelby Stephenson. Reprinted by permission of the author. "Hymn to the Tenants," from *Poor People*, © 1998 by Shelby Stephenson. Reprinted by permission of the author.

Julie Suk. "Waiting for the Storyteller" and "Sitting Out a War Once Removed," from *Heartwood*, © 1991 by Julie Suk. Reprinted by permission of the author. "La Dolce Vita," from *The Angel of Obsession*, © 1992 by Julie Suk. Reprinted by permission of the author.

Chuck Sullivan. "The Craft Entering the Body" and "Cooking the Books," from *Alphabet of Grace: New and Selected Poems, 1969–94*, © 1994 by Chuck Sullivan. Reprinted by permission of the author.

Maureen Sutton. "High Noon at the Matinee," from *To Encourage the Dawn*, © 1995 by Maureen Sutton. Reprinted by permission of the author.

Eleanor Ross Taylor. "Love Knows," "Ironweed," and "In Case of Danger," from *New and Selected Poems*, © 1983 by Eleanor Ross Taylor. Reprinted by permission of the author.

Rudy Wallace. "Woman in a Red Dress." Printed by permission of the author.

Thomas Walters. "Cowpasture Baseball No. 1," from *The Loblolly Excalibur and a Crown of Shagbark*, © 1976 by Thomas Walters. Reprinted by permission of Linda Walters.

Robert Watson. "God as Magician," from *The Pendulum*, © 1995 by Robert Watson. Reprinted by permission of the author and Louisiana State University Press. "Planet Eight," from *Selected Poems*, © 1974 by Robert Watson. Reprinted by permission of the author.

Carole Boston Weatherford. "Yeast Rolls and Water Biscuits," from *The Tan Chanteuse*, © 1995 by Carole Boston Weatherford. Reprinted by permission of the author.

John Foster West. "After Whippoorwills," from *Wry Wine*, © 1977 by John Foster West. Reprinted by permission of the author.

Michael White. "Postcard," from *The Island*, © 1992 by Michael White. Reprinted by permission of the author.

Carolyn Beard Whitlow. "Rockin' a Man Stone Blind," from *Wild Meat*, © 1986 by Carolyn Beard Whitlow. Reprinted by permission of the author. "Book of Ruth," from *The Kenyon Review*, Summer, 1994. Reprinted by permission of the author.

Jonathan Williams. "Enthusiast," "Credo," "Beaucoup Buttercups," and "The Flower-Hunter in the Fields," from *An Ear in Bartram's Tree: Selected Poems, 1957–67*, © 1969 by Jonathan Williams. Reprinted by permission of the author. "Aunt Creasy, on Work," from *Blues and Roots, Rue and Bluets: A Garland for the Appalachians*, © 1971 by Jonathan Williams. Reprinted by permission of the author.

Emily Wilson. "The Bread and Butter of Life," and "Temple-Building," from *Balancing on Stones*, © 1975 by Emily Wilson. Reprinted by permission of the author. "Memory," from *Pembroke Magazine*, 1998. Reprinted by permission of the author.

Anna Wooten-Hawkins. "Advice for Long Life," printed by permission of the author.

John York. "Eleventh Grade, 1971," from *Johnny's Cosmology*, © 1994 by John York. Reprinted by permission of the author.

Isabel Zuber. "For Her," from *Winter's Exile*, © 1997 by Isabel Zuber. Reprinted by permission of the author.

# Word
# and
# Witness

# Introduction:
# A Century of Poetry

### A Time for Reflection

The turning of a century provides made-to-order opportunities for reflection. Already prognosticators are predicting — usually with vast optimism — what may await us in the twenty-first century. As we complete this one, it seems only natural to also take a long look back and consider what has been distinctive about these one hundred years.

One undisputable distinction: North Carolina's remarkable rise in the literary world. At the beginning of the century, our literary reputation was, at best, pallid; only the hardiest dreamers would have predicted that less than ninety years later national commentators would herald this state for its remarkable outpouring of high-quality writing and for the astonishing numbers of serious writers working within these borders.

In no genre has this achievement been more notable than in poetry. North Carolina poets are being published by some of the nation's most distinguished firms; they are winning national competitions and receiving such major honors as the Bollingen Prize, the T. S. Eliot Award, the Tanning Prize, and the National Book Award. Membership in state-wide poetry associations have swelled to over 400, while local poetry groups have emerged in every corner of the state.

Recognizing this burgeoning activity, the North Carolina Poetry Society, oldest and largest organization devoted to poetry in this state, decided in the mid-1990s to commemorate the centennial with an anthology of North Carolina poetry throughout the century. This decision was in keeping with the Society's history. Since its inception in 1932, it has served as more than a support/critiquing group for members, sponsoring a wide array of activities to promote both the reading and the writing of poetry throughout the state. One year after organizing, the Society began monthly publication of the *North Carolina Poetry Review* — surely, in the heart of the Great Depression, an act of sturdy faith! Through intervening years it has encouraged writers, including students, with competitions, providing cash prizes, and publishing an annual anthology, *Award-Winning Poems*. It has produced other anthologies, including, to mark the state's quadricentennial, *North Carolina's 400 Years: Signs Along the Way*. Each year since 1977 it has presented an annual award (originally the Zoe Kincaid Brockman Award, now the Brockman-Campbell Award) to the poetry collection judged by a noted poet to be best in the state for the current year. In conjunction with Duke University's Continuing Education Division, the society in 1989 and 1991 organized two statewide poetry festivals featuring national poets laureate and internationally honored writers, as well as some of our state's most notable poets.

## The Making of This Anthology

The official statement for this project reads as follows:

> *The mission of this anthology is to provide for readers and writers an overview of twentieth century North Carolina poetry, including work which is representative of (1) our best poetry by our best poets; (2) the historical development of poetry; (3) geographic regions; (4) diverse cultures/ethnic groups.*

This statement has been the touchstone to which editor and board members have returned repeatedly as work proceeded. You will see that, in contrast to some earlier anthologies, this is a book about North Carolina *poetry*, not North Carolina *poets*. Of course the two cannot be completely separated, but the emphasis is important. This collection of course includes poems by our most acknowledged poets, those who have won national attention (and often national awards). But it also offers work by those with lesser reputations: poems marked by innovative form, voice, or unusual insight, or poems that explore unusual subjects—or old subjects in surprisingly new ways.

In short, this book cannot be *comprehensive*, for to include noteworthy poems by every good poet and a more complete survey of the work of our more prolific writers would require at least two volumes this size. Instead, it strives to be *representative*. Every effort has been made to represent our varied communities and the assorted concerns and aesthetics of our writers as the century moved forward. You will find here vast diversity of subject matter, approach, voice, tone, form, and technique.

Of course a major question was, whose work qualifies for review? Or, to put it another way, whom can we claim as North Carolinians? Rather quickly, the editorial board agreed that those eligible for review should have a strong North Carolina association that can be explained in one of three ways:

1. They are lifelong residents.

2. They were born and/or grew up here—they were shaped here—then moved elsewhere.

3. They were natives of another state or area, but while living here they have in their publication and/or work in the literary community, influenced North Carolina poetry.

Deliberately omitted were those just passing through—say, during their college years.

As work was reviewed, two groups were always in mind: readers searching for something that will illuminate and enrich their lives; writers who want to learn from others.

Every historian, including literary historians, should proceed with humility. We are fully aware that some poems now applauded as dazzling will seem ho-hum to future generations, and that reputations which currently glow will dull with time. We also recognize that the reverse happens. Furthermore, we will not be surprised if the moment this book rolls from the presses—just at the turning of the century—some new poet heretofore unrecognized will burst upon the scene with immense promise.

This collection is therefore not meant to establish a twentieth-century North Carolina canon or to certify the worthiness of certain poets; we have not been deputized to pronounce such certifications. We briefly considered naming poets not represented here, but of course then, too, we would inevitably commit major omissions. So we offer what is in our best judgment a reliable representation of what has transpired during this century. We leave it to readers and scholars to be alert to writers not included here, yet making distinctive contributions to our literature.

## How This Anthology Is Organized

Another decision involved how to present all this material. To demonstrate, perhaps dramatize, the changes that have occurred, we have divided the century into four periods

1. 1900–1916: Comparatively quiet years before World War I, which ended forever our nation's isolation from the remainder of the world. Poetry continues nineteenth-century patterns.

2. 1917–1954: Tumultuous years marked by major wars, economic upheaval and scientific and technical development. The beginnings of a groundswell for poetry and of marked changes in form and subject matter.

3. 1955–1979: Equally tumultuous years, distinguished by revolutionary social change which challenged long-held assumptions. Poetry comes of age in this state.

4. 1980–present: A period in which a rapid pace of change in all areas of human experience is taken for granted. A deluge of excellent poetry, much of it attracting national attention.

Within these sections, poems are placed approximately in the order in which their authors began major publishing. (*Note*: Many of our poets have written over a long span of years. Some of their poems in this collection may have been published in a period following that in which their work appears.)

Also included are aids for the reader: biographical notes about the writers, a selected bibliography, and a list of major state awards.

## Our Poetic Heritage

Of course poetry was written in North Carolina long before this century—202 years before, to be exact. In 1698—forty-three years after the first known permanent settler built a house near Albemarle Sound—Henry White wrote a long, untitled religious poem, the first piece of imaginative literature known to be composed in this state. In the coming years, three early governors wrote occasional verse, mainly patriotic in theme: Royal Governor Arthur Dobbs (1759), Governor Thomas Burke (1781–82), and Governor Alexander Martin (1789–92).

But the development of poetry—indeed, of any imaginative literature—in North Carolina proceeded very slowly. The first book of poems published by a single author—James Gay of Iredell County—did not appear until 1810. During the remainder of the century the verse printed in collections or newspapers was mainly undistinguished, though works by Edwin Wiley Fuller, Joseph William Holden, and Theophilus Hunter Hill won local attention.

The most notable achievement in North Carolina poetry during the nineteenth century went largely unnoticed at the time of its publication; indeed, only now, 170 years later, is it receiving the attention it deserves. In 1829, *The Hope of Liberty*, by George Moses Horton, an African American from Chatham County, was published—the first book by a slave in North Carolina, and, according to Richard Walser, the first by any southern black. Horton's poetry is remarkable not only because the poet was self-taught, but because he so honestly portrayed the slave experience. Joan R. Sherman has told Horton's unusual story and included a generous sampling of his work in *The Black Bard of North Carolina: George Moses Horton and His Poetry* (University of North Carolina Press, 1997).

## Poetry During the Twentieth Century

As pundits and scholars analyze the past hundred years, certainly they will focus on *change* as a—perhaps *the*—major theme. This century has seen exceptional innovations in science and technology, as well as remarkable political and social upheaval. Reflecting these developments, change has also been a dominant factor in all of the arts.

It must be noted that North Carolina poets have seldom been at the experimental forefront. To the contrary, early in the century they were slow to move from the models of Edgar Allen Poe and Sydney Lanier to those of Walt Whitman, Emily Dickinson, and Edwin Arlington Robinson. Even today they are not given to leaping onto the latest faddish bandwagons; they are much more likely to experiment in small ways, including adapting only those trends which seem harmonious with their own voices and congruent with their own aesthetics.

But very soon in the century changes did begin to occur, and by midcentury they were cartwheeling over one another. As we move through this collection, we see changes in

- *Form*: Poets have moved from strict rhyme, meter, and standard forms such as the sonnet to free verse, adopted forms such as haiku and pantoum, and original forms.
- *Subject matter*: Following Walt Whitman's principle that all human experience is fit for poetic expression, poets now write on every conceivable subject — personal experience, political events, social concerns — and they do so with increasing frankness.
- *Tone*: Whereas much nineteenth century poetry is uttered in an objective, sometimes almost detached tone, much twentieth century poetry radiates every emotion from rage to sexual passion. Irony is perhaps the dominant tone of the later decades, and its cousin, satire — sometimes savage — appears more frequently as the century moves forward.
- *Voice*: Rejecting the formal, elevated diction of previous centuries, today's poets speak in more conversational language. However, there is no typical North Carolina voice. Although some poems are written in one or another of our many dialects, often including local idiom, others employ standard English, but in less stilted ways than before.
- *Quality*: Reputation is neither the only nor the best measure of quality, but it may be used as one benchmark. At the first of the century, our poets' reputations were essentially contained within state borders. Today this state's poets have won some of our most distinguished national awards and affirmative critical attention.

More detailed explanations for these revolutionary changes will be included in the introductions to each of the four sections of this anthology, but in general the shifts can be accounted for by

- Cultural change: historic and social developments, improved education, and growing interest in all the arts, including literature.
- The influence of literary trends throughout the nation and—as education, travel, and worldwide communication familiarized Carolinians with poetry of other cultures—trends across the globe.

But not only has poetry changed; so have the poets themselves. In the first place, there are many more of them. True, few (here or, for that matter, any place in this country) earn their daily bread solely through poetry. But we have a large number of what we might call quasi-professional poets. Many teach at colleges or universities—a natural home for those interested in language and ideas—but others pursue careers in research, public relations, journalism, library services, government, etc.

Furthermore, a growing number of North Carolinians have adopted poetry as a major avocation. These are not simply dilettantes who turn to poetry the way they might choose croquet or bridge on a leisurely afternoon. They take poetry—both their own and that of other poets—seriously; it is not a hobby, but a passion. They enroll for classes and conferences, attend readings and workshops, buy and study books, join and work actively in writers' groups and associations, submit work for publication.

The population of poets has not only enlarged; it has changed in makeup. There are more women and more minorities writing, as well as members of disadvantaged groups: prisoners, patients, homeless persons. Writing poetry is no longer the province of an elite; it has become a common practice in most corners of our culture.

Some may ask if there is such a thing as "typical North Carolina poetry." Because of the wide diversity among poets and the variety of literary influences, the answer is a resounding *no*. However, many of the poems share characteristics which Guy Owen described in "The Renaissance of Southern Poetry," (*Southern World*, 1980): richly textured language, often including folk or regional idioms and allusions; attachment to place; a feeling for community; a strong narrative core, even in lyric verse; and a deeply-felt sense of the past.

## *The Power of Community*

In the introductions to the four sections we try to account—at least in part—for the burgeoning interest in poetry and the growing number of poets in North Carolina. We note a number of factors that support this trend. But for now let us concentrate on what we consider the most crucial factor: the exceptional literary community in this state.

In recent years a number of commentators, attempting to explain what is often called the "Southern Literary Renaissance," have cited such factors as dramatic social change and the love of land and heritage. True enough—but those factors apply to the entire South as well as to other regions. Why is North Carolina producing more poets—and more good poets—than any other Southern state? (Few would dispute that claim. Evidence: A major 1987 collection, *The Made Thing: An Anthology of Contemporary Southern Poetry*, includes sixty-one poets, twelve of whom have sufficiently strong ties to this state to be included in this anthology. That's twenty percent—a far higher ratio than can be accounted for by the size of our population.)

The secret of this astonishing literary production, we maintain, is North Carolina's strong literary community—fostered, yes, by cultural support (creative writing programs, writing awards, etc.), but depending primarily on writers supporting and encouraging one another. Literary history is crammed with gloomy reports of writers who jealously guard professional secrets and envy one another's successes. In contrast, many writers (not just poets) in this state have established a reputation for helping one another: they critique one another's manuscripts, share names of publishers, offer contact with agents, recommend publication outlets. Writer Georgann Eubanks speaks of our state's "tradition of generosity among writers to give back what they've received." Examples abound, but we might point to our two most recent poets laureate. Neither Fred Chappell nor his predecessor, the late Sam Ragan, has been content merely to revel in the honor of the title; both have worked tirelessly to encourage other writers, to help them develop their work and careers, to make readers aware of those writers, and to promote the appreciation of poetry throughout the state.

Indeed, North Carolina had a flourishing writers' network before it had an organized and marvelously supportive Writers' Network. This generous spirit has moved beyond writers to encompass readers. At the end of the twentieth century, this state has a *writers-and-readers* network sufficiently strong to attract eight thousand people to a Literary Festival on the Chapel Hill campus during one April weekend in 1998. As Shakespeare, the greatest of all poets who wrote in English, proclaimed, " 'Tis a consummation devoutly to be wished."

## *Why Poetry Matters*

And now, a final question: why does the burgeoning growth of poetic production and appreciation matter in this rapidly changing state at the end of a bustling century? It requires a hefty amount of intellectual and emotional energy for the poet to discover that "best" word or image, construct a suitable rhythm, compose the right linguistic melody, then pull all these threads taut to weave layers of meaning and feeling into a workable poem. Furthermore, as any reader of serious poetry can confirm, reading contemporary poetry is no simple task either. Readers must exert serious effort to delve beneath and between syllables, to free images, rhythms, and word-music to do their work, and to recreate the poem in such a way as to uncover the poet's intention — even perhaps to discover something the poet never consciously intended but, as if with a wand whose magic moves beyond his/her making, fused into the poem anyhow.

In our era, marked by the instantaneous in everything from food to electronic communication, the time and effort required for both the composing and the reading of poetry may seem unwieldy and burdensome. Wouldn't those hours, that energy be better spent browsing the Net, manipulating investments, jetting hither and yon in search of "the good life"?

For an answer, we might turn to poets themselves. Many of us are familiar with the lines of William Carlos Williams from "Asphodel, That Greeny Flower":

> It is difficult
> to get the news from poems
>      yet men die miserably every day
>            for lack
> of what is found there.

A large claim. Perhaps that claim is both clarified and justified by a commentary written by former U.S. Poet Laureate Richard Wilbur. In 1989, the North Carolina Poetry Society invited Wilbur to appear as a featured writer in a statewide conference, "The Poet and Human Values." Asked to make a preliminary statement on the topic, he wrote the following:

> Because poems are made out of our common language, they inescapably deal with the ways in which men have sought to order the world, and are inescapably engaged in examining the present force of all our concepts.... Poetry — as in Yeats, for example — can help us to live by eschewing propaganda and by focusing, instead, on the contradictions and incertitudes of human life. It can be enough, in short, for poetry to express us fully, and to rescue us in some measure from being inarticulate about our lot.

Enough, indeed. The poet struggles to halt the tantalizing flow of human experience, to secure its elusive essence, to untangle its tightly knotted secrets. When someone succeeds in doing so, both writer and reader experience a *hallelujah* moment. The use of religious terminology here is intentional; the moment is indeed religious, though not at all sectarian. For in this success we have not only encountered a truth, enormous or infinitesimal, but pronounced its name.

*Birthplace of John Charles McNeill*
*Scotland County, NC*

*Artist: Talmadge Moose*

# Word and Witness:
# 1900–1916

As this century began, North Carolina was still reeling from the devastation—physical, social, and economic—wrought by the Civil War, which had ended thirty-five years earlier. After all, during that conflict, more than 40,000 North Carolina soldiers had died from disease or wounds, and many who returned were maimed or psychologically wounded. Crops and livestock had been destroyed; railroads, bridges, homes, barns, and mills, demolished or severely damaged

Through the following decades, for most Southerners poverty was a fact of life. Although new industries—primarily textile, furniture, and tobacco—were developed, wages were often meager. Rural life, transformed by the sharecropper system, was no more promising: tenants earned only subsistence living, and various conditions contributed to general agricultural depression.

Furthermore, the public school system was in disarray: in 1900 the school term was a mere sixty days and only thirty-seven percent of children attended on a regular basis. Many were too busy working on farms or in industry to go to school. (In 1903, twenty-four percent of the state's textile workers were children.)

With widespread economic deprivation and sparse education, it is not surprising that the arts did not flourish. The wonder is not that there were few poets, but that any received sufficient attention to sell 1000 books in a year, as did John Charles McNeill, with his first collection, *Songs Merry and Sad*, in 1906. Three poets included here—Henry Stockard, Benjamin Sledd, and John Henry Boner—had published collections before the turn of the century and were still actively writing. The esteem they commanded is evidenced by the fact that new or reprinted collections of all three, as well as McNeill, were published several decades after their deaths. The six poets in this section, we may say with admiration, kept the literary flame alive in spite of severely adverse circumstances.

At the turn of the century, several heartening events occurred, among them the 1900 election of Charles Aycock, termed "the education governor" for his vigorous efforts to open more schools and lengthen the school term to four months. Three years later the first child labor law was passed—albeit a weak one, covering only children under twelve. That same year the North Carolina Literary and Historical Association was organized "to stimulate literary and historical activity in North Carolina...and [engender] an intelligent, healthy State pride in the rising generation."

The poems written during those years demonstrate that the poets abided by the expectations of their time regarding their craft. All are rhymed and metered. (The two unrhymed poems by Dargan were composed later.) Most of the earliest employ lofty language—*puissant, plangent, voidless ultimate*—and even sixteenth-century terms such as *'tis, saith, whate'er, e'en, thou art*. Such elevated diction testifies to the then-popular belief that poetry should be more eloquent than daily speech. On the other hand, when they wrote in dialect, John Charles McNeill and James McGirt followed the traditional policy of misspelling words to represent pronunciation—a tradition that would all but disappear by mid-century.

Many topics are also traditional: nature (both its inspiring and its terrifying aspects), love, death, the unpredictability of life. Although personal pronouns are frequently employed, there is seldom any indication that the *I* is more than a persona representing human response in general. Certainly there is no hint of the confessional mode which would become voguish in the second half of the century. Much of the work echoes that of Longfellow, Lowell, Whittier—certainly not Whitman or even Emerson.

Yet these poets began moving in new directions. Although he often wrote traditional verse, McNeill frequently swerved from the path of his mentor, Professor Sledd, to experiment with poetry about everyday concerns written in everyday language, even experimenting with dialects—Gaelic, African-American, Native-American, and poor white. Although some of this work may be considered condescending, McNeill also took the unusual—and, for his time, courageous—step of demonstrating empathy with the black community, especially in "Red Shirts," in which a black speaker expresses delight in all things red except the bright shirts worn by white men to intimidate black voters; a sharply satiric monologue, "Mr. Nigger," which targets white attitudes and practices towards African Americans; and, included in this collection, the poignant "Wishing." John Henry Boner takes a similar stance in "Swannanoa," in which a pleasant woodland stroll reminds the speaker of "all the woes and the oppression" of Native Americans who, "driven by relentless foes...and cruel hand" have sought refuge in the West.

It remained for Olive Tilford Dargan, who lived well past mid-century, to make the technical leap to free verse. *The Cycle's Rim*, published in 1914, is a series of traditional sonnets dealing with her grief after her husband's sudden death. But by 1922, she was experimenting with new forms and a more impassioned, more informal voice. By 1958 — ten years before her death at the age of 99 — she had clearly moved into the mainstream of modern poetry. Her experiments in her prize-winning final collection heralded the work which would dominate the remainder of the century.

*Henry Jerome Stockard*

## On Hatteras Bar

The night was wild, the breakers churned.
    In Heaven's vast shone not a star;
  Alone the light, mist-haloed, burned
    On Hatteras Bar.

From out the scabbard of the dark
    There flashed a sudden blazing brand,
  And, grasped by some puissant hand,
    'Twas thrust against a shrinking bark
  With so dire, deadly, damning might,
    'Twas broke to fragments dazzling white.

Then denser sunk the lurid air,
    And cries blent with the surges' jar,
  And, stabbed, the ship clung reeling there
    On Hatteras Bar.

The ocean massed its ancient strength,
    And hoarser raved the savage gale;
  To shreds was rent each helpless sail;
    A breaker swept the vessel's length:
  It lurched, and, ghost-like through the gloom,
    It shivered, vanished to its doom.

The souls that in the sad winds moan,
    Where lay at morn that shattered spar—
  That sob where plangent seas intone
    On Hatteras Bar!

*Benjamin Sledd*

## The Guerdon

What though the hurrying throng
Heeds not, whate'er I sing? —
Mine is the heaven a breath of song
Down to a life can bring.

Who knows but some patient hour
There cometh from within
The word whose instant power
Some listening ear may win;

Make glad some aching heart,
Failing feet make strong;
Reclaim a lamb from the spoiler's mart,
Or right some old, old wrong?

And so, unheeded, unheard,
Still must I sing, and wait;
If only at last song send the word
That opens Life's temple-gate.

## Twilight

A lost lamb from the meadows crying,
A lone bird through the shadows flying, —
Tears gathering for the day that's dead. —
A weeping heart that wills not to be comforted.

*John Henry Boner*

# By the Swannanoa

Sauntering alone one summer's day
   I wandered to the woodland where
The Swannanoa's dancing waves
   Make musical the mountain air.

While on the river's brink I lay,
   Regardless of the hours that flew,
And watched the sparkling ripples play,
   Fanned by the gentle winds that blew
Along the flowery shore, and heard
The song of many a sweet-voiced bird,
I grew so dreamy that the hum
   Of the wild woods-bees hovering near
Came like a distant Indian drum
   In rude, weird music to my ear,
And glowing woodbines here and there
   In graceful tangles thickly bound
   Appeared like warriors from the ground
Uprising, decked with plumage rare.
I sighed to think of all the woes
   And the oppressions of that race
Which, driven by relentless foes
From time to time, and cruel hand,
   Since Christianity begun
To civilize their native land,
   Sought at the last a resting place
   Far out toward the setting sun.

# The Wolf

The wolf came sniffing at my door,
But the wolf had prowled on my track before,
And his sniff, sniff, sniff at my lodge door-sill
Only made me laugh at his devilish will.

I stirred my fire and read my book,
And joyed my soul at my ingle-nook.
His sniff and his snarl were always there,
But my heart was not the heart of a hare.

I cursed the beast and drove him away,
But he came with the fall of night each day,
And his sniff, sniff, sniff the whole night through
I could hear between the winds that blew.

And the time came when I laughed no more,
But glanced with fear at my frail lodge door,
For now I knew that the wolf at bay
Sooner or later would have his way.

The Fates were three, and I was one.
About my life a net was spun;
My soul grew faint in the deadly snare,
And the shrewd wolf knew my heart's despair.

A crash, and my door flew open wide.
My strength was not as the beast's at my side.
That night on my hearthstone cold and bare
He licked his paw and made his lair.

*James McGirt*

## Life and Love

Life is a boundless sea, on which men float;
Succeed we may to ride the waves of Fate,
Yet still within our paths there surely lies,
The chasm death, the voidless ultimate.

Love is a sacred shrine, to which men kneel,
Succeed we may the blessing to attain,
Yet rest assured the hallowed joy it brings,
E'en though sublime, somehow is tinged with pain.

## Spring

I rise up in de mornin'
Early in de spring,
And hear de bees a hummin'
An hear de robbins sing;
Th're com' o'er me a feelin'
So queer I know not why.
I jus' sit down an' listen,
It seem I 'most could cry;
The win' has lost its biting,
Around' de vine de bees,
The air is full o' fragrance,
From blossom of the trees.
I stroll out in de garden,
An' take a look about,
I see de ground' a crackin,'
The seed has 'gun to sprout.
Beneath de vine a blos'om,
All dried an' curle' it lies,
A striped little melon,
Is hangin' 'fore my eyes.
Its den I 'gin a hummin'
An' j'in the birds and sing,
My heart is full o' raptur'
An' grandeur o' de spring.

*John Charles McNeill*

## Autumn

Heavy with sleep is the old farmstead;
    The windfall of orchards is mellow;
The green of the gum tree is shot with red,
    The poplar is sprinkled with yellow.
Sluggish the snake and leafy the stream;
    The fieldmouse is fat in his burrow;
Sun-up sets millions of dewdrops a-gleam
    Where the late grass is grown in the furrow.

Oh, the smell of the fennel is the autumn's own breath,
    And the sumac is dyed in her blood;
The char of the locust is what her voice saith,
    And the cricket is one with her mood.
Soft are her arms as soft-seeded grass,
    The bluebells at dawn are her eyes,
And slow as slow winds are her feet as they pass
    Her bees and her butterflies.

And when I grow sick at man's sorrow and crime,
    At the pain of pale womanly faces,
At the fever that frets every heart-throb of time,
    At all that brings grief or debases,
I thank God the world is as wide as it is,
    That 't is sweet still to hope and remember;
That, for him who will seek them, the valleys are his
    And the far quiet hills of September.

## The Counselor

My bairnies, touch no barleycarn,
For drinkin' makes an empty barn.
(They winna see me if I slip
Tae the big chist an' tak a sip.)

My ain bairns, never never fight:
The Book says brawlin' isna right.

(I hope they'll heed these gude words rather
Than imitate their deere auld father.)

Whan ye hae siller, dinna lend,
but hauld 't, baith frae faw an' friend.
(Ach! I had walth tae busk me bonny
Had I na gien awa' my money.)

Whan ye wad wed, hear na love's singin',
But mind what gear the wench is bringin'.
(My ain wife, Maggie, smiles at this,
For she had naething but a kiss.)

## Wishing

I wisht I wus a hummin' bird.
    I'd nes' in a willer tree.
Den noth'n' but supp'n' wut goes on wings
    Could ever git to me.

I wisht I wus a snake. I'd crawl
    Down in a deep stump hole.
Noth'n' u'd venture down in dar,
    Into de dark en col'.

But jis' a nigger in his shack,
    Wid de farlight in de chinks—
Supp'n kin see him ever' time
    He even so much as winks.

It's a natchel fac' dat many a time
    I wisht I wus supp'n' wil';
A coon or a' owl or a possum or crow—
    Leas' ways, a little while.

I'd lak to sleep in a holler gum
    Or roost in a long-leaf pine,
Whar nothin' 'u'd come to mess wid me
    Or ax me whar I's gwine.

*Olive Tilford Dargan*

## The Cycle's Rim: XXXVI

Today I went among the mountain folk
To hear the gentle talk most dear to me.
I saw slow tears, and tenderness that woke
From sternest bed to light a lamp for thee.
And "Is it true?" hope asked and asked again,
And "It is true," was all that I could say,
And pride rose over love to hide gray pain
As eyes tears might ungrace were turned away.
So much they loved thee I was half decoyed
By human warmth to feel thee near, but when
I put my hand out all the earth was void,
And vanished even these near-weeping men.
Thus each new time I find that thou art gone,
Anew do I survive the world, alone.

## Twilight

The mountains lie in curves so tender
I want to lay my arm about them
As God does.

## Birth

*In the Hollow*

The hills hover in their snow-shawls
Fringed with black, ragged firs.
In the hollow where three slopes
Touch their great toes together
A hut shrinks down and away
From a cold step-mother sky.
In the hut a woman with gray lips
Sits by a pile of ashes
With now and then a feeble wink
Of fading fire.

Very soon she will be dead;
But on the floor is a screaming baby,
Warm, red, kicking fiercely
With little male feet
At life that gives no welcome.

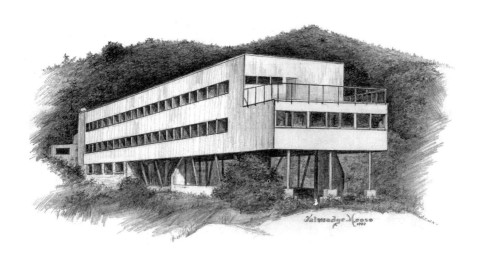

*Studies Building, Black Mountain College*
*Black Mountain, North Carolina*

*Artist: Talmadge Moose*

# Word and Witness: 1917–1954

Beginning in 1917, this country underwent four major upheavals in rapid succession: World War I, the Great Depression, World War II, and the Korean War. Yet despite the energies and resources demanded by these crises, literature began to flourish in this state. Perhaps, given enough compensating factors, upheaval itself provides impetus for both the production and the appreciation of serious literature.

Indeed, there were compensating factors. Before World War I, the United States was not only isolated, but isolationist; afterward, we began the gradual move toward full membership in and, eventually, leadership of the fractious community of nations. Ideas and aesthetic values as well as commercial products crossed the oceans on either side of us. Industrialization continued, and better roads promoted agriculture, commerce, and travel. Education improved dramatically, not only because of more schools and longer school terms, but also because of the growth and development of universities and colleges, and many more North Carolinians went to college, especially under the G.I. Bill of Rights after World War II. With such developments, we inevitably became a less insular, less provincial people.

In the years including and immediately following World War I, there were no notable achievements in poetry, but North Carolina writers achieved major national distinction in other forms. Within three years, two Tar Heels won the Pulitzer Prize for drama: Hatcher Hughes in 1924 and Paul Green in 1927. James Boyd's *Drums* (1925) was hailed as a new high in historical fiction, and in 1929 the appearance of Thomas Wolfe's *Look Homeward Angel* began what became a legendary, if sadly short, career. This national success must have heartened North Carolina writers of all genres.

In addition, during the 1930s, despite the grim economic state that gripped the nation, several noteworthy events signaled increasing attention to literature. In 1931, the Mayflower Award was established to recognize outstanding writing. In 1932, a group of writers in Gastonia organized the North Carolina Poetry Society and began publishing the *North Carolina Poetry Review*.

That same year on the Blue Ridge Assembly grounds near Asheville, Black Mountain College, a daring experiment in higher education and one which focused on the arts, opened with eleven faculty and fewer than two dozen students. The list of those who worked or studied there during the twenty-three years of its struggling existence reads like an honor roll of practitioners of all the arts. Examples: John Cage, Josef and Anni Albers, Willem de Kooning, Buckminster Fuller, Franz Kline, and poets Joel Oppenheimer, Denise Levertov, Jonathan Williams, and Charles Olson. Although never large— there were seldom more than one hundred students— Black Mountain, with its emphasis on free expression, exerted an influence far beyond its own borders.

Other marks of literary interest during this period included

- The establishment of three literary awards, including the Roanoke-Chowan Poetry Cup, and the official establishment of the title of Poet Laureate in 1935. (The position was not filled until 1948, when Arthur Talmadge Abernethy was named to the post.)
- The publication in 1941 of the first of Richard Walser's anthologies dedicated to North Carolina literature, *North Carolina Poetry*. It engendered sufficient interest to justify a revised edition ten years later.
- The establishment of John F. Blair, Publishers, which centered on books of regional interest, including poetry.
- The founding of another statewide poetry organization, the Poetry Council of North Carolina, in 1949.
- The organization of the North Carolina Writers Conference in 1950.
- The presence of master teachers of creative writing at major universities: at the Woman's College of the University of North Carolina, Randall Jarrell, whose students included Heather Ross Miller and Emily Wilson; at Duke University, William Blackburn, who taught James Applewhite, Fred Chappell, and Reynolds Price.

The writing of this period clearly demonstrates that our poets had finally read Whitman and Dickinson. Yes, many still preferred rhyme and meter, and Stewart Atkins and Zoe Kincaid Brockman were still composing sonnets, but Atkins was also breaking out of traditional forms and into a more conversational voice, especially in his "industrial" poetry. Free verse became a common choice for many, and some, such as Charles Edward Eaton and Frank Borden Hanes, were designing their own forms.

Subject matter, like technique, was evolving, moving beyond customary topics to encompass more areas of human experience: politics, working life, social protest, personal experience, daily routine. Tone and attitude included irony, satire, even anger. A dramatic example of this evolution is provided in the two poems by Paul Green included here, both dealing with his experience as a soldier in World War I. The first, "Men of America," is reminiscent of nineteenth-century form and attitude. It is an impassioned patriotic—and clichéd—hurrah, like jingoistic posters and such songs as "Over There." This poem was composed, as John Herbert Roper notes, by "an idealist in training to fight 'the war to end all wars.'" The second, "Stopping in Albert Behind the Germans," was written a little over a year later by a seasoned soldier who in serving on front lines had discovered the reality of battle. It is as impassioned as the earlier poem, but now the speaker questions and protests instead of blindly celebrating. These two poems demonstrate the transformation experienced by so many young men during that conflict, the disillusionment dramatized by Erich Maria Remarque in *All's Quiet on the Western Front.*

During these nearly four decades, one of America's most famous and beloved poets—Carl Sandburg—moved to North Carolina, and two poets who were born elsewhere but spent most of their working lives in this state, won national attention: Helen Bevington, whose neat, witty lines frequently appeared in the *New Yorker*, and Randall Jarrell, whose "The Death of the Ball Turret Gunner" is perhaps the most famous poem to come from World War II. With continued development as poet and critic, Jarrell, by the time he died in 1965, had established a reputation as a major literary figure. Poetry was beginning to make its way as a cultural force within our borders.

*Paul Green*

## Men of America
## (Aux Aimes)

Men of America!
The whole world breathless waits on thee
Arise and grasp thy vengeful steel
To save endangered liberty.
Remember how our fathers bled;
Remember thou our honored dead
Who marched to death thro' fields of red
    That all men might be free.

Men of America!
The war-lords of the earth arise
To trample down the fruits of peace
And raise their banners to the skies.
Remember now poor Belgium's cry—
Her honor taught her how to die
And there's a judgment writ on high
    Against her enemies.

Men of America!
Let loose the gun's red, wrathful flame
And blast the vulturous brood of war
Into the darkness whence they came.
Oh men of freedom prove thy worth
Till fires of peace light every hearth,
Till Tyranny is brot' to earth
    And slavery's but a name.

Men of America!
With every flag of war unfurled,
Are marching by in thundering hosts
To light a freedom to the world.
Across the seas our men shall sweep,
And monarchs of the world may weep
For all their glory in the deep
    Oblivion shall be hurled.

## Stopping in Albert Behind the Germans

Dark clouds, hang low to-night,
Let not the moon shine down,
'Twould sicken heaven's sight
With horrors of this town.

This fen's miasmic woe
Spues death upon the air,
Ah, that all men might know,
what war has gained them here!
The want and desolation
O hearts and hearthstones riven
Send up a protestation
That needs must reach to Heaven.

What fruits of fiendish scorn
Here in the graveyard lie!
Shafts, tombs, trees, bodies torn
Chaosed unutterably.
And see there in the gloom
Those slinking creatures steal!
Down in some blasted tomb
They'll take their evening meal.

O stars! shine not to-night,
O moon! look thou not down.
'Twould choke up Heaven's sight
With horrors of this town!

*Norman Macleod*

## The Bitterroots

In the Bitterroots were sapphire mines
And ticks were a menace to the cattle.

I followed the myths of mica and gold
And shared flapjacks with the grizzled

Prospectors. The cabins were of spruce
And pines were a forest along horizon.

The bald bench of the black mountains
Was above the snowline and ptarmigans

Were a thin white silence in the hills.
The beavers gnawed the edge of winter

Where jackrabbits zigzagged along the
Creek bottoms. My mackinaw camouflaged

A stag shirt and my breath was a frost
Sparkling like the skies on a blue day.

I hunted beneath the ridges for sheep
And the trails led from one cabin to

Another: there were no women for me
To look upon. The mountain men were

Starved from a wariness of body hunger
Until their skulls encased a hardness

No possible cold could ever penetrate
—I warmed my hands at many fires.

## The Spanish Loyalist

During the calculated, cool retreat
(The darkening drone of airplanes in the sky),

Our bayonets starched with moonlight—
Beyond Lerida and backing to the sea—

My eyes burst, and through them
I was drenched with death,

Beating staccato in the
Bitter blood of my brain:

But from that moment I could see
The cross of a black hand over me.

## Stride on the Desert

The desert is a long way in a day's journey.
One ridge is cut from the pattern of

The arroyo before it.
There is much time to wrap with my thoughts

A blanket around me.
The pace of the sand is as certain

As my stride on the desert.
I hollow my life and pick up the fragments.

I hold myself within the grip of my arms.
In firelight there is space for my smoke

To rise into starlight.
Morning or evening there is no yellow wind

Like my sorrow. I do not speak
Of this to another.

There are buttes and monuments for my grief:
I am no stronger than they are.

## In Memory: Northern Navajo

Like no other people to say
Beautiful to things not quite understood.
Between birth and four days of mourning
Lonely beneath a scarlet cliff
The color of independent grief
There is such for singing
The days are a requiem
To be intoned softly:
Beautiful.
It is better, the story that is told.
It is better for the sadness
Of comprehension.
The days are grey as sand.

*James Larkin Pearson*

## Fifty Acres

I've never been to London,
   I've never been to Rome;
But on my Fifty Acres
   I travel here at home.

The hill that looks upon me
   Right here where I was born
Shall be my mighty Jungfrau,
   My Alp, my Matterhorn.

A little land of Egypt
   My meadow plot shall be,
With pyramids of hay-stacks
   Along its sheltered lee.

My hundred yards of brooklet
   Shall fancy's faith beguile,
And be my Rhine, my Avon,
   My Amazon, my Nile.

My humble bed of roses,
   My honeysuckle hedge,
Will do for all the gardens
   At all the far world's edge.

In June I find the Tropics
   Camped all about the place;
Then white December shows me
   The Arctic's frozen face.

My wood-lot grows an Arden,
   My pond a Caspian Sea;
And so my Fifty Acres
   Is all the world to me.

Here on my Fifty Acres
   I safe at home remain,
And have my own Bermuda,
   My Sicily, my Spain.

## Homer in a Garden

A sheltered garden in a sheltered land,
   A pleasant seat upon the mossy ground,
A book of Homer open in my hand,
   And languorous sweet odors all around.

Then suddenly the ages fell away,
   My sheltered garden floated off in space,
And on some lost millennium's bloody day
   I stood with storied Ilium face to face.

The honeysuckle smells that would not fade
   Hung like a ghost above the field of red,
And every dreaming pansy-face was made
   The likeness of the faces of the dead.

Such wonders were abroad in all the land,
   Such magic did the mighty gods employ,
That every lily was a Helen's hand
   And every rose a burning tower of Troy.


## God

   When young Eternity was born
      In days that never can be told—
   In some far-off forgotten morn—
      Then God was old.

   When old Eternity lies dead
      The awful wreck of worlds among,
   And every sun and star has fled,
      God will be young.

*James Boyd*

## Song for the Silent

Down here the mule leans in the traces,
The plow swims through the loam,
And men at dusk turn quiet faces
To chimney smoke and home.
The roof is touched, then, by the first star's finger,
A lamp stands in the wall;
Inside the house, slow sparse words linger,
Slow shadows rise and fall.

Out where the tracery of trees is cool
The plow leans toward the shed
In whose black cave the mule
Lies on his rustling bed.
Deep dark and silence come,
The mule no longer stirs,
The house, the darkened room
Seem filled with whisperers:
No sound but quiet breathing,
No light but from the star,
Whose beams through starlight and dark forests weaving
Form webs to where there are
Some other breathers lost in woods and clearing,
Some other breathers in the starry night,
Living their days beyond all others' hearing,
Beyond all others' sight.
But not beyond the web that holds them
To plow, to mule, to star,
And with light, lovely majesty enfolds them
And all the earth's silent breathers, lone and far;
Breathers and brothers in the world's dark reaches,
Brothers at peace within the web of light,
Free of the day and all the ill day teaches,
At rest now in the silver of the night.

The manikins of state who scheme astutely
To blot each other's names from history's page
Forget that here in lonely cabins mutely
Men watch the feuds they wage.

But when through roads by ghosts of soldiers haunted
The crippled boys come back to mule and star,
If they shall miss the brotherhood they wanted
Our leaders may learn who the silent are.


## Long Distance, 1944

Lift the receiver. Hear the young word, "Hi!"
Feel the heart leap up and shout with joy,
Tumbling and crying to the brain: "The boy!
It's him! He has not had to die!"

*We just got in...*
*Well, it was quite a trip...*
*Oh, sure, I'm fine....*
*She's a good ship...*
*How's everyone at home?*
*...That's swell...that's swell,*
*Maybe a liberty...*
*We're not allowed to tell..."*

And all the while, old heart with his uproar
Keeps shouting, "Brain, why speak so calm, so slow?
Caper you fool, and holler! Don't you know
That this is him? That he is back once more?"
Until brain answers low,
"Hush, hush. I know, I know.
Back from that Distant Shore,
Once...more."

*Carl Sandburg*

## New Weather

Mist came up as a man's hand.
Fog lifted as a woman's shawl.
Fair weather rode in with a blue oath.
One large cloud bellied in a white wind.
Two new winds joined for weather.
Splinters of rain broke out of the west.
Blue rains soaked in a lowland loam.
The dahlia leaves are points of red.
Bees roam singing in the buckwheat.
Russet and gold are the wheatstraws.
Forgotten bells fade and change.
Forgetful bells fill the air.
Fog shawls and mist hands come again.
New weather weaves new garments.

## Love Is a Deep and a Dark and a Lonely

love is a deep and a dark and a lonely
and you take it deep take it dark
and take it with a lonely winding
and when the winding gets too lonely
then may come the windflowers
and the breath of wind over many flowers
winding its way out of many lonely flowers
waiting in rainleaf whispers
waiting in dry stalks of noon
wanting in a music of windbreaths
so you can take love as it comes keening
as it comes with a voice and a face
and you make a talk of it
talking to yourself a talk worth keeping
and you put it away for a keen keeping
and you find it to be a hoarding
and you give it away and yet it stays hoarded

like a book read over and over again
like one book being a long row of books
like leaves of windflowers bending low
and bending to be never broken.

## Personalia

The personal idiom of a corn shock satisfies me.

So does the attack of a high note by an Australian mezzo-soprano.

Also the face and body blow punishment taken by the boilermaker who won the world's championship belt.

I find majesty in the remembrance of a stump speech by John P. Altgeld explaining his act as governor of Illinois in the pardon of four convicts.

The simple dignity of a child drinking a bowl of milk embodies the fascination of an ancient rite.

The color of redhaws when the last driving rain of October sprays their gypsy crimson against the khaki brown of the blown leaves, the ankle-deep leaves—

If I should be sent to jail I would write of these things, lover of mine.

If I live to a majestic old age becoming the owner of a farm I shall sit under apple trees in the summer and on a pad of paper with a large yellow lead pencil, I shall write of these things, lover of mine.

*Helen Bevington*

## The Oceans of Dr. Johnson

I never take a cup of tea
But I consider pleasurably
That, poured a twenty-seventh cup,
Dr. Johnson drank it up.

Before that mighty thirst was quenched,
Pot by pot, his hostess blenched
And, marveling, took fearful count
To be exact in the amount.

Perhaps his dryness had diminished,
Say, when the twenty-first was finished,
Yet being in a social mood
He drank to thrust out solitude,

Extending the complacent hour,
The festive rite, by staying power.
And twenty-seven cups would be
His limit, his capacity.

## January Jasmine

Jasmine flower,
Brief and wary,
On the breast
Of January,

Yellow in the sun
And little,
Tentative of bud
And petal,

Quicker than the quince
Or cherry,
Enterprising,
Solitary,

Quicker to be out
Than spring,
Doubtful of
A welcoming.

## Postcard from Here

Here winter is winterspring,
And the Mayfly mates in April,
The time of the singing of birds
Is nearly all the time.

In this green world, the hoot owls
Live to the age of fifty.
The same well-being marks
The doves and dragonflies.

A May night brings the June bug,
The moths do turns and handsprings,
A kind of thriving stirs
The sweet and lovely air,

So I'm taking breathing lessons,
Hoping to smell the rapture
Here early like the Mayfly,
And emulate the hoot owl.

*Charles Edward Eaton*

## The Bright Plain

This has been a day
    luxurious and lilting and spun
    like a long-linked spool of brightness from the sun.

This has been a day
    like the first stanza: beginning rhyme
    of the song-drift (*da capo*: *da capo*) of importunate time.

This has been a day
    when life-long travelers through the glistening world
    found air lavish: prodigal: the landscape hurled

In glinting rock:
    sun-lake and long legato green.
    Joy was the way breath leaned

Like a fresh wind
    into day, barely ruffling the grass, the landscape's ease,
    leaving desire unhorizoned: the bright plain between distant trees.

## Witness for the Defense

Be a cardinal in a forest full of swallows—
The times need it, and, if it is your nature,
You will sustain the chain-reaction that nearly always follows.

Quick wing-motion and you are there yet out of reach.
Even the busiest parliament of fowls cannot condemn you wholly:
The court may even be a place where you can teach.

There is some circumstantial evidence, leaf by leaf,
The forest cannot subsist on brown alone—
The so-called criminal was called upon to give an elegant motif.

Perhaps it can all be settled out of court—
No one was really put upon, put down, or murdered
Though that red vitality may, at first, indeed have seemed a sharp report.

No one denigrated, no class distinctions overdone—
I do believe a brilliant bird can show us how
We charge the air without resorting to the gun.

Power-politics at every level? No doubt, no doubt, no doubt—
But I would rather be a swallow burnished by red shadow
Than one who put the cardinal to rout.

*Randall Jarrell*

## The Player Piano

I ate pancakes one night in a Pancake House
Run by a lady my age. She was gay.
When I told her that I came from Pasadena
She laughed and said, "I lived in Pasadena
When Fatty Arbuckle drove the El Molino bus."

I felt that I had met someone from home.
No, not Pasadena, Fatty Arbuckle.
Who's that? Oh, something that we had in common
Like—like—the false armistice. Piano rolls.
She told me her house was the first Pancake House

East of the Mississippi, and I showed her
A picture of my grandson. Going home—
Home to the hotel—I began to hum,
"Smile a while, I bid you sad adieu,
When the clouds roll back I'll come to you."

Let's brush our hair before we go to bed,
I say to the old friend who lives in my mirror.
I remember how I'd brush my mother's hair
Before she bobbed it. How long has it been
Since I hit my funnybone? had a scab on my knee?

Here are Mother and Father in a photograph,
Father's holding me . . . . They both look so *young*.
I'm so much older than they are. Look at them,
Two babies with their baby. I don't blame you,
You weren't old enough to know any better;

If I could I'd go back, sit down by you both,
And sign our true armistice: you weren't to blame.
I shut my eyes and there's our living room.
The piano's playing something by Chopin,
And Mother and Father and their little girl

Listen. Look, the keys go down by themselves!
I go over, hold my hands out, play I play—

If only, somehow, I had learned to live!
The three of us sit watching, as my waltz
Plays itself out a half-inch from my fingers.

## The Mockingbird

Look one way and the sun is going down,
Look the other and the moon is rising.
The sparrow's shadow's longer than the lawn.
The bats squeak: "Night is here"; the birds cheep: "Day is gone."
On the willow's highest branch, monopolizing
Day and night, cheeping, squeaking, soaring,
The mockingbird is imitating life.

All day the mockingbird has owned the yard.
As light first woke the world, the sparrows trooped
Onto the seedy lawn: the mockingbird
Chased them off shrieking. Hour by hour, fighting hard
To make the world his own, he swooped
On thrushes, thrashers, jays, and chickadees—
At noon he drove away a big black cat.

Now, in the moonlight, he sits here and sings.
A thrush is singing, then a thrasher, then a jay—
Then, all at once, a cat begins meowing.
A mockingbird can sound like anything.
He imitates the world he drove away
So well that for a minute, in the moonlight,
Which one's the mockingbird? which one's the world?

## The Death of the Ball Turret Gunner

From my mother's sleep I fell into the State,
And I hunched in its belly till my wet fur froze.
Six miles from earth, loosed from its dream of life,
I woke to black flak and the nightmare fighters.
When I died they washed me out of the turret with a hose.

*Frank Borden Hanes*

## Inner Ear

I've been out amongst the wordwinds:
heavy mouths that struck high decibels.
(I suppose their teeth still ring
like tuning forks.)

But should I pass among the men of silence
I would know them, greet them in a shy tongue,
see them through the deep heart,
read those lives they cry for without glare
        or gesture.
I, knowing mimicry then, watching benumbed
by that last great gratitude.

Until I could wish to stand hard, straining
high out on some barren eminence
and speak lock-jawed into a gale.

## Old Arrowhead Thoughts of a Late War

Soon
now it
will be done
like strains maroon
shifting from teeth that grit
at death to a hopped-up sax's run
All over but one good rumble for the throng
All done but the idiotic righting of the wrong

May
will come
a tiptoe virgin
doe-eyed from delay
molested by drums of Harlem
Let silent buddies lie beyond dirging
Don't we who pick a memory's tattered thread
make crowsfeet of the spool that binds us to the dead?

*Zoe Kincaid Brockman*

## Cardinal

One leaf, I thought, has turned bright red,
Autumn has sent a shining word.
And then it turned and skyward fled
To let me know it was a bird.

## Widows of Lidice

(Headline: *"Widows of Lidice See Frank Hanged"*)

Widows of ravaged Lidice
Stood where the noose swung high;
They stood in utter silence
As, clear and stern of eye,

They saw the man who robbed them
Of love and home and child,
Stripped clean of pomp and power.
Grim looks were not beguiled

To mien of shame or pity
As the dread trap was sprung;
Hearts were a walled-in city
Where tolling bells had rung.

Widows of mourning Lidice
Saw justice meted out;
They did not weep nor tremble,
They did not laugh nor shout;

But, as the frightened, loathsome thing
Twitched on the scaffold's arm,
Each missed, with anguished longing,
A man who tilled a farm.

*Stewart Atkins*

# Lynching

They swung him high on a hempen strand.
(Blood must wipe out blood.)
He had no chance at the witness stand.
The only justice they understand
Is sudden death with a sudden hand.
(Blood must wipe out blood.)

No chaplain sounded a prayer for him.
(Blood must wipe out blood.)
No weeping eyes with tears were dim.
Their eyes were hard and their faces grim.
They laughed as they swung him off the limb.
(Blood must wipe out blood.)

His soul they damned, but their own as well.
(Blood must wipe out blood.)
They wrote their names in the pits of hell.
His limp, black body rides the swell
Of the wind, which sounds alone his knell.
(Blood must wipe out blood.)

*Thad Stem, Jr.*

## Boy on the Back of a Wagon

I doubt he even bothers to suspect this world
May soon be claimed by fire. His legs dangle
From the rear and keep time to the slow rolling
Of the shuffling wheels. Now it's queer
He should have troubled to hail the wagon
When legs would do the distance to the creek
In almost half the wagon's time.

        Well, perhaps he holds it true
That prolonging the journey enhances the final joy?
Or maybe it's just to see the wiggling road behind him
Crawling around the green trees like an apathetic snake?
Or is it he blows his harp better sitting down
And can fuller serenade the crows this way?

But he didn't ask me to explain what needs explanation
No more than wild blackberries need sugar and cream.
I think he rides simply because he's going somewhere
and the slower the ride, the sweeter the trip.
The creek is merely a station at the end of the line
And the day is redolently precious with spice and mint,
And he senses something indecorous in plunging headlong,
Though he's not so smug a fool to go hunting reasons
For riding slowly through Maytime's secret heart.

## Blotting Paper

This bedlam is a cracked platter of cold fried eggs,
A short shirt with a button missing, and a handful
Of transfer tokens on a defunct trolley-line.

It's uneaten pears rotting on a grimy shelf,
A mantlepiece littered with faded photographs, and
A billion bumble-bees seeking something to strike.

It's a hangover and buttermilk dark with flies,
A host of lovers sinning behind hedgerows
To show contempt for springtime's wayward spices.

But yesterday a fool of a mockingbird blundered along
Without passport or any license to sing, blotting up
The loose ink from a million smeary odds and ends.


## Uptight

God, for a leader whose face is beautifully wrinkled
From quiet mirth, and from loud laughter, too.
God, for some top men who exude charming asides,
For ones who had rather be dead than solemn.

Today, we somber little people ape our elders,
And the face of every leader is so long and gloomy
A barber ought to charge him twenty bucks for a shave.
But the sky, if sullen and angry, at times, isn't solemn,
And trees, counting greenbacks or gold, or cold and naked,
Don't know how to be solemn, or pious, or pontifical.
Dogs, creeks, possums, rabbits, and jaybirds spit on solemnity.
Only men are solemn, and the bigger the job,
The more outrageously solemn the lock-jawed man.
      I say unto you, O, Front Street,
And unto you, O, America, we have more to fear from solemnity
Than from the Russians, Chinese, et. al. Look at the Pentagon:
From the hatchet-faced, imperious way it grimaces you'd think
It had been invited to a free, sumptuous banquet at the White House
But had left its false teeth in its attaché-case.

*The Weymouth Center for the Arts & Humanities*
*(former home of James Boyd)*
*Southern Pines, North Carolina*

*Artist: Evalynn Halsey*

# Word and Witness:
# 1955–1979

In their 1977 anthology, *Contemporary Poetry of North Carolina*, editors Guy Owen and Mary Williams wrote, "The last two decades have seen an unprecedented explosion of fine poetry in our state.... Not only is there an unusually large number of people writing poetry here, but an unusually large number writing very good poetry." *Explosion* was precisely the right word, and their estimation of the quality of the work was exactly on target. In North Carolina, poetry had indeed come of age, as is evidenced by the 103 poems in this section.

This period, like the previous one, was marked by upheaval: the civil rights movement, the women's movement, changing social mores, the Vietnam War and its accompanying internal turbulence. Many poets explored those stormy topics with disturbingly honest voices. Included here, for example, are an increasing number of poems by African Americans who addressed the struggles of their people, their history, their pride, and their outrage. More women, too, were writing. In the first seventeen years of the century, we claimed only one notable woman poet, Olive Tilford Dargan; in these twenty-four years, there are seventeen, and they were not hesitant to examine feminist concerns.

Like the rest of the country, North Carolina was becoming richer and more comfortable. Air conditioning and the establishment of business/industrial centers such as Research Triangle Park hastened urbanization, the generation of new commercial ventures, and the mushrooming expansion of colleges and universities. One important result: a dramatic influx of people — including poets — from other states: among others, Gerald Barrax from Pennsylvania, Ann Deagon from Alabama, James Seay from Louisiana. The cross-fertilization of ideas doubtless promoted the new flood of literary activity. The reverse situation of course occurred: some of our most talented — among them, R. S. Gwynn, A. R. Ammons, Jim Wayne Miller — left for flourishing careers elsewhere.

Many poets were involved in college teaching, frequently in new creative writing programs. Following the model of Randall Jarrell and William

Blackburn, these teachers helped their students develop significant reputations. Examples:

- North Carolina State University, Guy Owen (Among his most noted students were Betty Adcock and Robert Morgan)
- University of North Carolina at Greensboro, Fred Chappell (Among others, Kathryn Stripling Byer, Stephen Smith, Sarah Lindsay)
- Appalachian State University, John Foster West (Hilda Downer, R. T. Smith).

Workshops sponsored by colleges, libraries, and organizations such as the North Carolina Poetry Society blossomed throughout the state. Writers' groups began to form in almost every large community and many smaller ones. One of the most notable is the North Carolina Haiku Society, founded in 1979 by Rebecca Rust and others, and still going strong, with an international membership.

Beginning in 1971, poets had another professional outlet: the statewide Poetry-in-the-Schools program, which sent writers into public schools for week-long residencies. After the first experimental year, poet Ardis Hatch (formerly Kimsey) was appointed statewide director, and the program succeeded beyond expectations. Designed to involve children at all grade levels in writing poetry, it had other significant salutory effects: it also improved the students' reading and appreciation of poetry, and it acknowledged both the importance of poetry and the professionalism of poets.

Other trends fueled the burgeoning interest in poetry:

- The development of more small presses, including St. Andrews, Red Clay, Briarpatch, Carolina Wren, Jargon, Jackpine.
- The development and growth of "little mags" and literary periodicals such as *Southern Poetry Review, Crucible, St. Andrews Revew, Pembroke Magazine, Red Clay Reader, Greensboro Review, Tar River Poetry, Uwharrie Review, Appalachian Journal, Arts Journal, International Poetry Review.*
- The establishment of the North Carolina Arts Council, which provided grants to magazines, presses, and writers.
- The establishment of the North Carolina Awards, including one for literature, in 1964.
- The publication of two more major anthologies of North Carolina poetry—in 1963, Richard Walser's *Poets of North Carolina*; in 1977, Owen and Williams' *Contemporary Poetry of North Carolina*—and of Richard Walser's extensive bibliography, *Literary North Carolina.*

Behind these trends were energetic, creative, dedicated people: among them, Charleen Swansea Whisnant, the force behind *Red Clay Reader* and

Red Clay Books; Judy Hogan, whose Carolina Wren Press often published the work of writers in the margins of our culture, those who might never otherwise have been noted; John Dancy-Jones, who sponsored weekly readings at The Paper Plant in Raleigh and who made the printing of broadsides and chapbooks into a visually artistic endeavor; Bernadette Hoyle, whose annual Writers' Roundtable brought professionals and novices together for weekends filled with information and encouragement; Ronald Bayes, whose *St. Andrews Review* and St. Andrews Press became major literary outlets; Guy Owen, whose *Southern Poetry Review* became one of the most distinguished poetry journals in the nation; and a brimming handful of other individuals who poured their energies and often their money into small presses and magazines.

One of the key forces behind the poetry explosion was Sam Ragan. As executive editor of the Raleigh *News and Observer*, he published a poem in each issue. He also began a weekly column, "Southern Accent," which he took with him to Southern Pines when he became editor and publisher of the *Pilot* in that town; here he reported literary events, noted the emergence of new writers, and often prodded their careers by publishing their efforts. For years he led a writers' workshop at North Carolina State University. He was also the prime mover behind the transformation of the James Boyd estate in Southern Pines into Weymouth Center for the Arts & Humanities and the establishment there of the Writers-in-Residence program, in which writers spend up to two weeks taking advantage of the lovely estate and grounds as well as virtually complete privacy as they develop their work. Weymouth hosted an annual Poetry Festival; it also became the regular meeting place of the North Carolina Poetry Society and, in the 1990s, the site of the North Carolina Literary Hall of Fame, another of Ragan's projects.

The poetry that was stimulated and supported by all these factors continued trends noted in the second section of this collection. Now, for many poets, rhyme and meter were almost incidental; if, like Robert Watson and Robert Morgan, poets used traditional forms, they did so with the rhythms and vocabulary of everyday speech; like Robert Frost, they had learned that rhyme and meter need not be rigid and/or forced. Furthermore, as we move further into the century, we see less and less direct statement, more and more dependence on allusion, image, metaphor, rhythm, and connotation to thrust the poem towards meaning. This practice, plus the sometimes seemingly random juxtaposition of apparently unrelated images or ideas, of course places greater responsibility on the reader.

Reflecting the still-vigorous Black Mountain influence, some poets were clearly experimental, including Jonathan Williams, Charles Olson, and William Harmon. Others devised their own forms; see Elizabeth Sewell's "How, for love, no poem will do" and Hilda Downer's "Shadows That Steep in Dreams of the New Ground."

As for subject matter, the trend toward franker expression, including use of personal experience, continued; see, as two examples among many, Susan Ludvigson's "The Night We Sang" and Gibbons Ruark's "Singing Hymns Late at Night for My Father." When poets undertook old topics — the nature of God, for instance — they approached them from surprising angles; see Robert Watson's "God as Magician" or Betty Adcock's "Prophecy." No area of human experience was considered too small for poetic exploration: breadmaking, sandlot baseball, a day at the beach.

So the century, and poetry, moved forward.

*Jonathan Williams*

## Enthusiast

*literature*—the way we ripen ourselves
by conversation, said
Edward Dahlberg . . .

we flower in talk, we slake
our thirsts in a brandy of heated speech, song
sweats through the pores,
trickles a swarm
into the sounding keyboard,

pollen falls
across the blackened paper . . .

always idle—before and
after
the act:

making meat
of vowels
in cells
with sticky feet

## Aunt Creasy, On Work:

shucks
I make the livin

uncle
just makes the livin
worthwhile

## Credo:

I do
dig Everything Swinging (thinking

as I do:

ah, art
is fro-
zen Zen)

---

*Goethe said: Architecture is frozen music.*

## Beaucoup Buttercups

and   c o w     c o w     c o w
      o o       o o       o o
      w        w        w
   parsley   parsley   parsley

the way a
whole field looks
back at you

in Berkshire in
June

## The Flower-Hunter in the Fields
### *(for Agnes Arber)*

a flame azalea, mayapple, maple, thornapple
plantation

a white cloud in the eye
of a white horse

a field of bluets moving
below the black suit
of William Bartram

*bluets*; or "Quaker Ladies," or some say
"Innocence"

bluets and the blue of gentians and
Philadelphia blue laws . . .

high hills,

stone cold
sober

as October

*Eleanor Ross Taylor*

## Love Knows

Love knows but one story.
It sits in the corner with its book
and reads it over and over
lips parted, eyes shining—
how the face appeared at the window
how the door was opened
the eyes met
and the hands

Luckily, it is my story.

## Ironweed

In poverty of soil,
in death of summer,
I bloom—
decree to bloom—
And in the color of kings.

## In Case of Danger

I am sending my son
an emergency survival kit:
flares
to light up wild mountainous terrain to
searchers in planes;
inscrutably furled
space blanket, tested against exposure
at Everest by recent explorers;
small high-calorie ration to sustain
one really strayed to the edge of the world.

I include a candle for him to set
in a can of sand in the car. I have
read just so much heat will keep a stranded
motorist from freezing.

My son lives quietly, mostly browsing
in libraries in Iowa City,
lingering sometimes late at a bar
amberizing Freud and Philip Levine
with his friends; occasionally he
spends a morning at the laundromat.

But once when four he ran headlong
towards the edge of an unrailed deck
in LeHavre; a ship's guard jumped in front.
I was wearing a tissue wool suit
and brown hat.
              I had to sit down.
Again, at ten alarmed us all
rising to chart Jupiter's moons—
at four A.M., when a straggler
might have entered the dark house, or
he been molested by a milkman.
In London when he was so ill
I watched sea birds at sunrise flap
along the Thames beyond the obelisk,
and sick with fright by the deranged cot
prayed for this safe time.

I must write a letter of instructions:
            *When in Himalayas* . . . .

*Elizabeth Sewell*

### How, for love, no poem will do

No image serves
For this at-oneness,
Not even the figure
Of bodies loving,
No tendril of vines
How twined so ever,
Nor fish, suspense
Twin and all-touching,
Gravityless
In greensilk flood

*were I watersmeet*
*or woman with child*
*or that child itself*
*might I say what I mean*

As longboat cradles
Its form in air,
As object to shadow
When sun not shines,
As sap and fibre
The mutual flesh,
Bride and groom
Bathe and embroider—
With hint of between,
No image serves

*were I watersmeet*
*or woman with child*
*or that child itself*
*might I say what I mean*

*A. R. Ammons*

## The Yucca Moth

The yucca clump
is blooming,
   tall sturdy spears
spangling into bells of light,
   green
in the white blooms
   faint as a memory of mint.

I raid
   a bloom,
spread the hung petals out,
   and, surprised he is not
a bloom-part, find
   a moth inside, the exact color,
the bloom his daylight port or cove:

though time comes
   and goes and troubles
are unlessened,
   the yucca is lifting temples
of bloom: from the night
   of our dark flights, can
we go in to heal, live
   out in white-green shade
the radiant, white, hanging day?

## Zero and Then Some

We would not want to persuade ourselves
on eternity with an insistence of
our own, pre-empting narrowly or

warping out of centrality the nature of what is —
nevertheless we would not want to miss a
right praising, even if we had to reduce

the praise from substance and stand empty
in stance alone, an attitude merely or
willingness that would at least shirk

indifference in wanting not to avoid praise:
whatever forever is we would not want to be
unconjoined with it or only in the ways

the temporal and particular necessarily
fall short of staying put: there is
an ongoing we nearly cheapen by being its

specific crest, but humbly we know too it
bore us and will support us into whatever
rest remains: what if the infinite

filters through here ordinary as if it
were just taking place locally? that is,
though the infinite is quite impressive

it may be like a weak gravity field, the
least spectacular thing around, the
immediate's most trifling ingredient: we

probably couldn't detect it to redress or
address it, amass it to praise it, not with
regular human instrumentation: but addle

us enough, we will drop the whole
subject and invent for substitution "that
which is to be praised" and invest it with

our store of verve, not matter: the jay
will sometimes at dawn sit in the blue spruce
as if too blank to stir first and

piddle idly in song like a swinging
squeak or singing wheel: it could be praise
though how it works or why it's sung, we guess.

## Apologetics

I don't amount to a thing, I said to the mountain:
I'm not worth a tuft of rubble: I come from
nothing, that's where I'll go: you take, like, from

my elevation, everything rises, slopes with huge
shoulders barreling and breaking up as if out of
melt-deep ground: when I look out I don't see

a scope falling away under prevailing views
into ridges, windings, plots, stream-fields: sir,
the mountain noticing me below and fixing

me in view said, what you don't have you nearly
acquire in the telling, there is a weaving
winding round in you lifting you buzzardlike up into

high-windings: just a minute, I said to the
mountain: exaggeration is not your prerogative:
you have to settle for size: eminence is mine.


## Giving Up Word with Words

Isn't it time to let things be:
I don't pick up the drafts-book,
I ease out of the typewriter room:

bumblebees' wings swirl
free of the fine-spun of words:
the brook blinks

a leaf down-bed, shadow mingling,
tumbling with the leaf, with no
help from me: do things let alone

go to pieces: is rescue written
already into the motions of coherence:
have words all along

imitated work better done undone:
one thinks not ruthlessly to bestir again:
one eases off harsh attentions

to watch the dew dry, the squirrel stand
(white belly prairie-dog erect)
the mayfly cling daylong to the doorscreen.

*Charles Olson*

## Maximus, to Himself

I have had to learn the simplest things
last. Which made for difficulties.
Even at sea I was slow, to get the hand out, or to cross
a wet deck.
        The sea was not, finally, my trade.
But even my trade, at it, I stood estranged
from that which was most familiar. Was delayed,
and not content with the man's argument
that such postponement
is now the nature of
obedience,

        that we are all late
        in a slow time,
        that we grow up many
        And the single
        is not easily
        known.


It could be, though the sharpness (the *achiote*)
I note in others,
makes more sense
than my own distances. The agilities

        they show daily
        who do the world's
        businesses
        And who do nature's
        as I have no sense
        I have done either.

I have made dialogues,
have discussed ancient texts,
have thrown what light I could, offered
what pleasures
doceat allows

But the known?
This I have had to be given,
a life, love, and from one man
the world.

Tokens,
But sitting here
I look out as a wind
and water man, testing
And missing
some proof.

I know the quarters
of the weather, where it comes from,
where it goes. But the stem of me,
this I took from their welcome,
or their rejection, of me

And my arrogance
was neither diminished
nor increased,
by the communication

2

It is undone business
I speak of, this morning,
with the sea
stretching out
from my feet.

*Robert Watson*

## God as Magician

He yanks a whole Spring out of his top hat
Of night: warm air, leaves, violets, daffodils.
Or maybe wraps up the town in ice.

His wand moves and children tumble from wombs.
Or he makes things disappear, say grandfathers
and snow, entire cities under volcanoes...

He palmed the universe out of his sleeve
Like a grenade, exploding it "bang,"
A giant Fourth of July rocket. Behold,

Our earth, the heavens, the beautiful debris
Still soaring beyond telescopes, beyond....
It beats me. You flew, a bouquet from his wand

To me as I flew. I love you, I say
 Before he tucks us with his wand away.

## Planet Eight

We clambered down in airtight suits to the ground
Of Planet Eight where the temperature
For us was cold. The sky was green and windless,
Our feet sank into dust that felt like fur.

We marched toward mounds and tall stones we thought
Must be a town, marched through a plain of dust
Where nothing grew, no tracks of bird or beast.
Under the layer of dust was a crust

Of rock. Our mallets tapped the house-high mounds.
We bored holes. Our gloves rubbed dust from walls of stone.
We found no sign of doors, no carved words.
A light flashed from our capsule, then our phone

Clicked with orders to return. That was all
I saw on Planet Eight, that stillbirth
Or corpse: we would have welcomed rats or flies.
But on the long weightless flight back to earth

With my life's high point shrinking to star size,
I dwell on the dust, the stone mounds, a life
Without life. I land on our stranger planet:
I look out with hostile eyes.

*Lou Lipsitz*

## Word

Looking at my right hand, I can imagine
picking up the heavy, black, cast-iron skillet,
and lifting it quietly off the stove.
Her back is turned. I raise the skillet
 over her head and smash it down against
her skull. She crumbles,
falls toward the floor. I stand over her,
the skillet still poised,
my hand itching to do it again.

No, of course I don't do this. Instead,
I locate the word "fool." A simple word
that dances out along the fingers
of my left hand. The word is a tiny
person dressed in a wild costume—
one arm yellow, one arm red;
one leg green, the other purple.
He wears a blue cap decorated
with silver stars. His nose
is tinted orange. There are
bells on his woven black slippers.
He does somersaults in my hand. He jumps
and shouts. Look how entertaining he is!
I hold him out toward her. He wants to jump
on her shoulder and play
with her hair. O, watch out,
he has a little scissors!

*Guy Owen*

## Deserted Farm

I took a walk through woods and snow
Until I came to a garden row
Gone to sedge, then a gate of boards
Rotting beneath two martin gourds.

A roofless shed, an old turn plow
Said men were here, but not here now.
"Where have they gone?" I asked the pump
Rusting beside the light'ood stump.

Its handle swept toward the sky
(Whatever that might signify);
Its mouth was dry as chimney clay—
And if it knew, it didn't say.

## For James
### (1926–1965)

May there be basketballs in Beulah
and you bouncing arpeggios
looping in rainbow arcs
under hosannas of saints.

Let there be hunting in heaven, too
persimmons with possums dangling like fruit
and under your calm bead
bucks bearing trees of lightning
to fall in pools of painless blood
rising over and over.

I wish you basketballs and deer, James
you who left our hearts
like old leather     unlaced
unfit for game or chase.

# When We Dropped the Bomb
*(After John Hersey)*

When we dropped the bomb on Hiroshima
   it roasted pumpkins on the vine
   and baked potatoes nicely under the ground;
   deep in the vaults the x-ray plates were spoiled;
   men became sterile; women miscarried,
   but sesame and sickle throve in ashes and puke.

When we dropped the bomb on Hiroshima
   the soldiers' eyes ran from their sockets
   and smeared like honey down patient faces;
   unnumbered thousands lay in the streets
     in vomit and died politely
     under the darkened sky.

When we dropped the bomb on Hiroshima
   the wounded crawled to Mr. Tanaka's garden,
   retching among bamboo and laurel
   fouling the exquisite garden, the pools,
   staining the pools, the delicate bridges
     arching . . .
     (No one wept.)

All day the young wife rocked her swaddled
   corpse;
a burnt horse walked on the dying,
     trailing its entrails
   while Father Kliensorge scratched in ashes,
     seeking his melted Christ.

When we dropped the bomb on Hiroshima
   it worked; it was altogether good.

So we turned to Nagasaki.

## An Image of Lichen

At fifty-five the image of my life should be fixed:
all right, then, let it be settled once and for all.
I know that it is not a tree shouldering a patch of sky,
    nesting imperishable songs or casting shade for lovers,
And certainly not a flower, lily or rose,
nor saxifrage, rock-splitter (nor the stone itself),
not even the quiet dignity of mushrooms
    which, waiting for rain, split weathered cement or boards.

Let it be lichen then (surely no one will envy me that)—
...an image of lichen, yes, crusty and brown:
    one tuft on a stone at some desert's edge
where its secret acid bites
    turning dry rock to a spoonful of soil

*Paul Baker Newman*

## Skimmers

Where you see the undersides of their wings
the flock is white and flickering in the sunlight
above the sandbar and the blue water of the sound
and you can hear them crying and protesting
in the cool sea wind that blows across the channel,
and where the rest of them are turning toward you
they are all black and flickering in the sunlight
and they go swinging in a long Cartesian figure
like a twisted plane that lets you see its outlines
by its colors, the one half white and tilting away,
and the other half black and tilting toward you,
as they swing into the air and call you all the names
they can think of in the time it takes to rise
and get away, loping on their long black wings
so leisurely toward the sound behind the islands.

## Wreath

I dreamed the earth swept clear of life
knowing the greatest cruelty is self-pity.
All at once, a symbol is a leaf,
dry, hard and green, that thrusts unwithered
through the sand and blooms red berries,
splashing like a candle's flaming drops.
You see their crisp and crackling light
on cheerful leaves of hard dry holly.
Run your hand among their multitudes
and touch the crisp and piercing leaves
and pluck red berries and a branch of light
to make a symbol, cheerful, hard, serene.
Then trust it with those many flaming points
against that evil: earth swept clear of life.

*Robert Morgan*

## Audubon's Flute

Audubon in the summer woods
by the afternoon river sips
his flute, his fingers swimming on
the silver as silver notes pour

by the afternoon river, sips
and fills the mosquito-note air
with silver as silver notes pour
two hundred miles from any wall.

And fills the mosquito-note air
as deer and herons pause, listen,
two hundred miles from any wall,
and sunset plays the stops of river.

As deer and herons pause, listen,
the silver pipe sings on his tongue
and sunset plays the stops of river,
his breath modeling a melody

the silver pipe sings on his tongue,
coloring the trees and canebrakes,
his breath modeling a melody
over calamus and brush country,

coloring the trees and canebrakes
to the horizon and beyond,
over calamus and brush country
where the whitest moon is rising

to the horizon and beyond
his flute, his fingers swimming on
where the whitest moon is rising.
Audubon in the summer woods.

## The Gift of Tongues

The whole church got hot and vivid
with the rush of unhuman chatter
above the congregation,
and I saw my father looking at
the altar as though electrocuted.
It was a voice I'd never heard
but knew as from other centuries.
It was the voice of awful fire.
"What's he saying?" Ronald hissed
and jabbed my arm. "Probably Hebrew."
The preacher called out another
hymn, and the glissade came again,
high syllables not from my father's
lips but elsewhere, the flare of
higher language, sentences of light.
And we sang and sang again, but
no one rose as if from sleep to
be interpreter, explain the writing
on the air that still shone there like
blindness. None volunteered a gloss
or translation or receiver
of the message. My hands hurt
when pulled from the pew's varnish
they'd gripped and sweated so. Later,
standing under the high and plain-
sung pines on the mountain I clenched
my jaws like pliers, holding in
and savoring the gift of silence.

## Mountain Bride

They say Revis found a flatrock
on the ridge just
perfect for a natural hearth,
and built his cabin with a stick

and clay chimney right over it.
On their wedding night he lit
the fireplace to dry away the mountain
chill of late spring, and flung on

applewood to dye
the room with molten color while
he and Martha that was a Parrish
warmed the sheets between the tick

stuffed with leaves and its feather
cover. Under that wide hearth
a nest of rattlers,
they'll knot a hundred together,

had wintered and were coming awake.
The warming rock
flushed them out early.
It was she

who wakened to their singing near
the embers and roused him to go look.
Before he reached the fire
more than a dozen struck

and he died yelling her to stay
on the big four-poster.
Her uncle coming up the hollow
with a gift bearham two days later

found her shivering there
marooned above a pool
of hungry snakes,
and the body beginning to swell.

## Vietnam War Memorial

What we see first seems a shadow
or a retaining wall in the park,
like half a giant pool or half
an exposed foundation. The names
start a few to the column at
the shallow ends and grow panel
by deeper panel as though month
by month to the point of opposing
planes. From that pit you can't see much
official Washington, just sky
and trees and names and people on
the Mall and the Capitol like
a fancy urn. For this is a wedge
into the earth, a ramp of names
driven into the nation's green,
a black mirror of names many
as the text of a book published
in stone, beginning almost
imperceptibly in the lawn
on one side and growing on black
pages bigger than any reader
 (as you look for your own name in
each chapter) and then thin away
like a ledger into turf again,
with no beginning, no end. As though
the black wall uncovered here a few
rods for sunlight and recognition
runs on and on through the ground in
both directions, with all our names
on the hidden panels, while
these names shine in the open noon.

*Pauli Murray*

## from **Dark Testament**

**2**

America was a new dream and a new world for dreaming.
America was the vast sleeping Gulliver of the globe.
America was the dream of freedom,
But the dream was lost when campfires grew,
The Bible twisted as white men threw
The Redskins back to mountain pass,
The senses dulled with whiskey flask,
The arrow broken by searing lead.
"Better to die," the Red Man said.

The white slave ran away too soon,
Followed the path of dying moon—
A face forgotten in frontier shack
Where none asked questions, few turned back,
Here was a place where a man could stand
Holding free earth in scrawny hand.
Here was a world where freedom was won
By the hand on an axe, the hand on a gun.

**7**

Trade a king's freedom for a barrel of molasses,
Trade a queen's freedom for a red bandanna,
Or Cherokee-mulattoes in North Carolina,
Or a Creole mistress in Louisiana.
Sell a man's brain for a handful of greenbacks,
Mark him up in Congress—he's three-fifths human,
Mark him down in the record with mules and mortgage,
Sell him long! Sell him short! Cotton's a-boomin'.
Take a black's manhood, give a white God,
Send him 'way down in the dismal woods
Where a black man's tears will not embarrass
A white man's juleps and lofty moods.

A black man down on his knees in the swamp-grass
Sent his prayer straight to the white God's throne,
Built him a faith, built a bridge to this God
And God gave him hope and the power of song.

**8**

Hope is a crushed stalk
Between clenched fingers.
Hope is a bird's wing
Broken by a stone.
Hope is a word in a tuneless ditty—
A word whispered with the wind,
A dream of forty acres and a mule,
A cabin of one's own and a moment to rest,
A name and place for one's children
And children's children at last . . .
Hope is a song in a weary throat.

> *Give me a song of hope*
> *And a world where I can sing it.*
> *Give me a song of faith*
> *And a people to believe in it.*
> *Give me a song of kindliness*
> *And a country where I can live it.*
> *Give me a song of hope and love*
> *And a brown girl's heart to hear it.*

*Harold G. McCurdy*

## Goldfinches

Now, in July, goldfinches
Drop lolloping down to feed
On golden coreopsis
Going to seed.

Among the tangled flowers
Their own gold's scarcely seen,
As, earnestly and in silence,
They search and glean.

So quietly they forage
One could suppose a breeze
Was stirring among the flowers,
Not birds like these.

O the delightful shock,
When, suddenly upspringing,
The whole lyrical flock
Takes off, singing!

## Lizard

Reality? A lizard on a fence
Pants in the sun; the split pine-rail drips gum;
Over his beady eye the sky's immense.
Reality is here, throbbing and dumb.

Upon which actual scene our words intrude,
Speaking of hormones or the meddling State:
A tragic or a comic interlude.
The lizard in the great sun waits, will wait,

Ambassador of life base as our blood—
Baser, since all his heat's the sun's direct.
Reality? We've never understood,
Although we talk, cry havoc, and suspect.

*Gerald Barrax*

## Strangers Like Us:
## Pittsburgh, Raleigh, 1945–1985

The sounds our parents heard echoing over
housetops while listening to evening radios
were the uninterrupted cries running and cycling
we sent through the streets and yards, where spring summer
fall we were entrusted to the night, boys
and girls together, to send us home for bath
and bed after the dark had drifted down and eased
contests between pitcher and batter, hider and seeker.

Our own children live imprisoned in light.
They are cycloned into our yards and hearts,
whose gates flutter shut on unfamiliar smiles.
At the rumor of a moon, we call them in
before the monsters who hunt, who hurt, who haunt
us, rise up from our own dim streets.

## Whose Children Are These?

### I

*Whose children* are *these?*
*Who do these childen belong to?*
With no power to watch over,
He looks at them, sleeping,
Exhaustion overwhelming hunger,
Barely protected with burlap from the cold
Cabin. Fear and rage make him tremble
For them; for himself, shame that he can do no more
Than die for them,
For no certain purpose. He heard about the woman,
Margaret Garner, in spite of the white folks' silence.
How she killed two of hers
To keep them from being taken back.
Killed herself after the others were taken back
Anyway. So she saved
Two. He couldn't save his Ellen and Henry.

Who do these belong to?
He doesn't dare kiss them
Now, but stands dreaming,
Willing these five back
To a place or forward to a time
He can't remember or imagine.
All he can do is find the place
He knows about. Leave now
Before dawn sets the white fields raging
And murders the North Star.

## II

Grandsire, I kissed, blessed, chewed, and swallowed your rage
when I stood over the five you sent, warm in their beds,
and force-fed my stunned dumb soul to believe someone
owned, someone bought, someone sold at will
our children, Grandsire, I held them, I held them
as you could not, and revered that fierce mother
whose courage and whose solution I could not.
But we have not rescued them altogether.
We moved them through one dimension, from one killing
field to another on history's flat page,
1850s' slavery to 1980s' racism and murder.
Baraka has told us "They have made
this star unsafe, and this age, primitive,"
and it is so. I stood over each child sleeping
and looked at each child and wanted to know
who decides to break our hearts one by one by one.
The Greeks named it Tyche and made a goddess of chance.
Here they call it this god's "mysterious Will."
I have the children, but we have not saved them
from this primitive star, and I can't forgive.

10 September 1985

## Something I Know about Her

She touches when she talks—
must touch to smooth out syntax with her fingertips,
must lay on her hand to hear her echo,
to feel the words you don't speak
below the ones you do.

What she means by it is warm;
if she touches you, listen:
to surprise her at it
   would be like waking a sleepwalker
   between two dreams—
would trap her in this tedious
world of mere
          jive
            words.

*Rebecca Ball Rust*

## Carolina's Boat People

Is the land so unloving,
so hostile a host,
that they choose this gnawed hull
and the anarchy of the sea?
So many, so many
ride the splintered ark,
press the bow, jam the stern.
Their bones scrape the deck,
the oils of their bodies mingle,
one flesh quickening.

Heavy they ride, rise and fall,
their hopes, the sea.
With each oncoming wave
the throat of the sea widens,
swallowing, swallowing.

## Haiku

early summer morn
sunlight travels a web's lone strand
between two cornstalks

*William Harmon*

## Redounding

Responsively
Our whole house shakes to the thunder's psalm,

Windows react
To the wind's offices, and I am turned all the way around

By the bold sound
That represents, in one sense, almost nothing at all

But, in another sense,
The presence of an old God — popular,

Avuncular
Gullible, petty, sports-minded, omnipotent, girl-crazy,

But nothing now
But noise, with some nominal vestiges of awe. One

Could tell it to
Roar on. Byron told (James said "besought") the deep blue sea

To roll
Longfellow told the flower of the lily to bloom on. Romanticism

Did things
Like that. Redundant. So, what the hell: throw

Your hammer, Thor!
Thunder, thunder. Be yourself. Provoke apostrophes. That's it.

## Memory in February

Dandelions everywhere
                  are asterisks of yellowness
for butterflies to hesitate
    & children to pull off shoes & socks
to wade & to sail the wafer stones
      across the waves that toss (as seals
poise balls from nose to nose, all balanced)
              and the tremendous citric sun
whose Chinese face has smiled all day
             liquifies my lemon sherbet
all down my sweet neglected sleeve
          for lovely lovely lovely girls
in infinitesimal bikinis
           green, burgundy & tangerine
& polka with room for just one dot
       to laugh at with their eyes & tresses
& superlative disporting of
      nice sunburned calves and unburned breasts
me turned and churned to country butter
           like the tigers in the Sambo fable
or upward helium balloons
          into the toy-engulfing sky
becoming absolutely blue
        and slowly lovely vanish!

*James Seay*

## Cisternal Anecdote

According to my Uncle
Damon the only decent
cistern was double-lined,
the rock taken by hand
down into the earth and
placed piece by chosen piece
in the bell-shaped flare until there
was the double wall of stone for sweeter
water and self-respect. And when the reservoir
filled with rain off the tin roof, he took his sense
of what was decent and self-respecting one step more:
the single          goldfish          he slipped into the water
for the country summer. And naturally why and why one,
I asked. It feeds on mosquito larvae, he said,
and doesn't breed. Don't gag; it kept
the chosen drink of my summer
visits cool and clean and
I am here telling this.

## The Weather Wizard's Cloud Book
*(to LDR, Jr.)*

Of the clouds your father
photographed, you must remember most
those that day in the drizzle
as you stepped down from the trolley
and found him with his camera cloaked
and angled toward that part of the firmament
he needed to fix and leave with us,
his own record of weather's quirky provenance.

And how the weather of your youth
must have turned suddenly gray and sodden
within you, this man your father,
hunched over in the middle of the street,

photographing the worthless sky—or the rain
itself for all she knew, the girl you'd brought home
to meet the family, to somehow impress,
there, O lost, on your arm, a rigid adolescent silence.

Last month I touched a stone
that Thomas Wolfe's father had worked
into a doorstop for his bride-to-be.
J.E.W. FROM W.O.W. 1884
was all it said, and we can read
into that the coming remoteness that drove them
to Dixieland, by which I mean her literally
to her boardinghouse and Tom to the found door

of fiction. By which I mean too
you couldn't have known, there on the street
with your miserable teenage angst,
in what ways clouds were his meaning, likenesses struck
in black-and-white and Kodachrome for his book.
Nor could you have known your turning away was old hat
as sons go—sky, wet leaves and tarmac, red scarf all a book,
one book always a door to another, our story of loss never lost.


## Valentine with Hyphens, for CLS-S

Without your warmth or laugh or hyphened-name,
what would my love be like , or worth,
cast so-lo and umbral on valentine's path?
The rose would be the rose and smell the same
by any ol-factoring, except my own.
The sun would sponsor light across the spectrum,
but I, both shadow and shadowed one,
would see the world in mo-no-chrome,
gray to gray to gray, and still more gray
invading every cell and bright nerve.
Knowing this, I walk in-love into the day
with keenest sense of how the one one loves
is almost everything, and would be all
if not for halfness, which I offer whole.

*Robert Waters Grey*

## Topsail Beach/Columbus Day

My main life left
far inland, I forgot
how old I was until
I read the tides.

Watching night surf
break from darkness,
wondering when to expect
the shift back out from in,
I scanned the charts,
discovered the date
and remembered the day's
highs and lows were tied
to my birth. One year
more means one year
less. I stared
from the edge
of a new world
grown cold.

Slowly, slowly
rising from under
the full moon's
choppy sheen,
dark troughs curled,
deepening darkness
until each wave
into itself fell
breaking into light.

*Gibbons Ruark*

## Singing Hymns Late at Night for My Father

While our mother, your dark-haired lover,
Lay paralyzed with polio,
We heard your crackling voice recover

A lost tune on the radio.
Never a singer, you nearly sang in time
"You Are My Sunshine," one more blow

Struck gladly for the March of Dimes.
Sister and I called up and pledged
Five bucks to hear it five more times.

For though on Sunday mornings you edged
Back from the pulpit microphone,
At home you offered like a cage

Of swallows your hopeless monotone.
By the old piano out of key
You sang too early, stopped too soon.

Last time I saw you, you had only
A seamy lyric in your ear,
Dandling the baby on your knee

To words you never let us hear.
If now, far from you in the close
Of night, we falter out of fear

Or out of tune or out of too much whiskey,
Bear with us, even in distress,
And when we raise the raucous noise

Of "Come Thou Fount of Every Blessing"
We will make an everlasting
Music with something missing.

## Nightmare Inspection Tour for American Generals

Though you tear the medals
From your chests and pray
Not to go, though you whimper
And shrink in a cold huddle
Of dogs crying *Semper
Fidelis*, I come to say

It is your solemn duty.
You have seen the yellow
Babies bombed back to their
Leaking bones, the whole air
Wild with the fluting
Or their mothers lost in woe,

You have seen the dead shoved
Into their sleeping bags,
The wrecked boys lowered from
The choppers, a left arm
Gone or a shredded leg,
And you have not been moved.

You have seen everything,
You have seen nothing.
I have come to take you
Somewhere out of my mind.
I am not one of you
And yet I am your kind.

I never laid down any
Body's life, but I have
Paid you to, I have laid
Down on the line good money
Made from poetry and love
For you to count the dead.

So I will take you where
We are damned to go,
Through the dreamed hospital,
Ranks of white beds fatal
And blank as graves of snow,
Through the stone bunkers clear

Of everything but cold
Muzzles slanted for the kill,
Down the edge of a field
You will believe you know
Until it suddenly wells
Up with a light so

Fierce we can see nothing
But what we came to see,
Hunched over like burnt stacks
Of entrails under a black
Flap of night like the wing
Of a buried banshee

Angel, hugging their bones
In the cold or clawing
At their chests for medals,
Huddled on the ripples
Of an undug grave, knowing
Their only lives are gone

Far from them in a deep
River of tears beneath
Their blackening deaths,
The dead pride of our own
Mother country, weeping
To be let down.

*Fred Chappell*

### Fast Ball
*for Winthrop Watson*

The grass raw and electric
as the cat's whiskers.

3 and 2.

At second the runner loiters,
nervous as the corner junkie
edgy for a connection.

Hunched like a cat, the batter:
his prehensile bat
he curls and uncurls.

The pitcher hitches & hitches.

At last the hitcher pitches.

"It gets about the size," Ty Cobb said,
"Of a watermelon seed.
It hisses as it passes."

The outfielders tumble like kittens
back to the benches.
Baseball's a game of light-speeds.
And inches.

### A Prayer for the Mountains

Let these peaks have happened.

The hawk-haunted knobs and hollers,
The blind coves dense as meditation,
The white rock-face, the laurel hells,
The terraced pasture ridge
With its broom sedge combed back by wind:
Let these have taken place, let them be place.

And where Harmon Fork piles unrushing
Against its tabled stones, let the gray trout
Idle below, its dim plectrum a shadow
That marks the stone's clear shadow.

In the slow glade where sunlight comes through
In circlets and moves from leaf to fallen leaf
Like a tribe of shining bees,
Let the milk-flecked fawn lie unseen, unseeing.

Let me lie there too
Aand share the sleep
Of the cool ground's mildest children.

## Grace Before Meat

Bless, O Lord, our daily bread.
Bless those in hunger and in need
Of strength. Bless all who stand in want.
Bless us who pray, bless us who can't.

## The Stories

The story of lovers torn apart by war is a thousand pages long.

The story of lovers whom money separates fills all the
    stiff ledgers of Europe.

By the light of a single candle I read the tale of lovers
    grown old together, climbing faithfully to the darkened
    landing of the stairway.

## Earthsleep

It is the bottomless swoon of never forgetting.

It is the foul well of salvation.

It is the skin of eternity like a coverlet.

It is a tree of fire with tongues of wind.

It is the grandfather lying in earth and the father digging,
The mother aloft in air, and the grandmother sighing.

It is the fire that eats the tree of fire.

It is Susan in the hand of sleep a new creature.

I am a new creature born thirty-five years to this earth
Of jarring elements, its fractuous hold
On the man and woman brings
Earth to bloodmouth.
                            Here where I find
I am I founder.
                            Lord Lord
Let this lost dark not.

Who's used?
Who's not scrawled upon
By the wilderness hand of
Earth and fire and water and air?

How simple simple blessèd simple.

It is the fathomless noon that blossoms after midnight,
And daybreak at the margin of the oaks
Begins to sculpt our sleeping bodies
In the wimpled bed.

What shapes may we take now
where destiny unfurls its roots of fire?

Let it then be flesh that we take on
That I may see you
Cool in time and blonde as this fresh daybreak.

No one no one sleeps apart
Or rises separate
In the burning river of this morning
that earth and wind overtake.

The way the light rubs upon this planet
So do I press to you,

Susan   Susan

The love that moves the sun and other stars
The love that moves itself in light to loving
Flames up like dew

Here in the earliest morning of the world.

*Ronald Bayes*

## Makura-Kotoba

Our coming together from far ends
amazes us both,
neither knowing the other
was cowardly too,
two years ago,
now we confess it, laughing.

We joy in such presence
my cynical dear:
we are in love,
knowing it usually passes
with flowers and years—
still honoring it.

———————————

On waking at four
by your beautiful person
I listened
to your heavy breathing
two hours with no wish to sleep:
I refused to sleep.
With sun through shades
at nine I woke again,
saw the perfect flower
of your ear on my inner arm,
pressed into it. Celebrated
quietly another hour.

———————————

Now we part with hot coffee
and without grief
planning, instead of tears,
outrageous attacks on future years
to keep our hearts as dry as wit
whatever our eyes think of it.

## General John Meditates on Being Lonely

Absence makes
the heart grow
teeth.

## But to Tell the Truth

As for flavor
it's hard to best
a rib
said my butcher to
me,
and I thought about
Eve.

*Amon Liner*

## Things That Are True of Blue

More devious than violins,
blue
performs well as a singing cancer;
vaster than purple,
blue conforms well to the principle
of empty skies;
cooler than green,
blue covers well all possible statues of weeping.

Political as God,
blue
sings well when harmonized with flesh & wrapt body;
colder than the lyrics of compulsion,
blue with mustache is heroic;
smaller than moon,
blue burns with its own light.

Things that are true of blue
are true of the universe too;
words apply to those who
become their symbols;
go wherever your speech exceeds you.

*Sam Ragan*

## October Statement

Written in a clear hand
In black ink and xeroxed,
It said:
Purchase of $19.57.
That was all the store sent me
Of its "October Statement."
But I have my own
October Statement to make—
And I find it difficult to contain
In such conciseness and clarity.
For October is a haze,
A blue sky and a cry
Of unnamed things that wing
Beyond the hill that flares
And taunts the eye,
Of stumbling feet, running
To catch something,
Something that was there, but lost,
Lost a long time ago.
But I keep on running—
Running into October.

## That Summer

That summer when the creeks all dried up
Except for a few deep holes
Under the caved-out roots of oaks
Now leaning toward the water's edge,
The catfish clung to the mud.
But now and then a perch was caught
In the oatsack seine.
Even the Tar was a trickle
And I could walk all the way across
On the rocks, and the place
Where we had swung from limb to water—
Splashing below surface and rising sputtering

Was now no more than moist mud
From which a turtle crawled.

They sat on the porches
And talked of the weather,
And Herbert Hoover,
Cursing both, and every son of a bitch
Who had voted for him.
Even if the Baptists saved any souls
Worth the saving
Where in the hell would they find the water
To baptize them.

A wild turkey flew out of the woods
And even if it was out of season
He fed a family for two days.
And it was better than that mud turtle
That looked like mud and tasted like mud...
that summer when it didn't rain.


## Seasons

From dogwood white to dogwood red,
That's the way the summer's fled.


## The Girl in the Green Bathing Suit

The girl in the green bathing suit
Swings in a swing near the sea.
I watch from my window.
There's a tree bent by the winds
That hangs over the roof of the house.
I can see through the tree's limbs,
Beyond the girl
In the green bathing suit
Beyond the sea oats and sand
Where the sea rolls,
Breaking white, as far out
As where the fishing boat
Sits motionless in the sun.

## The Marked and Unmarked

I cannot say upon which luminous evening
I shall go out beyond the stars,
To windless spaces and unmarked time,
Turning nights to days and days to nights.

    This is the place where I live.
    I planted this tree.
    I watched it grow.
    The leaves fall and I scuff them with my feet.
    This is the street on which I walk.
    I have walked it many times.
    Sometimes it seems there are echoes of my walking—

In the mornings, in the nights,
In those long evenings of silence and stars

    —the unmarked stars.

*Heather Ross Miller*

## Breadstuff

I've had enough of making bread go around,
slapping it, pat-a-caking me to death. But.
Nowhere do I find me so painstakingly
real and rising, leavening each hour
but in this salt, yeast, and cool unblanched flour.
Over the dough bowl, my loony face sifts,
takes shape and lifts. My thumbs search
the elements and my fist blends
the taste of a real presence.
I'd like to waste it, starve people,
go to bed and sleep a year. But.
The oven heats up right
and I wait wait wait.
Crumbs and little bones, sweet dark-curling peels
pile my table, seal the plates. I set out more,
pour cups, catch fish, rob bees to fill up
hungrier, hungrier brothers, nursing all these
on my one lovely body. Never enough.
I make myself go around. Starting over,
I measure and stir, punch the blind stuff
to make it grow. Somebody's tears fall in,
teasing the helpless dough.
Stop it, brothers.
I've got life up to the elbow.

## Seventh Grades

We spread in the grass and slit clover
with a thumbnail, slid one stem
through another, hinged like long lovers,
locked death mates, sucking
the tight white knots
of dead persistent flowers.
We said we'd have it all,
bridesmaids, babies,

hot abundant nectars
the magazines promised like Aretha
singing off our mother's radios,
chainchain-*chain*!
   chainchain-
*chain*! Chain of *fooooools*!

That was our flowering period,
unlucky three-leafed,
each one an unwed
troublesome weed
of a girl
growing April through October,
chaining clover, easy as cattle
in good pasture.

## Loss of Memory

Things were going to come out of her mind someday.
Big loud things. And soft ones. Ones smelling
like honeysuckle bright in the shade, sweet,
strangling.

Things were going to take hold.
The soft blond hair of her children,
her face in their hair, her mind swelling,
the taste of salt. She would remember
her children. She would remember
the honeysuckle. She would remember
the big loud things, letters of some alphabet
and bright obnoxious multiplication tables, *and*!
the voices of her own mind shouting back at her
*A B C D*! Then the blond,
the soft strangle,
the unsayable sweet tangle
of her mind.

*Marion Cannon*

## Grammar

My generation, old as all the nineteen hundreds,
Was reared on strict and hard obedient lines:
Our inspirations paragraphed,
Our philosophy grammatical,
Our impulses punctuated,
Our fantasies in metered rhyme.
It is hard for us to liberate our language;
Hard not to parse our fervencies,
And for our every thought not to scan
In iambic pentameters.
We still make love in fourteen lines of sonnet,
And end a love affair with terse rhymed couplet.
And those of us who are not yet completely deaf
Envy the beat, the dissonance, the free form
Of the unrhymed young.

*Jim Wayne Miller*

## Brier Losing Touch with His Traditions

Once he was a chairmaker.
People up north discovered him.
They said he was "an authentic mountain craftsman."
People came and made pictures of him working,
wrote him up in the newspapers.

He got famous.
Got a lot of orders for his chairs.

When he moved up to Cincinnati
so he could be closer to his market
(besides, a lot of his people lived there now)
he found out he was a Brier.

And when his customers found out
he was using an electric lathe and power drill
just to keep up with all the orders,
they said he was losing touch with his traditions.
His orders fell off something awful.
He figured it had been a bad mistake
to let the magazine people take those pictures
of him with his power tools, clean-shaven,
wearing a flowered sport shirt and drip-dry pants.

So he moved back down to east Kentucky.
Had himself a brochure printed up
with a picture of him using his hand lathe,
bearded, barefoot, in faded overalls.
Then when folks would come from the magazines,
he'd get rid of them before suppertime
so he could put on his shoes, his flowered sport shirt
and double-knit pants, and open a can of beer
and watch the six-thirty news on tv
out of New York and Washington.

He had to have some time to be himself.

* "North of the Ohio River, migrants from the southern Appalachians are known as Briers." — Jim Wayne Miller

## Restoring an Old Farmhouse

He kept coming here.
On the low-skied landscape rolling behind his eyes
country feelings, settled and gray
as weathered farmhouses left leaning in Kentucky fields
among broomsage and cedars.

He kept coming here
a deer drawn again and again to a salt lick.

Pulling away a warped, split board, he found beneath
it another just as old but seasoned and straight,
sawmill fresh. He drew a rusty-headed nail,
found its shank bright as the day it was driven.

Dismantling country feelings.

Tearing down, building up again
from what was salvaged.

In that farmhouse, under that low sky in November,
he read his past like a salt-caked sheet of newsprint
used once to paper a smokehouse shelf.

A coming shape, a new room and view,
rose from old flooring.

Two times mingled. Fresh sawdust
spumed yellow as sunlight from old timber.

*Susan Ludvigson*

## Some Notes on Courage

Think of a child who goes out
into the new neighborhood,
cap at any angle, and offers to lend
a baseball glove. He knows
how many traps there are—
his accent or his clothes, the club
already formed.
Think of a pregnant woman
whose first child died—
her history of blood.
Or your friend whose father
locked her in basements, closets,
cars. Now when she speaks
to strangers, she must have
all the windows open.
She forces herself indoors each day,
sheer will makes her climb the stairs.
And love. Imagine it. After all
those years in the circus, that last
bad fall when the net didn't hold.
Think of the ladder to the wire,
spotlights moving as you move,
then how you used to see yourself
balanced on the shiny air.
Think of doing it again.

## The Night We Sang

The night we sang until 3 A.M.
my back hurt so much
I thought splinters were lodged
near my spine, reminders
that floors, like certain beds,
can be dangerous. Yours, for instance,
though in fact that time the cause

was undramatic: I'd merely
leaned to pick up a pillow.
After dinner, drunk by the fire,
we remembered the piano—
first Bach, and then show tunes,
then old southern hymns.
We distressed the air
in those proper rooms
like ghosts encountering
uncovered mirrors,
their souls lost forever.

I reminded you of our first night
together, how you'd shamed me with all
my Sunday School talk,
making me sing a childish verse
that proved, you said,
what a prude I was.

When we found that old book
with its tattered cover, its black notes
like birds on the autumn sky,
the music absorbed our reckless voices
(we were hoarse for two days), absorbed
my pain, your desire, the dark
we hadn't seen coming in.

*Roger Sauls*

## First Instruction in Prayer

Once, when departing birds
rose from the elms in thrashing vowels,

I learned to make my own speech
a perfection of o's. At night

on my knees I'd repeat words from the big
black book I had, its pages

rippling with joyous sentences.
O my God, I'd say

I could feel the heart
inside me turning. I remembered

the way my bicycle felt
under me when we glided,

how sometimes I fused
with the continuous downpour

of its blue metal.
With so much motion

in me it was impossible
not to believe. O, I could see myself

being carried off by angels
and dropped in the sky like a twig to grow.

*Lance Jeffers*

## When I Know the Power of My Black Hand

I do not know the power of my hand,
I do not know the power of my black hand.

I sit slumped in the conviction that I am powerless,
tolerate ceilings that make me bend.
My godly mind stoops, my ambition is crippled;
I do not know the power of my hand.

I see my children stunted,
my young men slaughtered,
I do not know the mighty power of my hand.

I see the power over my life and death in
another man's hands, and sometimes
I shake my woolly head and wonder:

> *Lord have mercy! What would it be like . . . to be free?*

But when I know the mighty power of my black hand
    I will snatch my freedom from the tyrant's mouth,
know the first taste of freedom on my eager tongue,
sing the miracle of freedom with all the force
    of my lungs,
christen my black land with exuberant creation,
stand independent in the hall of nations,
root submission and dependence from the soil of my soul
and pitch the monument of slavery from my back when
I know the mighty power of my hand!


## On Listening to the Spirituals

When the master lived a king and I a starving hutted slave
    beneath the lash, and

when my five-year-old son was driven at dawn to cottonfield
    to pick until he could no longer see the sun, and

when master called my wife to the big house when mistress
    was gone,
took her against her will and gave her a dollar to be still, and
when she turned upon her pride and cleavered it, cursed
    her dignity
and stamped on it, came back to me with his evil on her thighs,
hung her head when I condemned her with my eyes,
what broken mettle of my soul wept steel, cracked teeth in
self-contempt upon my flesh, crept underground to seek
new roots and secret breathing place?

When all the hatred of my bones was buried in a forgotten
    county of my soul,
then from beauty muscled from the degradation of my
    oaken bread,
I stroked on slavery soil the mighty colors of my song:
    a passionate heaven rose no God in heaven could create!

*Reynolds Price*

## First Christmas

Two early Christmases in my mind—
The first dim as a post-op drug haze
(Our jittery terrier eats a pill
Father drops at bedtime and greets us
Dead beneath the tree when we rise
For Santa; I'm three years old), the second
Gleaming a little higher like a lantern
Smoking in a room under fog (my main
Gift a Dopey doll from Disney's
*Snow White*, 1937; so I'm four
And take Santa's sooty broad thumbprint
On the white plate where we'd left him a biscuit
For testimony at least as real
As a face-to-face sighting at my bedside).
    Another year before I'm given
The plaster set of the Holy family
With assorted guests and attentive beasts,
All their eyes betraying the legend
Stamped on their bottoms—*Made in Japan*—
So till then, and the learning that starts with the sight
Of their two blissed-out faces yearning
Toward the mangered boy, I have no model
For boundless love but my luckless stone-broke
Tall young parents:
                    an adequate stop-gap
Spectacle still burning here fifty-seven
Years on, though selfless as water,
Their steady eyes.


## A Heron, A Deer—A Single Day

A dull tin noon and, struck down on us
From the crest of pines, a heron—the one
That's brought me each winter solstice
For twenty-six years now whatever code

I've earned for the past year, need for the next:
Vast as a stork in a child's old reader
And fierce in the head as a demon deputed
To pluck out human eyes in vengeance,
Bolt them down hot.
                              Yet our two faces
Broaden—eased, assured once more
Of witness at least: our names and precise
Address still known to Guidance Central.

Midnight mist and roaring cold,
We roll toward home from Christmas-eve dinner;
And there in the glen, frozen at the verge,
A six-point buck, young in eye
And grace of joint but flat-eternal
In steady witness. We slow to spare him—
Or think to spare a soulless thing.

He spares us. Sustaining our glare
A long instant of still composure,
His eyes consume whatever we show.
Then in a solemn choice to leave,
He melts a huge body, graceful as girls,
Through two strands of vicious barbed-wire.

We pass unscathed, drive in silence
A last slow mile, then both laugh sudden
At the sight of home. *Seen,* well-seen
But spared to pass.

*Ann Deagon*

## Hitting the Old Mark

When I was ten
my country uncle came to town
to take me to the fair and plunked down quarters
to see me flatten galleries of ducks
bison and tigers splat in no time flat
and cracked his kneecap chortling at the stares.

When I was twelve
he tricked me to the country
lost me in a wood spongy with spring
and at a sluggish pond shadowed with catfish
set me on to slaughter, doubled up
choking with knowing how the wily green
undulant liquid gulps your bullets down
by sleight of water while the catfish peer
in a grey puzzlement at crack and chortle.

I swung the rifle up.
My uncle straightened
his laughter drained away into his boots
a grey man puzzled out of his element
only the air between us and my eye
sighting along the barrel, gave a leap
worthy of dolphins down into the slime-
laced ignominious but grateful ooze.

We walked back silent
aged beyond our ages
his clothes and my imagination dripping
with some genetic holdover some slimy gene
that marks us all and makes us killing kin.

# Augury

Tonight my father cupped his hands and blew
into their hollow sphere and brought to life
the long wild resonant cry
of country boyhood, owl-haunted evenings
and the dark modulations of distant hounds,
fluttered his fingers throbbing into memory
those sobbing whistles hunting down the rails
my childhood dreaming in the restless city.

And as my children wondered cupping their hands
to capture that primeval mimicry
of all that haunts and heightens our precarious sense
of living rooted in immemorial time,
I saw my father new, and shared his knowing
the secret of our give and take of breath:
live long enough to know that we are dying,
hand on with tenderness and dignity
our resonant art
the long learned call
of trumpeter man.

*Betty Adcock*

## Box-Camera Snapshot

She stands sharp as a plumb line beside the flowerbeds.
That's July melting the starch in her dress.
Yard dust grits the air, fuzzes the zinnias.

Straw-yellow plaits pulled so tight the eyes slant,
eyes grey as an owl's *who*, she'll wait
among those feral flowers that can grow anywhere.

I can't remember her dream—that ladder
collapsed inside like the skeleton
of some resident starved animal, rib after rib letting go.

She's the one I poke for with sticks,
after the family burials, after the housefires,
in the rubble and smoke of return.

Whose true name couldn't stay, this child's
name nicked and cut back, eked out what is left.
It coats my eyes like ashes or milk.

To see nothing but through this
string figure, lost shoe, puppet broken
out of the play, is less

and more than enough. Out of my hands
the zinnias pop and range, the sun of that year
pumping orange, scarlet, yellow over old ground

nothing should thrive in, the unseen in black-and-white.
She thrives and wears me like a dress. Her speech
is my sleep, all night the colors of loss discovered.

She will have her desire,
whatever that bone was, even love
counting its missing fingers.

## Prophecy
*with a borrowing from Stevie Smith*

The poets have gone out looking for God again,
having no choice,
disguising as typeface, mirror, theory's fretful counterturn
the old search in the voice.

The trees still wave, green as a summer sea.
the grain still makes in the ear
a richness we can almost hear.
And the world still comes to be. And not to be.

*Nothing has changed, really*, we whisper,
though all we trumpet is the changing stir.
And the air is emptied where they were:
spirits, gods, demons, with whatever

named them gone like fallen wind.
Did we imagine they had wings?
Perhaps they thought they did,
until we learned and flew ourselves, singing.

They went out the way stars do, slowly
the long centuries of flight
unspiraling from them. They melted quite
like Icarus or those figures of ordinary

murderers and monarchs remade in wax museums.
Like these, they lack all metaphor
to tell what they were for.
And we lack any means to ... any means.

What we do have is light. See how they are still burning —
all those classical noses, Coyote's laughing muzzle,
Shiva's raised foot, Christ's cheek, the dazzle
of leafy-armed women darkening, ashy-turning.

With this candle to see by, the poets are calling
and calling, much further out than they thought,
not kneeling but falling.

## The Clouded Leopards of Cambodia and Viet Nam

They are gone, almost, into the music of their name.
The few that are left
wait high and hesitant as mist
in the tallest trees where dawn breaks first.

Their color of mourning kindles
to patterns of stark white, random
and sudden as hope or a daydream.
Moving, they could be mirrors of the sky,
that play of masks
behind which the ancient burning continues
to dwindle and flee.

Thousands of years in their bones
leap blameless as lightning toward us.
To come close to what they know
would feel like thunder and its silent afterword.
We would turn slowly on our shadows, look up
again to name the shapes of the world:
*monkey, temple, rat, rice bowl, god,*
images echoed in the smoke of village cookfires,
in the drift of memory on the faces of elders.
We would stand in the clean footprints of animals,
holding like an offering our hope
for the lives of a handful of people,
a rain that is only rain.

*Maya Angelou*

### A Good Woman Feeling Bad

The blues may be the life you've led
Or midnight hours in
An empty bed. But persecuting
Blues I've known
Could stalk
Like tigers, break like bone,

Pend like rope in
A gallows tree,
Make me curse
My pedigree,

Bitterness thick on
A rankling tongue,
A psalm to love that's
Left unsung,

Rivers heading north
But ending South,
Funeral music
In a going-home mouth.

All riddles are blues,
And all blues are sad,
And I'm only mentioning
Some blues I've had.

*Emily Wilson*

## The Bread and Butter of Life

Phyllis makes magic:
add, stir, knead, and
under a light cloth
life rises, waits.
She brings perfection
to the table, without
fanfare, lets it speak
for itself.
If God were hungry,
he'd have Phyllis for his wife!
She has the touch
no man
can do without.
Her bread's
the envy
of the neighborhood
and rises
in the dreams
of other women.

## Memory

A long avenue of houses
an alley of boiling washpots
and a narrow yard

where sun strikes a match
to the crepe myrtle tree
and my body bursts into bloom.

## Temple-Building

I make for you
a new shape
of words
placed in exact
order, hoping
to join
earth and sky.

My long reaching
extends from this
morning to an
earlier time without
you and to a later
time when you are gone.
I touch

each word, feel its
motions, and bring it
in its flame
to you to keep burning
for me. May this small
but certain shape
light up

the sky, rooted in dark
earth, until cloud and
root move. And wherever
you are, I am, will be
the place of the burning
temple, giving off steady
warmth and light,

to see by, to live by.

*Chuck Sullivan*

## The Craft Entering the Body

*"... until an apprentice is hurt by his tools*
*the craft has not yet entered his body."*
              *—Simone Weil*

At last
the Master
of His trade

Christ
was the
complete

union man
the incomparable
carpenter

so skillfully
nailed
to the Sacred

Heart
of His
Art

by the crafty
hands of His
own Mystical Body.

# Cooking the Books

*"Due to illegally locked and chained fire doors, at least 25 workers died trapped inside the Imperial Food Plant in Hamlet, NC."*
—The Charlotte Observer

Imperial in Hamlet an equal opportunity
employer caught between thought and action
for its welfare mined in nuggets cut
from plump dead pullets kept locked

The doors of its tragic floors
beneath the majestical roof fretted
with golden fire capping the fate
of those poor working stiffs
living on chicken feed
who took the fall fell
down on the job
and died in the heated collective

Bargaining of the flames
from each according to his ability
to each according to her need
blackened screams coming to know
in the sweatshop of their chained ashes
that bosses live only to fire them
first with the sins of their wages
and then in the end with the flash
of a severance that debits their flesh
into being the surplus value
of their lives cooled into the misty

Coalition of smoke-cleared ghosts
a host all business now haunting
like a wispy assembly line the gutted
risk of the unshared profit margin
as apparitional now as the premium
of their faces filed with the facts
and figures shaded among the pages
of the shaky Insurance claim

From which the familiars of that bare
ruin'd choir burnt of blood chant
in urgent languor their dirge
"An honest day's work for an honest
day's wage!" —while sweet Hamlet
the sleepy town itself listens
a mad burg of antic disposition
that wherefore of o'er late has lost
all its mirth in the Imperial wake
of laissez-faire's foul and pestilent
congregation of vapors gathered
to a scrooged shape bent on playing
chicken with the picketing spirits
staring them down until they blink

In the ledgered face of management
laboring to cut
its plotted losses and kindle
restitution in the burning
of the names vanishing in the corporate
heart's pit of Imperial's quick lime
bottom line cooking the books
of the Dead to balance
like nobody's business but God's

*James Applewhite*

## A Forge of Words

I
Moths crowded streetlights revival evenings. The teenaged
Lingered long outside, reluctantly gathered.
The first hymn calling to sinners, bitter-mellow and lonesome,
Would detach us one by one from circumferences of light:
Circumscribed with shadow by a brim of tin, through leaves
Minnow-live in the wind. Still free among moths, we scraped
The wet sidewalk with reluctant soles, our shoulders flickered over
By magnified wings, like fluttering shapes of our sins.

At last to resist no longer we moved up concrete
Steps, abandoning the afternoon's rain in our thoughts,
To chastize our gesture, flip away bravado like cigarettes.

II
To gather up later. Now to fit sensibly in a pew.
I see my thighs muscled wide in the trousers.
The reverend's eyesockets hollow under eventime lighting.
We weight his voice with our responses; as we bend in singing
We empower his beseeching.
                              Kneeling in shame at the altar,
I sense on the back of my neck that repentance is for women.
I turn and encounter the resolve in masculine faces.
Bill Tyson's leather folds and slab-flat cheeks
From his road-building weather. John Grimsley an ashed-over coal,
His face to front the seasons of farming unabashed
By salvation. My own father's jaws locked tight on the names
Of his sins, hardly bowed on his wrestler's neck;
This company of Christians grim like underworld gods.

From the anvil of Christ, I receive my hammered name.

## The Morning After

As our President sleeps I see (in the dream
He cannot remember) industrial suburbs.
Petrochemical refineries isolate themselves in a glamour
Of lights by the Delaware, the James, the Savannah rivers.
Fumes fly like flags from catalytic towers.
Burnt stumps, half-extracted, rim strip mine cavities.
Hard-hat men watch bulldozers consuming pastures,
Streams run mud like the aftermath of Gettysburg.
The meaning of this carnage of flattening and poisoning
Is these blocks with the family grocery closing,
These thin card houses to be swept away
And set up again by the car-blast of freeways.
The meaning of this sacrifice of clear running
Drink without metallic pollutants is the trail bike
For eleven-year-old boys, the reverberation
Of lawnmower engines against the brick walls
Of disused schools. The meaning of this poisoning
And dulling of the land is a poisoning and
Dulling of the mind, a satiety with televised
Violence and beer, a dull stupor of
Desire for desire like lava-colored underground
Coal fires eating their way toward our children.
Undetermined substances leach deeper into Love Canal.
The outgoing tide leaves mud flats mounded
With feces, dead birds coated with oil.
He smiles, asleep, his expression comforts,
He mouths unconsciously the names of our
Accomplishments, athletes and astronauts
Chewed with the bodies of Marines and underfed
Children in a saliva striped like the flag.

## Storm in the Briar Patch

In obedience and ignorance, okra
     stalks, gaunt as prisoners, stand
where screens only keep the flies in.
     Dry season and the boy's father
slaps him for no reason it seems—

rutted landscape fallen to ruin,
pokeweed veined like a hand
    where the scraps of laundry hang,
flap like the wrung-necked rag of
    a chicken in its arcs. Storm
seems a long time coming and strong
    when it dooms down. Spark
crack connects the sky and land
    with copper-green scar in the eye,
as the cat trembles, the three fish
    wait to be cleaned. The lean-tos
lean into the wind, lean as bean-
    poles, the beans dangling, jangled
like wind chimes, while farmers damn
    the hail as it holes tobacco: broad
as banana leaves, like small roofs but
    pierced now, a punctured infantry.
After, he goes the rounds of his fields, each
    hill shredded, a mimic-man, a sham of
what life might be—ghost of a crop to go
    up from a match in cloud and
gesture, not shiver here, broken, long
    hours of raising ruined in his eyes.

## A Leaf of Tobacco

Is veined with mulatto hands. The ridges extending
Along crests of the topographical map from the stem
Marking a mountainous ridge encounter wrinkles
Where streams lead down toward coastal pocosins.
This time-yellowed scrap of a partial history
Features humans driven on like mules with no reprisal.
The grit your fingers feel exploring this pungent terrain
Is fragments of a Staffordshire tea service
Buried from Sherman in fields near Bentonville.
The snuff-colored resin on the ball of your finger
Crystallized in the corners of seventy-five-year-old lips,
On the porch of a shotgun shack, as she watched her grandsons
Crop lugs on their knees in the sun. This leaf has collected,
Like a river system draining a whole basin,

The white organdy lead bullet coon dog Baptist
Preacher iron plough freed slave raped and
Bleeding dead from the lynch mob cotton
Mouth South. Scented and sweetened with rum and molasses,
Rolled into cigarettes or squared in a thick plug,
Then inhaled or chewed, this history is like syrupy
Moonshine distilled through a car radiator so the salts
Strike you blind. Saliva starts in the body. We die for this leaf.

*Thomas Walters*

## Cowpasture Baseball # 1
*(for J. T. Oliver)*

goofy j.t.   gangly   gauging   badbounces
like a tobaccochewing beagle    lusting onto rabbits
stomping private sockhops   in last year's   cottonstalks
all shirttails   and greasy hair   he   good   God
amighty   he   he could evermore grab   grab and fling
a baseball    but never bothered to wipe it off
i mean   you know   could sure enough   manhandle
and muscle   that mother   all the way   in   from
where he   lived   was moving   at the center.

he could crouch   and leap   like i would read   and
learn later   a gazelle   trap the horsehide
and   let fly   hey hey hey   in   over second
my head   my upraised signaling   arms
the stitches   singing   razzing   edges of air
sandspurs   and   cowcrap   popping off into sunshine
like   landscapes of tan stars and   green clouds

after his lines in the play   j.t.   didn't give
a damn   or a beltbuckle for the script   just kept   dancing
spinning   still following through on the throw
spinning   and   spitting   and laughing   high
he was high   yeah   high as hell is low   high
on interception   retrieval   return   privy-ugly
blunt as a billboard   he was all   him   and self
made the game   made our team   hum   from the hit
the rush   and   the known beforehand   outs at home.

*Linda Beatrice Brown*

## I Want to Make the Drums Talk Again

I want to make the drums talk again
to make the shower of sounds fall down around you
I want to call the spirits from the trees
and take the beads
from around the plaster stands of museums
make them shake and rumble
dance your mind blind
with sound of some god who's got free.
I want to make the drums talk again
tell it all, tell it till a snake walks
it feels so good to be listening.
I want the dust to cloud up your nostrils
and I want to see the earrings swing
with each syllable of zebra skin
and some mountain ancestor gone on to the next land,
come down from his rest to sit and listen and
marvel that there is still a heartbeat
he can wipe his tears to.
I want to make the rains come
I want to ripple the waters
I want to send my dry mouth to my lover's innocence,
and have it filled by pulse, by time, by distant sound alone.
I want to find the place where God blinks in rhythm,
and the birds sing counterpoint in their sleep, the place
where touch was born.
I want to make the drums talk again.

*Grace Gibson*

## Myth: To the Fourth Generation

*We face the past; it may be shadowy,*
*but it is all there is.*
                    *—Northrop Frye*

No one lives in the house on that rocky
hill since the last child died, but I sometimes
go back with my sons and in dreams, real to
me as myth. Old photos glimpsed in albums
children open like Swiss music boxes
for their tinkling tunes implode in sudden
recognition. See that aquiline nose,
how that eyebrow flares, dark curly hair that
comb and water cannot slick down; boys in
brass-buttoned uniforms posed on the front
stoop with laughing girls in long white dresses.
We are theirs. They gaze at us like mirrors.

The snapshot group breaks up, turns away from
the box Kodak. They grow older, change, turn
into trees, become fixed stars, sow dragon's
teeth, cast thunderbolts, make the weather of
this place. For my boys the hollow house, like
some serene museum, preserves the empty
stage of an ended world. I can still hear
the cannon, caught in the crossfire, see old
battles won or lost, hear the silence hum.
To defuse our day, we look for those yet
to be born, their faces looking back like ours.

*John Foster West*

## In Memoriam—for Guy Owen

In the liver-spotted cathedral of Sienna,
I lit a candle for a stricken friend,
for two lira, watched over in hushed gloom
by the skull and fingerbone of Saint Domenica,
the long-dead patron saint of Italy's devout.
    As for a lira's mundane worth,
my act meant little, I later learned,
because by then concern was in vain;
but the simple act briefly relieved me,
a devout outsider concerning incense,
incantations, genuflections, origins lost.
So there was little left to do but grieve,
for, practically speaking, my deed was meaningless,
since the voracious crab, like stones falling,
had not been stayed.
    But it was good to feel right in an act,
though merely a gesture, nonetheless sincere;
for he too had known that candles lit
are much of what we have
to protest or petition whatever powers
may or may not deign to respond
to our moth-light
flickering in the cursed dark
out here between stars.

*Sallie Nixon*

o
believe
in the stirring
embryo of wonder
whatever can quiver
whatever can tremble
whatever can shake us
to set
it
spinning

### Blue Hosanna

On this last day of June
the fragile morning glories
are giving praise:
Here, they reach
to first light,
stretch their cups
for earliest grace.

I learn from them:
In this still place
I open my own thin blueness,
take deep into myself
the thrust of day.

*Ruth Moose*

## Dowry

Mother seamed my legs together,
said run but don't step on the grass.
She made me a cap of bridal lace,
fitted it with wire. This will
keep you warm, she said, and your
thinking straight. She taught me
to count to 28 and back, to depend
on the moon, chart tides, make my face
a clock. Showed me how to pour tea,
service always with a smile. She folded
my arms to hold babies and brooms.
Put pebbles in my mouth and said swallow.
She coaxed my voice to sing all the notes
of content. At her elbow, she taught
me the ways of fire, its principal use
to keep a man home. She never showed me
how to count coins, nor fitted my shoulder
for a gun. She didn't tell me the words
to save my life. Instead, I was made
to whisper quiet mumblings
to a white fur muff.

Mother,
today making my bed, I found the pea.
It was under the mattress seventh
from the floor. I knew from the first
and would have cried each night
except for numbness and the fact
that for years I have knotted sheets
of lasting escape.

# That Sunday

After church
we circled the cherry table
my grandfather had built.
His table served us
graciously smooth
as the words
we'd mumbled in hunger
and haste. Our manners
made, we ate the cold lunch
my grandmother yesterday
steamed and stirred and baked.
My uncles' hands, raw
in their farm boy ways,
lifted glasses of milk,
sweet and cold to lips
only hours past some neighbor
daughter's kisses.

Outside the window
dusting snow
spread wide the stubbled fields.
While in the new ground,
stumps still smoldered
gray and red and black
under the healing white.

From the domed Philco,
buzzy brown and full of sputters,
we heard the hum of light,
but didn't believe. Words
like Pearl Harbor, the Battleship
Arizona , which I knew was a state
and not in the Pacific.
But here was the President
holding us all in his lap.
Holding us all

as close as fear.

## When the Water Wore My Face

That day the dove came back
with nothing in her beak
I thought I'd die.  The sight
of the sea, endless, endless,
was almost more than I could
stand another hour. Water
smooth as glass, but darker.
Underneath lay the life I knew
while the boat rode on and on
to nowhere with none of us
seeing anything, even Himself
with the glass to his eye hourly.
He who knew all the answers
wouldn't let others take a watch
and only He decided when
to send out the doves.
Doves who came back wet and weary,
their wings torn. If the doves died
what would go next? I doubted
the weather, the water, but most
of all, I doubted God. I hated
the water I'd had such faith
in before. Keeping us out of what
was below. And it always felt good
in the bath, let our clothes
come clean which is enough
to get you through another day. But oh,
for the sight of a tree, the cap of a hill.
Anything but water the color of lead.
Sea of no hope. Sea of sameness. Sea of loss.
If it had not been for the stars which moved
and made patterns I don't think I could
have survived. When we were lost from
them, I felt so alone on the ship,
alone forever, the last woman
in the world and the water
wearing my face.

*Kathryn Bright Gurkin*

## Meditation

It is not death I fear, but disillusion.
All I know of dying is an aftermath—
the few sad sticks of furniture
and baubles hawked by auctioneers
because nobody cares that these cheap cups and saucers held
strong tea and sugar, comfort
for a day gone wrong or right,
that this chair mattered to a mind
which had no answers to the human plight
but patience and a bowing of the head.

I want to die upright, on my two feet and fighting
like Elizabeth the First,
to shake my fist at Chaos as she brandished dreams
of empire in the teeth of night.
I want to die upright,
even if held up by hirelings,
shouting dire and needful poems
into the ether, making light.

*Hilda Downer*

### Shadows That Steep in Dreams
### of the New Ground
*To Branch*

Dream, dream to sleep.
Rock infant softness to my shoulder.
Dream of not only the land we give you,
but the mountains' blue trill toward words.
Dream of not only the river's bordering lace,
but the gold glint of trout easing a sheer of sun.
Dream of not only the boulder's wrinkled prune shape,
but its cave's delicate moan of cool air;
of not only the wood's shadows folding light,
but the walnut's deepest fingernail-press of bark.
Dream of not only the field's claim to smooth green,
but the wild carrot giving itself to goldenrod and infinite running;
of not only the primitive road's melancholy color,
but the wild turkey and deer prints, molded to fit future walks;
of not only the stream tingling down the sloped vertebrae,
but its bright stone collection and slippery pungence.
Dream of not only the wind thumbing a ball across the yard,
but branches quietly weighed with the feather sleep of a breeze.
Dream, dream of not only the distant tree line's serration,
but eye level pins marching upon the mound of a pin cushion.
Dream, dream, dream of not only the open pond of sky,
but the clouds interpreting the landscape's jumbled code.
As my voice turns to cotton
as words loosen themselves like gloves,
allow the essence of what we cannot
convey in a poemtime,
the dream of the land we give you.

*Shelby Stephenson*

## When January Is Cold

In this ice-edged hour, this January of hog-killings,
I see the whipped creak of trace-chains
slipping under wrinkled snouts,
pigs' lashes like drawn shade-tassels hanging from closed lids,
know the running blood, the trembling
jar of heads and ears on sleds mule-drawn to the barrel
sliced in two bubbling with scalding water
triple rainbows in the sun—
I turn from the morning, and I believe
In the first dying made in pleasure or pain and I feel the goneness,
the sacrifices piling up in the fire
growing around the lightwood knots under the vat
and in the ice melting in dribs down hanging trees
and I long for whole days of understanding
the going-out lights, the washed-in-and-out of things
in a January coming onto an old gallows tree
when hogs are shot, cleaned and carved
and salted in a box or hung up to the ceilings
in smokehouses on nails and wires to cure,
tongues dripping a language I hear.

## When in the Sun I Dream

Blackbirds oar the horizon
dipping their wings over grainland
easy as a groomed crew.

On the tops of trees wind stirs.
Dry ninth-month grass abides no rain.
I gaze at dead limbs of pear
where a mockingbird turns tail to open air,
giving webbed twigs of black
a jackknife of feathers and blowing.

## Tobacco Days

The rows almost ridge themselves, shaping the year again
towards seasons that let the dust of sandlugs
fall into yesterdays lost in failed crops, quick dreams.

———————

I lay on the warm ground of the Mayo barn at four in the morning
hoping Brother would oversleep.
The flatbed trailer bounded across the ditch,
    the Farmall Cub droned.
"Morning, boys." I climbed the tierpoles.
Taking the top, I handed down four sticks at a time to Lee to
Paul who packed the trailer. From my perch I
stirred the sun through airholes under the eaves.
The barn emptied, we walked through dew to breakfast.
Dreams drifted awkwardly, Brother's Big Man chew
rolling over in sand-dust.

———————

The tobacco greens for the farmer who dives into the dirt,
renewed in the smell of warehouses,
golden leaves in the lightholes bringing the legged sunlight in.
Dew in dust, a musk in mist,
the tobacco tips one more time on the prime,

a sea of blooms
bobbing in ninetyfive degree wisps of heat,
adhesive tape slipping over blisters.

My bare feet burn on the ground and I shuffle
toes into dirt for moisture, inching stalk by stalk
down endless rows in the ten-acre field where short rows
fade into plumbushes and shade.

The mules on the drags
relax through the hot, climbing
July days, the frying dust, and you wonder if you'll ever
get the gum off your hands.

# Hymn to the Tenants

I will learn the blues
and go down the tobacco-middles with little pay
climb the tierpoles in the curingbarns
go down to the creek where the stray dog
hunts a piece of meat
where the blind man cries How we do, Sweet Jesus!

Old Man Pip Fellers
who worked for the Johnson Boys across the creek
lived in a rambly, shackly, unpainted plankhouse
grown over by sweetgum and honeysuckle
there right to the left of the old Sanders Place
where Lewis Sanders lived
telling me how there were bloodstains—
slave-blood—on the railing going up stairs
and when I go back home
between Cleveland School and McGee's Crossroads
I will ask the old people to tell
me what happened to these people—Marcelline and Marcelleach
and I hear how
they could sing to make the tobacco button out better
and in their presence I could not sing at all.

*The White Cross School*
*(home of the North Carolina Writers' Network)*
*Chapel Hill, North Carolina*

*Artist: Thomas W. Whisnant*

# Word and Witness
# 1980–1999

If *explosion* aptly described the state's poetry scene during the previous twenty-four years, what word will suffice for the end of the century? During these two decades, the development of poetry here has been not incremental, but exponential. In both the 1941 and 1951 editions of his anthology *North Carolina Poetry*, Richard Walser had enough room to include passages from Thomas Wolfe's novels (poetic prose, absolutely, but prose) and Paul Green's plays (poetic moments, yes, but not poetry). Today's anthologist, faced with the daunting array of currently published poetry, agonizes in recognition of the excellent material that cannot be included, the good poets who cannot be acknowledged, lest the book become too ponderous a tome. Reviewing the increasing number of poets and the expansion of interest in poetry throughout this century, perhaps we can adopt a new maxim: poetry begets poetry.

Of course this situation doesn't hold true only for North Carolina; since 1980, poetic activity has proceeded at a nearly frenetic pace all through the nation. These have been affluent times, with more of everything: technology, education, travel, interweaving of cultures, attention to the arts, insistence on individual rights. The cultural ferment which began in the conflict-ridden sixties continues, with both happy and discomfiting results. On one hand, the culture as a whole is enriched and its perspectives broadened by the contributions of so many sub-groups; on the other hand, the nation is frequently split into *us* versus *them*—blacks (and other racial and/or ethnic groups) vs. whites, women vs. men, gays vs. straights, fundamentalists vs. mainstream religions. The dialogue is not infrequently divisive and antagonistic.

But, as we said earlier, perhaps upheaval itself provides impetus for the creation of serious literature. At any rate, such literature is being created— and in an increasingly friendly atmosphere. Friendly, it undeniably is. Movements which began decades ago have not only continued, but grown. For example, still more small presses appeared—among them Persephone,

Scots Plaid, North Carolina Wesleyan, Mt. Olive—and new literary magazines, including *Charlotte Review, Asheville Review, Mt. Olive Review, North Carolina Literary Review, Wellspring, Sandhills Review* (formerly *St. Andrews Review*). Still more creative writing programs are thriving at colleges and universities, led by notable writers, including poets such as Peter Makuck (East Carolina University), Betty Adcock (Meredith College), Michael White (UNC-Wilmington) James Applewhite (Duke University), Ronald Bayes (St. Andrews Presbyterian College), Kathryn Stripling Byer (Western Carolina University), James Seay, Alan Shapiro, and Michael McFee (UNC-Chapel Hill). UNC-Greensboro, UNC-Wilmington, and Warren Wilson College now offer the Master of Fine Arts degree. Many high schools and some middle schools also offer creative writing classes and publish annual literary magazines. Writing groups and writers' workshops continue to proliferate. The Writers' Workshop in Asheville has been a vibrant ongoing enterprise, and in 1998 the Friday Noon Poets in Chapel Hill celebrated twenty active years. Poetry readings, formerly infrequent occasions, have become everyday events in larger cities, sponsored by libraries, colleges, museums, and bookstores—particularly the plucky independent bookstores, which often shower local writers with attention. Forums and symposia centered on poetry abound. The North Carolina Poetry Festival, held each summer since 1980 at Weymouth Center for the Arts & Humanities, continues under the sponsorship of the North Carolina Poetry Society as Sam Ragan Poetry Day, named for its founder.

That poetry has moved from the fringes and into the main warp-and-woof of our culture is evidenced by two North Carolina-based enterprises with similar names. Poetry Alive!, a theatrical group that specializes in readers' theater, not only carries its programs to colleges, schools, libraries, and other cultural centers throughout the nation, but sponsors a biennial poetry conference in its home city, Asheville. Meanwhile, WUNC-TV has produced not one, but two series of *Poetry Live*, a program of interview/readings featuring North Carolina poets.

In 1980 Ann Deagon, poet and professor at Guilford College, organized Poetry Center Southeast, a nonprofit agency to aid and promote writing. It provided impetus for the organization five years later of the North Carolina Writers' Network, with poet Robert Hill Long as its first director. After the inevitable struggle of any new organization, the Network, under the direction of Marsha Warren for the next nine years, flourished into a major resource center for writers and others interested in the state's literature, providing writing competitions, a bi-monthly newsletter, specialized workshops, and an annual conference with presentations on every subject from composing to marketing. Presently boasting over 1800 members, the Network, now directed by Linda Hobson, also oversees the North Carolina Literary Hall of Fame, sited at the Weymouth Center for the Arts &

Humanities. Thus far, of the twenty-one writers who have been inducted, six are primarily poets and the work of two others includes distinguished poetry.

Like the population of the country, the population of poets in the state is more and more diverse. Migration both in and out of state continues: North Carolina has gained poets such as Julie Suk, Michael Chitwood, and Stephen Smith, while natives such as Earl Braggs and R. T. Smith pursue their careers elsewhere. More and more poetry is emerging from the African-American community, and writers from other ethnic groups — Hispanic, Asian, and Native-American — are beginning to make themselves known. An especially noteworthy development is the organization of the Carolina African American Writers' Collective, founded and directed by Lenard Moore in 1992. At monthly meetings, members critique one another's works and study marketing and contemporary literature. Moore's monthly newsletter provides marketing suggestions and announcements of special events. By 1998 many of the 35 members had published poems in anthologies and journals and read at literary festivals.

Most notable is the increase in women poets. If this sampling is typical, women have become dominant in numbers, accounting for forty-five of the seventy-six poets included in this section. Several have won major publishing awards, and in 1997, Sarah Lindsay was a finalist for the National Book Award. Although many of these women address gender-specific issues, none would be characterized as simply feminist poets; their interests are far too broad.

As to the nature of the verse being written today, here at the end of the century we see no startling changes such as were apparent in earlier years. Yes, experiments continue in both form and content, although even when Black Mountain College enjoyed its strongest influence, North Carolinians were not generally members of any avant-garde. In content we find still more autobiographical poetry, satire, and social protest. Language continues to echo everyday speech. One of the most notable trends is a move back to rhyme, including slant rhyme, and form — both traditional (Carolyn Beard Whitlow's "Book of Ruth" and Michael McFee's "Phantoum") and self-designed (Steve Lautermilch's "The Canticle of the Skeleton" and Debra Kaufman's "Dialogue Concerning a Blue Convertible.")

Of the 138 writers included in this collection, 122 are still alive and actively writing and/or serving the literary community — a vibrant community indeed.

*Julie Suk*

## Waiting for the Storyteller

Once more we wait for the storyteller
to step into the margin and reveal intentions:
why the first letter flowered,
spiralling down the page with intricate designs,
the hand translating what the tongue began.

Clues drop, mostly forgotten,
so on and so on stacked like bricks,
crumbling when we look back,
a voice once close now a stranger.

All through the book we wild-guess the villain,
so deceived by this one or that
we look for reprieve, a surprise ending,
the page turning to a house in the woods,
dogs locked up, gun put away.

In the still forest of words,
where the hidden appears in its season,
hills darken and move in.
Like lean horses that have rocked a long way home,
they circle the pool of our hands.
A deer riffles through leaves, then a bird
sings *begin again, begin again.*

## Sitting Out a War Once Removed

It stormed a lot that summer—
brute cloudbursts, pane-rattling thunder.
Open the front door and a bolt might rip
the length of a hall.

It was days of card games,
a battery of rain at the window.

The weeks racked up a list of disasters:
strikes on the golf course,
drownings by undertow.

A man on our block took to his boat
and never returned,
but the war took most,
bit by bit someone,
no one, we knew,
the way ants peel away from remains,
hauling off piecemeal
legs, thorax, wings.

We were left wings, oak leaves, stars,
and a box of photos—a gallery
of uniformed figures in knocked out places
we could only conjure from books.

Villagers, flowers, ruddy cheeks—
what did we know?

Caught in the steady drizzle of our lives,
we hardly looked up from the game
of high-card-take-all.


## La Dolce Vita

The woman steps down from the bus
into a swarm of paparazzi,
a new dress under her arm,
not a cloud smearing the sky.
She has yet to learn
her children and husband are dead.
Murder.  Suicide.

Story after story, the same
sun-bathed day,
muted guns at the border,
women berry-picking in a field near town.
*I gave my love a willow sprig* they sing.

A few kilometers away, the enemy
slips through the forest.

Say happiness is suspect,
reason enough to knock on wood
before the axe swings.
Barbed questions catch us
trying to escape.
Were the women left sprawled
across rows of blood?
Were the children asleep
when the father raised his gun?

Say we're incapable of certain acts.
Say it again.

Boxcars rattle through the countryside,
crammed with the fear
that this is not just a change of camps.
The pitch night swells with screams,
the ground between trees
strewn with owl pellets,
those indigestible remains
of lives swallowed whole.

*Thomas R. Hawkins*

## The Yankee King

Far from the diamond of life,
the arc of a deep centerfield hit,
fouled, walked into doldrums of neglect
where you once took soaring crowds
around baseline ecstasy,
now you dodder helplessly drunk
trying to find your restaurant table.

For those made perfect, plain life plays a travesty.
No tribe hangs by the million radios on every play
as dust flies from the plate.
No hush strangles the air as you swipe
with swordstroke practice swings.
No cymbal rings as your tobacco quid
hits the sod.

No chain of boys sanctifies your shadow
in this tomb of ordinary life.
The lordly powers of your impassivity
now echo in the maw of stadium void.

You can't hit this darkness.
You play this night game without lights.
The hide laced around the ball is your own.

For a sport played on flat ground
who'd have thought to fall so far?
Money is a lesser game for lesser men,
 a surrogate for the holy innocence
of sport, extended immortal boyhood joy.

Drunk enough you still round homerun bases
and the stands' Greek chorus roars and roars,
every heart and face your loving own.

So gloat, you men who've settled life on kinder terms,
who enjoy whatever success might bring.
Feast then on the disaster glory can exact.

How many others arouse such meditations?
Who else's staggering mirrors destiny more?
A mortal hero struck by time's lightning pitches,
out.

## Hospital Ship:  Cua Viet

the shell had dressed him out like October
venison, left for dying five tropic days,
small in the bandages we unwrapped
as a runover cat, and we hunted the end
of intestine that should have been clipped
    to the edge of the wound.
a nice guy from Nebraska, cheerful and polite.
we scooped out maggots with a spoon.

*Stephen Smith*

## How the River Took Daughtry McLamb

A cloud shadow came dark over the water
& Daughtry was gone

along with that paint-manged rowboat
he bought for fishing in the summer
of '54. I recall how he scraped & sanded
& caulked & finally in mid-river
went down in one minute. Baskin Cole
& I watched from the Peachbottom Bridge
as the current took him away, his
hands gripping the gunnels, his scared-
pale face blurring the sycamores
that shaded Crains Point.
Then that cloud shadow came over
the water & he was gone.
Quick as that.

They crated Daughtry up in a cedar box
& at the Peachbottom Baptist Church
we lowered him down into that sweet-Jesus
earth. It wasn't two days later Hazel
came through & that river went into
the graveyard & took Daughtry again.
But this time we didn't find him.
No box or nothing. At Crains Point we
searched among the toppled sycamores
& found a few drowned cats, a hen house,
a bloated sow or two. But no Daughtry McLamb.

He'd gone off down the river
to wherever it goes.

## The 1950s

To know how it was in the fifties
go to the nearest pay phone,
deposit a dime
and call home when you know
no one is there.

While the phone is ringing,
shut your eyes and imagine
at the other end of the line
daffodils and sunlight
(it is always a spring morning
in the fifties).

Recall whatever pleases you:
pineapple upside down cake,
Rosemary Clooney, Glass Wax,
a blue checkered tablecloth,
Almond Roca, HaloLights,
Gunther Beer, I Like Ike
buttons, Pablum, Ann Blyth,
tangerines—

but you must allow the phone
to ring for ten years.
When no one answers,
you'll know you've dialed
the right number.

## Whatever There Was to Say

*A sky the pallor of hands folded in a casket.*

You are driving south on Church Street this November
afternoon, and as you approach a railway crossing,
you notice a family, or what you believe
to be a family, walking the road—a man, a woman,
a boy, and a small girl, who is maybe eight.
The girl wears a blue print dress and is barefoot
in this late chill. And because the sky is the gray

of your grandmother's hands, you recall how that
old woman embraced you years ago as you sat in the
Avalon Theatre watching the movie news, the face
of a shivering child, a girl about the age of this
small girl, waiting beside a death camp railway.
Your grandmother put her arms around you there in
the darkness and you were embarrassed, felt awkward:
an old woman clinging to you, a child of eight,
in a crowded theatre. But your grandmother is a long
time dead and you have come to understand that shoeless
children are, these days, simply shoeless children:
you've see so many and so much worse.

Yet there is something about this family,
this child, her straight yellow hair cut
at such a ragged angle, the thin face, eyes set
deep in shadow. And her brother in a green cap,
her father, tight-waisted in blue trousers,
the mother in a heavy, white-flecked overcoat.
They carry plastic bags filled with aluminum cans
gathered from the roadsides and ditches. And haven't
you seen these very faces in photographs of Jews,
Gypsies, Poles, eyes blank with resignation, fatigue,
awaiting the gas chamber, clutching their belongings—
as if those few scraps of cloth could be of some value
where they were going? You wonder about this family,
wonder if the future of this small girl is as clear
as the past in photographs. Wonder how these church
steeples dare to rise straight into the smoky skies
of this most terrible of centuries. How neatly they
weave themselves among the bare branches of oak and
sycamore! And haven't you finally come to understand
that whatever there was to say cannot be said?
Which is probably what your grandmother was telling
you in the darkness of that long ago matinee
when she held you hard against her as you watched
that child shivering beside the death camp railway.
Remember how you tried to pull away and how she held
on tight as if that simple, desperate gesture
might make a difference in such a world?

*Marie Gilbert*

## On Watching Challenger
*January 28, 1986*

The crew of seven seeks
the ultimate stretch
out beyond the strings of Earth

to find whatever waits
for man's bringing home
to pyramid science.

Half the State of Florida stands
face up on a clear, cold morning
to watch in animal numbness

as awesome surge of red
bleeds orange
colorless

a cloud of vapor
grows long fingers that grasp
for Earth in the habit of gravity.

Inch of bone, shred of sock wash ashore
dredges haul debris from ocean depth —
outgrown shell discarded.

The cloud of vapor floats free
in pure space beyond tomorrow.

*Jeffery Beam*

## Snake in Autumn

I could have stood there
                                    until
                  the creek dried up.
Coiling
                  and uncoiling. I
was that happy and that
                                    terrified.


                  The snake silent.

The coiling and uncoiling.
                                    Silent.
Both blessed and troubled—
                                    I
radiant in my
                  red and blue heats
                  before him.

The yellow came from him.
                  A golden mesmerizing eye.
Between us
                  the creek flowing.
Coiling and un-
                  coiling.

*Grace DiSanto*

## The Eye Is Single
*(For Mother, July 1, 1896–August 28, 1977)*

1.  Mother
I want you young
when
your flesh was unused
tissue,
your eyes Balinese bells
your hair crackled
wheat
and your mouth spilling
merlin—magic, kings and knights,
queens and wizards, fairies
and elves.
Mother I want the time
we both thought death
a unicorn.

2.
Mother, my eyes quiver,
my heart stares.
Like an umbrella
death stays a net
above your head.

*Shirley Moody*

## A Whole Different Spin on the Ball

There are perhaps only two or three times
in a lifetime
when we leave our nice warm beds
thinking nothing in particular
then suddenly
the old patterns crack like aged leaves,
the balloonman in the sky rattles his strings
and we discover ourselves
in clover by a juggled moon,
the mist almost thinned to transparent
like close looking at things,
the squawks of geese scattered
like spray against a slippery rock,
and we find ourselves
reborn in an unexpected world.

## Women on the Pamlico

Waters flow around and under the newly-boarded piers,
sweet-scented rafts of floating dreams.
The river, like many blue-green chiffon scarves
smoothed and drying across a mirror; thin,
threadbare patches releasing shiny glints like mica.

With private witching-wands seeking
separate river secrets, we gather like lost
messages in bottles, corked tight and bobbing
amid the calling gulls—those wise-winged fishers
perched and watching on pilings, above teasing
silver sinkers of light that pull us gently,
gently tempt us into many dappled reflections.

*Mary Snotherly*

### Birthright: To Catch the Light

Married at twelve,
mother at thirteen,
she made her mark with an *x*
and never read
about crippled Laura Wingfield
living in that zoo-like dream
with all those tiny shining animals,
and never got close
to that chill darkness
swelling the nave, every cloister
at Westminster Abbey,
King Arthur flickering tall there
in stained glass glory, Candlemas,
cloisonné vases at the altar
holding scarlet Canna lilies,
to the Crown Jewels—

but she lined those jars and bottles
across her kitchen window sill,
all colors, shapes and sizes,
washed those dust-catchers once a week
in hot soapy water,
dried them, set them back—
watched for that certain moment
winter afternoons
when sun struck.

*Agnes McDonald*

## Text

For no reason, we are getting into
a small boat, off a vessel we were never sure why
we were on in the first place,
going some place of importance
we were never made aware of, from some
other place we had never been.

We are dropped weightless from stars
into some life we never knew we owned.
Or are found crawling half-clad and ragged
at the center of a frozen pond in snow
where nothing waits but the very thing
we need most.

We read our lives wherever we can,
even the sad or long or badly written.
A sudden turn of the head is all
it takes to miss what we might
spend the rest of it,
looking for.

*Margaret Boothe Baddour*

## What Color Is the Sun?

My mother was an ash blonde
too smart for flowers.

But in the spring
we carried armfuls
gold-bursts of forsythia
and puffs of baby's breath
up the long drive

Clipped the stems
with neat scissors
for oriental arrangements
and in a house so dark
it echoed
there were always yellow flowers.

One springtime
she stooped
lithe and blonde
picked a daffodil
spoke clearly in my dream mind
of a daffodil's bright life
and withering death.

My mother
smarter than flowers
went up in flames
returned to yellow ashes.
What color, what color
is the sun?

*Peter Makuck*

## After

In the low afternoon light,
a row of cottonwoods led us out of Santa Cruz,
a small cemetery off in the desert.

That day, a few days before Christmas,
your father in front with me, I kept seeing your mom
not there in the back beside you

and him, as I drove, stare through
the passing mesquite to some other place perhaps,
silence enforcing a distance.

Lame, he had held my arm,
looked down at the unhealed turf, then crossed himself,
thin shoulders quaking. I looked

beyond the wall, across
the creosote flats, and watched a coyote drag something
limp toward a culvert.

Back in the car, I kept seeing,
tethered to stones, all those mylar balloons—"Feliz Navidad"
or "Te quiero" in the shape of a heart—

emblems of another culture,
telling us how far from home we were, the balloons
tormented in the desert wind.

Before houses again rose up
and the lights of Phoenix hid a perfect indigo sky
where stars began to glimmer,

we stopped at a crossroads light,
emptiness everywhere but this rancho of cracked adobe,
chickens and a single goat.

In front of the corral,
a Mexican sat on a kitchen chair, his face tipped back
and bronzed like a mask.

We watched a young woman
trim his hair, then lean down for a whisper and a kiss,
their faces wrinkled with laughter,

making me ease the car ahead
to center and frame them in the open gate at our side,
while we waited for the light.

Your father turned
and watched them too, and though his face was shadowed,
I saw his features tighten and focus.

After the woman ran her fingers
through her husband's long dark hair and trimmed again,
your father closed his eyes and smiled.

Their voices came inside
but they never looked our way as we watched, oblivious
as a family photo

finished by a boy in a red bandana
entering from the right, chasing a black chicken
and making it fly.

Before we left that crossroads
with whatever it was we needed, the light went green
two or three times, I think.

## Dogwood Again

Home from college, I'd leave my reading,
climb the hill through trees behind the house,
listen to a rough wind suffer through
new leaves and, too aware of myself, ask why?

The answer could have been *stone wall,*
*wind* or some other words. In April, our house
lived in the light of those first white petals
and now I think more about hows than whys—

how, whenever we fished at Pond Meadow,
my father dug a small one up, carefully
wrapped the rootball in burlap, and trucked it
home until our yard blazed white all around,

and how, at Easter, those nighttime blossoms
seemed like hundreds of fluttering white wings.
Again that tree goes into the dark loaded
with envy, those leaves full of light not fading.

And this morning, a fogbright air presses
against the blank white pane and would have us
see the way mist burns from within, shimmers,
slowly parts, and flares upon an even whiter tree,

tinged now with orange, and how a soft fire
runs to the farthest cluster of cross-like petals,
each haloed with clear air, finely revealed.

*Bruce Piephoff*

## Honky Tonk Stradivarius

The name he gives is 'Sea Dog'
as he hoists to his chest an ole Martin D-28
like an ancient weathered Stradivarius found in a bar.
Pick guard ripped away, names carved into the spruce top,
mahogany & rosewood back…"Waylon Jennings, '72!"
Toes tap & fingers dance like ballerinas in a quadrille,
¾ time across the steel strings;
words come rushing, magical winged messengers
to keep away the dark.
News of St. Valentine's—tangerine and eiderdown,
wooden soldiers driving back the "bogey men,"
protecting babes in Toyland,
cheering up the lost
& slaves in shades on cloudy days.
The minstrel has built a fortress
against seedy trappings; arcade junk furnishings
in a gaudy nightmarish world.
His songs—like cathedrals made of popsicle sticks
by old men with broken teeth in jail—to combat the boredom.
A wall of noise roars back
yet the minstrel plays on;
his joy—the power of flowers,
black pearls in the gutter.

*Mary Kratt*

## A Memory Not Quite Abandoned

Wrung from my silent wandering
a ringing churchbell tilts me back:
hoisted from the bare oak floor
father helps me reach and pull the bellcord
hard and heavy as a muscled arm
then lifts me to a quiet swinging
sound surrounded
could I have caused
the ringing that calls out to countryside
                come    come
all these years I have been listening
                come    come
for bells to ring me home
to something larger than a sound
a skylight opened to the past
like sharp intake of woodsmoked winter air.

## Of Mother and Father

I call you early sometimes to tell you
anything. At eight o'clock you stand
in your slippers, the pink robe
you'll not throw away, a woman who collects rocks
from Walden, Rio and Rome, who still remembers
Latin endings. And how Father makes a list each morning,
not too long, not too short. In January
with seed catalogs, his mental ground ready,
weather is his eye. There are few earth places
he could not make do. I learn the memory,
how we three buried your son, my brother.
What could be hard after those long nights?
I am used to you: two familiar trees
I see far in the distance.
Like an only child now in the best room
in the house, I forget to say the good things.

*Stephen Knauth*

## The Runner

We are always merely passing by
when sorrow, the dark lily, blooms.
Around the flower, a broken halo of faces, figures.

The crooked hands of my father are folded there,
hands that gripped my head each Sunday,
combing my hair like a farmer plowing uphill,

his silence flowing in heavy currents
down the back of my shirt. When he died
I sealed his eyes with a kiss.

He would have preferred a salute
from across the field, distant shotguns of farewell.
I can hear them playing clearly now,

the orchestras of the Second World War,
the June bugs beating the screens of the florida room
where we sat together that long last evening,

fogged in, less by the weather
than the years of misalignment. An old story
written into ruin: father & son,

the proven design,
like opposing strides of a runner
passing in a blur toward the same destination,

like the staggered branches of these sad inscrutable pines.

*Mab Segrest*

## Winter's Secrets

I have wanted
winter's secrets:
what the tree leaves
the limbs to know
against an open sky

what the snow covers
why red suns glow
at moonrise
I want a share
in the reflection

you moon who climbs
the paling sky
o spill my roof
my gutters freeze
with moonbeams.

## Grandfather's Mandolin

A fugue of teak and pine
mahogany, rosewood
and from the rosewood
blossoms, mother-of-pearl,
twined down its neck
and over frets
like ivory trellises

and when he played,
his fingers plucked the roses.

*Harriet Doar*

## Cats at Twilight

*All cats are gray in the dark*

visible, secretive
hungry
they disappear at twilight
gray into gray
ghost into mist

materialize
at dawn
familiar, full, domestic
self-satisfied and round as rolls
set warm to rise

hearth-sleepers
baking slowly like good bread.

## Around the Block

Dark streets, or lighted streets; it does not matter.
Lighted windows behind which people must be
Happier than you. The stars burn fiercely
And move in orderly fashion; if one would shatter
That one would be you. But it does not matter.

Move down the street; speculate on the houses
Where the light turns on and off. It is pretense
To assume in light and dark no difference.
Darkness is kinder; light points to you, arouses
Fear in you. Speculate on the houses.

Memorize the night. Remember the lonely
Pattern of lighted window and dark; the print
Of barely moving leaves that the lamp has lent
To the wall; the austere stars that are only
A little farther than these.   Remember them, lonely.

*Michael McFee*

## Shooting Baskets at Dusk

He will never be happier than this,
lost in the perfectly thoughtless motion
of shot, rebound, dribble, shot,

his mind removed as the gossipy swallows
that pick and roll, that give and go
down the school chimney like smoke in reverse

as he shoots, rebounds, dribbles, shoots,
the brick wall giving the dribble back
to his body beginning another run

from foul line, corner, left of the key,
the jealous rim guarding its fickle net
as he shoots, rebounds, dribbles, shoots,

absorbed in the rhythm that seems to flow
from his fingertips to the winded sky
and back again to this lonely orbit

of shot, rebound, dribble, shot,
until he is just a shadow and a sound
though the ball still burns in his vanished hands.

## Cold Quilt

Our clear-eyed guide said it is the slick
cotton that makes quilts cold. I wonder
if it isn't the enduring dowry of bitterness
stitched into them that makes us shiver,
as in that quilt (unfit for hanging) handed
down to me from my father's mother, begun
the day her husband died, a lifelong lament

composed of old suits and shirts he'd worn,
threaded to her leftover dresses, its design—

each pane a basket of memorial flowers,
a dozen loud triangles tipped on their sides—
a stiff pastiche of grief and the solitary
nights spent trying to transform their bad luck
into something useful, used. No busy bee

touched that quilt. Her life became a patchwork
of quilted plenty, her backyard a dormitory
of vegetable beds, her table a dazzling pattern
of cakes and pies. But she stayed skinny
and wrapped herself in the plain handmade cocoon
of that death-quilt every night, even when
she began to fade in her children's spare beds.

At the funeral home, my uncle the soldier
draped her coffin with it, prayed, then handed
that life's flag to me, compactly folded, her
crooked stitches and nearly-rotten panes still
tenacious after half a century, the sheep
I count now in the inherited dark, her cold quilt
a poultice I spread on my chest before sleep.

## Phantoum

Where are the phantom words that got away,
the ones I knew I'd never see again,
the ones I thought would change my life
with a little more luck and a lot more time?

The ones I knew I'd never see again
wait like huge fish just below the surface.
With a little more luck and a lot more time,
they would've fed a grateful multitude.

---

* In the *pantoum* (a rhymed Malayan verse form) lines two and four of each stanza
are repeated as lines one and three of the subsequent quatrain; the final stanza again
repeats lines one and three of the first stanza.

Wait! Like huge fish just below the surface,
perfect words tease the end of this line:
they would've fed a grateful multitude,
but now they're gone, a ghostly cryptogram.

Perfect words tease the end of this line.
If only I'd been more patient, or maybe less!
But now they're gone, a ghostly cryptogram
never to be deciphered in this world.

If only I'd been more patient, or maybe less . . .
Plato thought all reality was phantom,
never to be deciphered in this world.
There's an aching where something used to be.

Plato thought all reality was phantom.
Is he the hunched figure stealing my words?
There's an aching where something used to be,
an amputated phrase, a friend, a father—

is he the hunched figure stealing my words,
the ones I thought would change my life?
An amputated phrase, a friend, a father—
where are the phantom worlds that got away?

*Jaki Shelton Green*

## things break down

things break down in different ways
like love
it's been ten years since
i've been thin
things break down in different ways
like the absence of his smile
things break down in different ways
like the meadows of the skin
apples spoil
meat rots
aspirin takes care of toothache but
things break down in different ways
like the last time he praised my art
stood in my mirror
things break down in different ways
like sunday morning blues
getting sung out at the altar
i said things break down
in different ways
like my clock stopping
one morning at 3 a.m.
he crashed his car into the river
things break down
     his toothbrush is still
beside the mirror

## praise song

You woman tree woman one
swaying to unheard of winds uninvented air streams
you woman sky with palms broad enough to hold egypt
who taught me to walk
slow and deliberate
like i had somewhere to go
who taught me stories
that needed telling

to love men and women who needed
who taught me to fetch life
out of the depths of rivers
taught me the words
that the tree branches sang to wake
the sun and bring morning home
who taught me to love loving
with my eyes wide open
who taught me to dance and smile
in rhythm
to clap with an open heart

## the griot's song

this man on the edge of the sun
speaking with truth-laced tongues
calls my name
he is the one who met me
in the dust storm
i was riding on the wind
into the mountains when i
heard his shadow
scream
suddenly canyons grew out of rivers
and the sunlight
    became a throb
    a drum beat
the veins in his heart
    dusty but full of fire
gave shadow to the new sun

*Rudy Wallace*

## Woman in a Red Dress

To get down that deep to the earth's center
To find that fire color, to descend in a mining shaft
Elevator, hard hatted, with a battery lamp beam
Leading the way, and the air so scarce it feels like
Somebody pinching your nose, and you're mouth-breathing,
Coughing, from the dirt you're swallowing.
Is that how you got that
Earth-core red?

Unless you had one of those science fiction,
Space age, state-of-the-art mole-machines
That can dive through earth like a submarine.
Anyway, I know you didn't dig thousands of miles under
With pick and shovel to shop for that
Earth-core red.

And when you dyed the cloth and made a dress
With that crimson from the earth's volcanic crust,
Why did you not use it to caress your figure
In your house, washing your family's dirty clothes,
Or to scale and gut fish, or scrub floors?
Though not to climb a kenip tree
In the name of decency.
That would have to be
In short shorts, but still the dreaded
Earth-core red.

Instead, you traipse up and down Main Street
In that infernal frock, a total pyromaniac,
Heating up and scorching, and blinding folks without
Sunglasses, who did not look away in time.
Behind the dark of tinted windows in a parked car,
I watched, and that's how I was spared from your
Earth-core red.

Red is hot and full of action,
Full of passion
And aflame with love,
Especially, earth-core red, on you,
Like fire on fire
Like two suns burning.

*Charles Fort*

## Prose Poem for Claire Aubin Fort
*January 7, 3:23 a.m., 1985*

Winter brings my wife a child, and your birth arrives
with the morning tide like wings alive in a jar. The
sunflower seeds and thorns bloom in your hands, Claire,
and we walk in the mist and draw circles in the sand.
I read your palms like a map, and there are small islands
and mountain roads rising in your summer eyes. Is my daughter
the dancer, actor, artist, gifted in language or song? I
search the form and proper length to write one impossible verse
to place into your hand. The unspoken metaphor falls like a
meteor into this simple throne of time I have built for you, and
your birth arrives with the morning tide like wings alive in a jar.

## For Martin Luther King
*In Memoriam, April 9, 1968*

Black swans with wings
draped over their eyes
move across a wooden bridge
and flourish in their song.
The freedom riders crawl
into America's backyard blues
against a stout sheriff and water hose.
They march with arms attending arms
toward foes with their empty hands.
They push their fingers
into the soil, and brush over
the brow and mouth of Martin's mask.
America, does it take a stagecoach
ambulance, moist engine of fear,
to call out his name?

*Nancy Simpson*

## Night Student

It is the first shooting star my eyes have seen
breaking blackness above the university parking lot.
I am impressed with Jones,
the spectacular mark he made on my paper.
I have it beside me two hours from home.

Truth is up there over the steering wheel,
keeping up, 60 mph on Franklin By-Pass.
Socrates said so. I would like to ask
the Know-It-All what makes stars break.

I drive slow on Standing Indian Mountain
and count the times Jones asked in class,
*Is it logically consistent?* Ten.
On the radio, static reception,
Linda Ronstadt is singing about a broken lady
waiting to be mended.

I see my face in the rear view mirror,
not a wife anymore, not a mother,
a thirty-eight-year-old freshman
chewing leftover cheese crackers
that crumble on my fingers, star showers
into the floorboard.

What was it I saw up there, white against black,
like white hairs in brunette,
like the white line on pavement?

What is it at two minutes past twelve,
this funnel cloud in me, this song of Forsythia
makes me stop my car at Shooting Creek
to search in space above trees
where headlights do not reach?

Star, one cut with your sword,
you have sliced the night open for me.

*Shirley Anders*

## The Words

Only when it is very quiet do they creep out
from the brush, from their fur-walled wombs,
come close, rest hands on our knees,
trust us. If we have waited, not in blinds,
wearing no camouflage, bearing
no arms, then they may
rouse, knuckle sleep's crystal residue
from their eyes, blink
in the soft dark, and come
by twos and sevens, bring
strands for us to knit. One small chorus
murmurs "Once on a hovel by the Irish sea,"
another "Always he waked in the night,
cold" ; a third, "She remembered
that she had been touched here,
and here." If, like Odysseus, we pour blood
on the earth at the mouth
of their lair, where we saw them last,
they may stumble out, touch lips to soil,
drink. If they do,
we will be their servants.

*Joseph Bathanti*

## Sneedsborough

*In the sweat of thy face shalt thou eat bread, till*
*thou return unto the ground; for out of it wast thou taken:*
*for dust thou art, and unto dust shalt thou return."*
                                        —Genesis 3:19

There is no traffic on 1829
north of Whortleberry Creek;
no tracks on the path leading into Sneedsborough,
made legend by fever and bad seed.
A phantom sun sluices through pine
and jacklegged balsams
spare as Confederate infantry
the year Kilpatrick torched the ghost town
timbers and left the flames
to the Pee Dee flood tide.
The cemetery is all that's left of the town.
Seven tombs and a black stone wall
are the only architecture:
the Johnsons, the Pearsons;
and, in a row under cracked granite
slabs and ponderous epitaphs—
each dead at 33—the Harris brothers
and John Hixson, a Canadian.
In this clearing,
prior to these bones and periwinkle,
letters were posted and men loved women;
wayfarers laid down at the Knox Inn
and dreamt of the future.
Genesis was read Ash Wednesdays
with wild promise, sackcloth donned
and gray hair plucked.
Nearly two hundred years ago.
This is all we can know
of their disappearance.

*R. S. Gwynn*

## Body Bags

### I

Let's hear it for Dwayne Coburn, who was small
And mean without a single saving grace
Except for stealing—home from second base
Or out of teammates' lockers, it was all
The same to Dwayne. The Pep Club candy sale,
However, proved his downfall. He was held
Briefly on various charges, then expelled
And given a choice: enlist or go to jail.

He finished basic and came home from Bragg
For Christmas on his reassignment leave
With one prize in his pack he thought unique,
Which went off prematurely New Year's Eve.
The student body got the folded flag
And flew it in his memory for a week.

### II

Good pulling guards were scarce in high school ball.
The ones who had the weight were usually slow
As lumber trucks. A scaled-down wild man, though,
Like Dennis "Wampus" Peterson, could haul
His ass around right end for me to slip
Behind his blocks. Played college ball a year—
Red-shirted when they yanked his scholarship
Because he majored, so he claimed, in Beer.

I saw him one last time. He'd added weight
Around the neck, used words like "grunt " and "slope,"
And said he'd swap his Harley and his dope
And both balls for a 4-F knee like mine.
This happened in the spring of '68.
He hanged himself in 1969.

### III

Jay Swinney did a great Roy Orbison
Impersonation once at Lyn-Rock Park,
Lip-synching to "It's Over" in his dark
Glasses beside the jukebox. He was one
Who'd want no better for an epitaph
Than he was good with girls and charmed them by
Opening his billfold to a photograph:
Big brother. The Marine. Who didn't die.

He comes to mind, years from that summer night,
In class for no good reason while I talk
About Thoreau's remark that one injustice
Makes prisoners of us all. The piece of chalk
Splinters and flakes in fragments as I write,
To settle in the tray, where all the dust is.

*Anna Wooten-Hawkins*

## Advice for Long Life

Keep simple, as simple as you can.
Like the heron who stands one leg on the sand.
Like the maple who stands one leg on the land.
Like the robin who, thirsty, gargles the worm.

The spider is simple if the web is not.
The tern is simple in a watery spot.
To be flexible, fluid, adored as a druid,
cryptic, mystic, blessed, lurid,
love simple as you can.

Plural by purpose, design, and make,
the effort to give is the urge to take.
Keep a hambone of joy at your right side.
Live broad, long, deep, wide,
but ride simple as you can.

Imitate wind and creep of dark—
as much as you can, the natural stark,
sun-driven crops and gradual shoat,
a frog spilling basso from a plum-blue throat
at river's edge. Be simple if you can.

*Evalyn Gill*

## Blue Ridge Parkway

We speed through Craggy Flats,
the tunnel's end of light dilates,
explodes to open sky.
A carnival of fall rolls by on either side,
parade of pheasant colors,
gold and apricot among rich darker greens.
And overhead sienna leaves
confetti the air like coins
showering wealth upon us.

We climb through Pisgah Forest
to Craggy Pinnacle.
Cloud mist floats in layers,
milky fog enveloping, receding.
We penetrate opaqueness,
hunt our way through muted brilliance.
November limbs are penciled charcoal
on a hazy scrim, autumn pattern
stenciled through gray void.
Scenes of blankness pique our sight,
evoke the spangled splash of pointillist,
suggest all height, all depth we ever knew.

*Carolyn Beard Whitlow*

## Rockin' a Man, Stone Blind

Cake in the oven, clothes out on the line,
Night wind blowin' against sweet, yellow thighs,
Two-eyed woman rockin' a man stone blind.

Man smell of honey, dark like coffee grind;
Countin' on his fingers since last July.
Cake in the oven, clothes out on the line.

Mister Jacobs say he be colorblind,
But got to tighten belts and loosen ties.
Two-eyed woman rockin' a man stone blind.

Winter becoming angry, rent behind.
Strapping spring sun needed to make mud pies.
Cake in the oven, clothes out on the line.

Looked in the mirror, Bessie's face I find.
I be so down low, my man be so high.
Two-eyed woman rockin' a man stone blind.

Policemans found him; damn near lost my mind.
Can't afford no flowers; can't even cry.
Cake in the oven, clothes out on the line.
Two-eyed woman rockin' a man stone blind.

## Book of Ruth

*Whither thou goest...*

I learn to live by guile, to do without love.
I'm not scared. I wait in the dark for you,
Sleeping to avoid death, tired of sleep.
    The withered dyed rug fades, dims, fades, recolors,
        Warp frayed, weft unraveled; as light looms dark,
I doubt I'm happy as can be in this house.

Outside no one would guess inside this house
I learn to live by guise, disguise my pain. Love
Dinner served by pyre light, sit doused by dark,
        Cornered in my room, wait in the dark for you.
        The bureau melts to shadow; that unraveled, uncolors.
Sleeping to avoid death, tired of sleep

        I avoid the mirror, the lie of truth. You sleep
Downstairs, chin lobbed over, chair rocked, spilled, house
Distilled in techtonic dreams of technicolor,
        Mostly golf course green and Triumph blue. I love
        Earthpots, cattails, a fireplace, no reflection of you.
While you sleep, I sip steeped ceremonial teas, dark

        As coffee, your swirled wineglass breathing dark
Downstairs fumes in the living dead room. Sleep
Comes easy, comes easy. I'm not scared. For you
        I curtsy before your mother, say I love this house.
        I love this house, this room. I love this. I love.
The traffic light blinks black and white. No color.

        Come Monday, I'll dustmop, repaper with multicolor
Prints, zigzag zebra stripe rooms, fuchsias, no dark
        Blue or somber gray, none of the colors that you love.
        Insomnia is sweet, I think, the once I cannot sleep:
        I'm not scared. I'm not scared. This is my house.
Illumined by darkness, I watch my dark mirror you.

        *No.* No silent hostage to the dark, I know you
Cast a giant shadow in a grim fairy tale, colors
        Bloodlet, blueblack, spineless yellow trim this house;
        Escaped maroon, I emerge from a chrysalined dark,
        Succumb, mesmered under a light spring-fed sleep,
Nightmare over, giddy, without sleep, with love.

        The colors of the room fade into dust, house now dark.
I'm not scared. I learn to live without you, with love,
        To do without sleeping to avoid death, tired of sleep.

*Kathryn Stripling Byer*

## Mountain Time

News travels slowly up here
in the mountains, our narrow
roads twisting for days, maybe years,
till we get where we're going,
if we ever do. Even if some lonesome message
should make it through Deep Gap
or the fastness of Thunderhead, we're not obliged
to believe it's true, are we? Consider
the famous poet, minding her post
at the Library of Congress, who
shrugged off the question of what we'd be
reading at century's end: "By the year 2000
nobody will be reading poems." Thus she
prophesied. End of that
interview! End of the world
as we know it. Yet, how can I fault
her despair, doing time as she was
in a crumbling Capitol, sirens
and gunfire the nights long, the Pentagon's
stockpile of weapons stacked higher
and higher? No wonder the books
stacked around her began to seem relics.
No wonder she dreamed her own bones
dug up years later, tagged in a museum somewhere
in the Midwest: American Poet—Extinct Species.

Up here in the mountains
we know what extinct means. We've seen
how our breath on a bitter night
fades like a ghost from the window glass.
We know the wolf's gone.
The panther. We've heard the old stories
run down, stutter out
into silence. Who knows where we're heading?
All roads seem to lead
to Millennium, dark roads with drop-offs
we can't plumb. It's time to be brought up short

now with the tale-tellers' *Listen*: There once lived
a woman named Delphia
who walked through these hills teaching children
to read. She was known as a quilter
whose hand never wearied, a mother
who raised up two daughters to pass on
her words like a strong chain of stitches.
Imagine her sitting among us,
her quick thimble moving along these lines
as if to hear every word striking true
as the stab of her needle through calico.
While prophets discourse about endings,
don't you think she'd tell us the world as we know it
keeps calling us back to beginnings?
This labor to make our words matter
is what any good quilter teaches.
A stitch in time, let's say.
A blind stitch
that clings to the edges
of what's left, the ripped
scraps and remnants, whatever
won't stop taking shape even though the whole
crazy quilt's falling to pieces.

## The Backwoods

*Great-grandmother* carried the cadence of Genesis.
Girl cousins up late at family reunions,
we made her an Indian, although her forebears
were Irish. Before her lay darkness, the empty fields
barren as desert until she came forward,
the sweat on her high cheekbones gleaming like eyes
we imagined surrounding her, bob-cat and red fox,
the last of the sleek, singing wolves. Every evening
she shouldered her hoe and walked home
through the tasselling corn. The Good Lord only knows
what bare feet stalked the backwoods in those days,
what waited behind every woodpile! She brought forth
a daughter with black hair that never curled.
Shy as a fieldmouse, that girl fell in love
with a man scything hay in the twilight. They kissed

twice. A moment she stood in her white dress
and smiled back at us, then she grew fat and sighed
in the kitchen. Four daughters she bore,
and the three who survived scarlet fever
wove grass in their brown hair and danced every night
with the fireflies. They galloped on wild horses
bareback until they got married and gave birth
to us, Southern Belles who could sit in a parlor
all evening and never complain. We could faint
in a handsome man's arms. We could charm
a stone wall. But we never forgot the back door,
how to disappear into the darkness, our crinolines rustling
like cornstalks between our legs. We told
this story so well, we inherit its black earth
where women hoe all night, inscrutable as Indians.

## Diamonds

*This*, he said, giving the hickory leaf
to me. *Because I am poor.*
And he lifted my hand to his lips,
kissed the fingers that might have worn
gold rings if he had inherited

bottomland, not this
impossible rock where the eagles soared
after the long rains were over. He stood
in the wet grass, his open hands empty,
his pockets turned inside out.

*Queen of the Meadow*, he teased me
and bowed like a gentleman.
I licked the diamonds off the green
tongue of the leaf, wanting only
that he fill his hands with my hair.

*R. T. Smith*

## Second Waking

Birdflash and birdsong
the morning after storm.
I can still hear the tornado's
freight train, see its lightning
in forsythia frenzy.
Black sticks littering the lawn,
overturned trash bins,
uproot, downfall, a scatter
of ripped tin. The dream
I was first stunned from—
was it midnight's billions
of milky stars extinguished,
the surge, a broken covenant
in the firs? Or was it
dawn's cardinal motionless
in the stripped willow,
that red catch-of-breath,
that stillness with no song?


## Vet

Afternoons Pete speaks to the birds
as they flock to his makeshift
feeders. Plastic milk jugs swing
from the hardwoods, and the yard
is alive with warning and song.
In the dust-feathery dark of his
den, he listens to their chatter
or talks to himself of nights
on watch in the North Sea, his
crystal radio tapped to a steel
guywire that brought Axis Sally
coldly into the shell of his ear.
No birdsong for months, for leagues;
he watched the waves, fascinated,

as he would stare for hours
at the strafed beach of Omaha, where
*The Herndon* was first in after
the landing craft. A mockingbird
stands on a low magnolia limb
baiting trespassers. Rival sparrows
scrabble for the wealth of seeds,
while Pete mutters of the black
ocean's cold. In memory, he swims
toward a receding shore, his old
nightmare of wolfpack, torpedo
planes diving, *his* war. He whistles
from the chair a veery's rich call,
then reaches for the radio dial,
but halts. Outside, does a fighter
tilt bright wings in a pilot's
salute to victory? "That Harper boy
was our first ace." He strokes
a worn flag's star, then sleeps.
Hawks ride the wind. Crows quarrel
with their past in the pines.

*Sally Buckner*

## Embroidery

After dark closed its door on a day
as predictable as a loaf of light bread,
with supper dishes, scoured and dried, assuming
their proper stations in the cabinet,
and all homework completed and approved,
we settled into the February night.
Daddy studied prospects for the Dodgers
while, snugly wrapped in flannel and chenille,
Sister and I huddled before the heatrola,
cherishing the reliable warmth it rumbled.

Perched directly under the ceiling light,
Mama firmed an oval of white muslin
across narrow wooden hoops. Squinting,
she threaded skeins of floss through wide-eyed needles,
then fashioned delicate rosy filaments
into graceful petals, coaxed pale green
to glossy leaves, persuaded gentian blue
to flight in the shape of songless birds.

Outside, beyond the wind's blowsy boast,
stars stitched their dazzle into night's black void.
Inside, on a stretched-taut field of cotton
as plainly vanilla as her hours,
Mama, armed with steel and pastel silk,
wrought a garden forever impervious
to late-March frosts, June's voracious beetles,
and the quenchless thirsts of August.

*Robert Hill Long*

## Piece by Piece

The war wasn't over, it was already lost. I grabbed
a thirty day leave, spent twenty-five tracking Julie:
we played chess in a Denver bar and the old days
ambushed me like the first rush of bad acid,
desire cramping my gut. Without meaning to,
a jukebox guitar amplified the month-old screams
of farmer-guerillas fried on our perimeter wire.
Then a beer got dumped on some recruit's shaved head
and the head bobbed through the violet smoke and laughter,
a peeled apple at a birthday party, but I ignored
the symptoms: nudging my queen's pawn to a safe white square,
I tried to recall the first time Julie and I made it
—Mount Tamalpais, sunrise, sunset?—
somebody launched a bottle against the jukebox.
"Run!" I shouted as sirens and red flares whirled closer
and I ran, everybody ran, but the soldier out front
exploded and when I came to, there was nothing
but a hand scratching at the roadside dirt
as if its final impulse was to bury itself.
And I remembered my orders: to pick up the pieces,
splint them, sedate them, suture them, stack them up.
Scooping the hand in a trashbag, I crawled back
to the other bodies. For the rest of my tour
I dreamed only two dreams: the first
was a fat Viet baby who sat waving at me,
the bloodless, blown-off hand in his hand;
the other was Julie, naked, knocking over my king
with her king, picking it up, knocking it over. . . .
Where have all the flowers gone? we sang,
grilling rainbow trout on green twigs in the Rockies;
daisy petals spilled from Julie's hair and in two days
I knelt by a palace pond in Hue to wash off
the confetti of bone and scalpeled flesh.
A dragontailed goldfish flickered to the surface,
inhaled each bit, and vanished in the scum.
The white king dangled between Julie's fingers
like a stubbed-out cigarette: I remember each move

she made, taking the game piece by piece.
After Saigon fell I signed on as an orderly
in a vets' hospital in Vermont. Between rounds
I traced Julie through the phone company
and when I found her voice it was winter,
an old ranch house in the Rockies. She was
renovating, had a beautiful little boy. She promised
to send me a few of his fingerpaintings
and a family snapshot. In the long pause
preceding the click of goodbye, I listened to the hiss
of snow falling on everything I couldn't say.

*Rebecca McClanahan*

# X

Summers over tic-tac-toe I crossed out
whole afternoons, slow to see
that X marks the place where victims fall
as well as buried treasure. Years later in school

I learned a blond hair from an Iowa woman
formed the cross-sight for Hiroshima.
When I questioned my father, he nodded
slightly, sadly, and kept on plotting

the quadrants of my algebra homework,
tracing for the third time that night
the puzzling intersection of x and y. *One
chromosome*, my friend is saying. *That's all it takes.*

We are sitting outside in old-fashioned
lawn chairs that press against the backs
of our thighs, forming an intricate latticework.
Inside the house, beneath the marionette strings

of a circus mobile, her baby sleeps,
his slanted eyes and dry fissured lips
linking him to thousands of genetic brothers,
and I think of childhood Bible schools,

the missionary banner — "Christ for the World" —
stretching from the wooden pulpit
to the earth's four corners. Once I stood
in four states at once. My mother still has the photo.

There I am, seven years old, splayed like a starfish:
a hand in Colorado, another in Utah, one leg each
in Arizona and New Mexico. Around us miles
of turquoise sky where, a hundred years before,

smoke from tepees rose. *Everything
an Indian does is in a circle*, the great
Sioux chief said. *Everything tries to be round.*
Documentary cameras were clicking. He stood

inside a square reservation house and pointed
to the corners, saying *That is why we died.*
My grandfather's last month was measured
in x's of the fence he hammered

on the farthest acre of his land, while upstairs
my grandmother collected x's in her lap,
canceling the empty muslin with thread and needle,
one stitch by one stitch, until a flower boomed.

## Teaching a Nephew to Type

Because you lag already
years behind the computer-and-
otherwise-literate boys with fathers,
and your handwriting is a tangle
the teachers have grown weary
of unraveling, and because you are as close
to a son as I can manage, though nothing
about you is manageable anymore,

I am teaching you to type. The trick
is to look anywhere but down.
Your fingers are dumb birds pecking,
just follow the chart I've made.
We'll begin in the thick of things,
the home row to which we'll always
return. Little finger on *a.* Then tap
your way next door to *s.* Now

you've made *as.* Don't think, I say.
Just watch the chart:  dad  sad  fad
a flash  a flask  a lad had.  Tomorrow
we'll move on to reach and return
and the period key, but for now
just use the comma, it's like catching
a breath, or you can type a colon,
double dot, old snake eyes, luck
in your future, meaning *watch this space:*
something is about to follow.

*Judy Goldman*

## Between Losses

There is a time between losses,
days with blank pages, when clapping
is permitted and singing and dancing,
even the kind of madness
that tells you to wear fireflies in your hair.
I am talking about the time
when no one is dying
and journeys are something to be planned for.
It is nothing like your dreams
which only remind you
of the strangeness of things,
I mean the dreams of the night,
not the dreams you are born with.
Sometimes it takes awhile
before you can say the names of the ones
who have left, before you can be sure
nobody else is thinking of turning away.

This morning you slide in beside me
and as I listen to you breathe
I think of our wedding
and the two young people
who ran down the steps of my parents' house.
We thought that day was a conclusion.
Nobody told us it was simply a time
between losses, when rice was something
to be held in the hand
before letting it fly for the camera.

*Lucinda Grey*

### Letter to No Address

Tonight
the trouble in your country
casts a shadow on the moon.
Your village no longer sleeps
peacefully at the foot of a mountain—
its name Meih Meih cries
through the olives.
Looters swarm the streets.
In what was your house,
a boy, perhaps, plays
the music box you left
and finds it out of tune
to his ear.
He burns the house
and all the foreign connections.

And so the days of war
follow each other like brothers;
the wail of weeping women
floods the sated air.
Wherever
neighbor turns on neighbor,
children stare from rubble—
surprised by nothing.
Your eyes, warm as honey,
have seen what I can only dread.
Months ago
when you wrote,
you described a boy
putting down his gun
to chase butterflies.
Last night I dreamed
we hid together in a crypt.
Where else could you hide last night
if you are still alive?

*Alan Shapiro*

## Mud Dancing
### —*Woodstock, 1969*

Anonymous as steam, in the steam teased
from the mud-hole at the field's edge
where we were gathered, the unhallowed dead,

the herded up, the poured out like water,
grew curious about us—naked as they were
once, our numbers so like theirs,

and the air, too, a familiar newsreel
dusk of rain all afternoon.
It could almost have been themselves

they saw, except that we were dancing
knee deep in mud, in the muddy
gestures of their degradation,

unpoliced and under no one's orders
but the wiry twang and thump
we danced to, sang to, yowling

on all fours, hooting on backs and bellies,
smearing black lather over our own,
each other's face, arms, hip

and crotch till we were sexless, placeless,
the whole damp mesh of who we were that made us
strangers to each other, the shalts and shalt

nots of you and me, mine and not yours,
cast off easily as clothing
into the blurred shapes of a single fluency.

Was this some new phase of their affliction?
The effect of yet some new device—
to make them go on dreaming, even now,

some version of themselves so long accustomed
to their torment that they confused
torment with exaltation, mud with light?

*Frau History, they asked, is this the final
reaving of what we loved well, that we should
swarm now in the steam over the indistinguishable*

*garments scattered everywhere in piles, that
we should need, even now, to sort through them,
to try to lift in our vaporous hands*

*the immovable rough granite
of this sleeve or collar, that vest,
those sandals, the flimsiest top?*

## Turn

Speech is the candle here — see the dark made mobile
now about its tongue, the gathering dark of voices
earlier than ours, and others still earlier, voice
ringed on voice out to the first rough filial hue and cry.
Here, we say, I'm here, turn to me now. Who is it speaking
in the circling namelessness? By whose breath is the flame fanned?
Speech is the candle I hold up to see you
and the night bent down to cup us in its giant hand.

*Isabel Zuber*

## For her

he cut locust poles
   in the woods,
    peeled, notched,
    joined and set them
    as an arbor,
planted a vine
   of pink grapes
   that she loved,
helped with the windows,
   she on the inside,
   he out, wiping spots,
smiled at her
   through shining glass,
brought her whatever
   he found strange or
   lovely—the first
   dandelion, a snail
   shell, whispering
   grasses' ears, bird's
   specked egg, a clear
   fine shaped stone—
fixed breakfast,
stayed near seventy years.

*Mary Belle Campbell*

## Pine Lake at Twilight
*Whispering Pines, NC 1975*

In the afterglow of February sundown
I hear the honking of two migrating ducks
over-flying our home—
fore-flyers of the flocks to come.

They swoop down over the pine-rimmed lake,
land on water, join the wintering mallards,
the pintails and widgeons feeding here
on the corn we spread at water's edge.

The air tonight is soft as the lapping water,
sweet with songs of indefinable
pre-spring waking, quiet as the maples
lining the inlet to the pine-rimmed lake,

their branches reddening, swelling to liven
with starbursts of strange red-brown
tree flowers. Something of last year's
dying is in the air, swelling to ripen anew.

Even as we do. We go from one year,
one love, one life, to another,
knowing spring will unfold us, summer
fly us, autumn flay us, till our veins

burst with longing to understand,
and we drop down—to lie with mosses
and fungi—under layers of leaves,
flexing our muscles on stone.

*Becky Gould Gibson*

## Putting Up Damson Preserves

You were right. I've never seen
such fruit, knobs the size of a man's thumb
clustered blue on every branch.
That old scrawny-necked tree shawled
in lichen lace I thought dead
you brought back, spread manure under
every spring till you died. Each year
it yields a few more pints. Your daughters
are grown, your sons have taken your place.

That's Marie at the sink seeding plums,
splitting each one along the crease.
You watched me watching the fruit,
taking it down to its sweetness.
You liked to lick foam from the spoon,
recalling the color of the dance dress
I wore in those cleaned out rooms.
But I'm not the girl you knew, nor
the woman either, here in the kitchen
with you gone off like steam.

Where your hands went I'm still smooth.
When you first came to me in the dark
I was scared, then you brought me close,
I thought I would fall, but where
you took me I could not fall enough—
split, unseeded, beyond blue to purple,
black, back to white, fruit to flower,
bee, beginning of the world.

Now I keep summer in jars, shelved
for pale winter tongues.
Sometimes I take one down, taste
the blue sweet all over again.

*Earl S. Braggs*

## I'll be calling you up tonight

Standing here smoking my seventy-second cigarette
in twenty-three hours, staring into the face
of every woman who passes, I think perhaps
I should apologize. Looking for you
in their fleeting eyes, I know I won't.

The night air down here is cool avenue blue.
Looking up I can only imagine you standing there
by the light of your window thirty-five stories above
this street level man you loved those twelve years.
There is a full moon out tonight so maybe I will cross

this street of mad traffic blues into our small town
and find us racing across perfect cornfields.
You in shorts and your brother's shirt
years too big and me in raggedy jeans.
That was the year of the Merrygo Carnival

with bag leg circus clowns smiling purple
smeared smiles. I loved you more than that '57 Chevy
Tommy left when he went off to war.

So many years have passed and we have pushed the memories
into the goodwill corner of some forgotten woman's blue room
like unwanted toys we've outgrown.

Remember that diamond princess ring I stole
for $17 and how we laughed and laughed
when it turned your finger green and yes
the children are almost grown now.

Yesterday the circus came to town and I dreamed
I was the blue wind that took your loverman's hat
but it didn't fit the way it did when I was just a kid,

Seventeen awkward wearing my father's shoes. Tonight
I am wearing a faded Yankee blue baseball cap
and an overcoat. My collar is turned up tight
to fight the nightwind that's trying to steal my mind.

And yes my dear Angelina, I know you won't answer
but I'll be calling you

from this dusty blue corner street phone
that smiles at everybody passing as it eats
my last quarters without saying "thank you for using AT&T"
in the voice of a sweet woman.

## The Sunday Facts of a Partly Cherished Life
## (Life in a Narrow Blue Room)

One day someone would ask "What about your family?"
She would ask herself what about my family
home waiting and wanting pork chops for supper
instead of naked bones and not-enough rice to go 'round
a tiny table of three half-empty dishes at dinner?
What about her family and what about Grandmama

standing in front of an ironing board steaming her life away
Monday through Friday from 7:30 'til the quarter 'til 3 bus
pulls away leaving a cloud of black smoke to settle
over the suburbs of the Forest Hills lifestyle
Grandmama loved like a man for 35 faithful years?

I was to understand by looking into her tired, weak eyes
that she enjoyed spending her golden years ironing
white shirts and cotton sheets for the Vanderbilts
while Mrs. Vanderbilt read the morning newspaper
over black coffee and sweetcakes. In the afternoon she'd take tea
and talk on the telephone to whoever would listen
to the same story over and over again about her fine sons.

And what about Grandmama's own son, Tally Junior, who grew up
        watching
a black and white television that watched him to sleep
every night because his working mother couldn't afford

a colorvision set? Now at 35 candles and living at home
he finally realizes the facts of colored life
down by the docks where his father works.

I was to understand that he loved loading and unloading
fish boxes in fish houses all over this fish city
living his idle days in the back room waiting
and rolling dice for roasted peanuts and sweet potatoes
while the boss was not watching.

What about this man who is not my grandfather,
who worked hard all his life but drinks more than he makes
even when the work is good "He ain't gonna 'mount
to a hill of beans," Grandmama's mother used to say.
Grandmama remembers. She was 17, prim and proper
and Tally was the prettiest boy in town.

"Now our little town is a city," she thinks back
as she smooths the wrinkles in her handed-down silk
skirt. She can't bring herself to iron this Sunday
morning. Today she will sing. The congregation always listens
to the choir.

I was to understand by looking into her tired eyes
that Mrs. Vanderbilt asked about the Sunday facts
of Grandmama's life every Monday morning,
but time has told Grandmama one time too many
that Mrs. Vanderbilt doesn't really want to know

how anyone can cherish the smallest corner of a life
without a hallway mirror leading to the narrow blue room
atop a stairwell that Grandmama will soon be too weak
to climb.

*Anthony Abbott*

## Evening Light

The trees undress slowly from the top.
Bare arms arc brownly into the sky. It is
sunset. Orange skirts swirl in an awful
dying light. The ground is littered gold.

I stop the scene with the shutter of my eye—
stop and hold and mark—this blue, these reds
and holding greens—those rusts upon the ground.
I stoop and pick and hold this one dry leaf.

It crumbles in my hand, and I see a picture
from the morning paper speak as if alive.
Five Turkish children killed by earthquake
lie upon the ground, seemingly asleep.

The mother screams above, mouth horror ravaged,
while in Kentucky and Ohio other mothers weep
into clean white handkerchiefs as taps are played
and flags are placed into their hollow laps.

Hats do not suffice. The time is never right.
Beauty is always almost gone. This dress, this
cock of the head, this touch, this curl of hair,
this graying beard, that look over the shoulder.

We are taken so suddenly, the breath goes
in white astonishment. If I had known is not
enough. Say it now. Say it now. Say it now.
Before the shutter clicks once more and closes.

*Gladys Owings Hughes*

## Survival

Sitting on the steps, I could see
him come at sundown, hurrying
from fields of ten-cent cotton.
Magic was needed. Maybe F.D.R.
would show up waving that cigarette
holder like Aaron's rod to spread
benediction across the rocky acres.
Or listen to a father of seven
orate about fear itself.

He was the only man I ever saw play
harmonica and piano at the same time.
We'd scramble for turns to reach
round his balding head to hold the harp
while he played a yahooing rendition
of The Fox Hunt. After the hounds
resounded through the house and out,
he'd bow to lusty applause, turn
with a flourish to seat Mama
and she played Love's Old Sweet Song.
We'd sing halfway through
The Yellow Book. Lambs safe
in the fold again.

One spring day he lifted me to marvel
at a marsh hen on her nest — my legs
pressed tight against his big chest
caught his heart's pulse of joy.
He knew ways to drown drudgery —
surviving, by God, to plow and plant
a wide swath straight through
his want and the mire of Depression.

*Steven Lautermilch*

## The Canticle of the Skeleton

Blessed are the bones of the feet,
   they have rhythm and walk on the ground.

For heel to toe is a leap and an answer,
   every step is a dance up and down.

Blessed are the anklebones,
   they hold the hinges of uprightness and speed.

For they are the hammer, they are the anvil,
   they forge the wheel, they run on fire.

Blessed are the bones of the knees,
   they know the way of the Lord.

By bending and breaking they are made perfect
   until they have no need of words.

Blessed are the thighbones,
   they are the cradle of song.

Lyre and lullaby and story by the bed,
   girl and stranger, they are mother and death.

Blessed are the bones of the hip,
   they are a valley of honey and milk.

Pasture and meadow, blossom and seed,
   they are the winepress, they are the wine.

Blessed are the backbones,
   they take the heat of the day.

For the shoulderblade is the relic of a fledgling,
   its dip and swing are the image of flight.

Blessed are the bones of the breast,
    they weave the wicker cage of the soul.

For only the foolish think the spirit is weak,
    in time it breaks free and is gone.

Blessed are the shoulderbones,
    they bear the cross.

For they draw the spear, the bow, and the lance,
    they take the shock of the gun.

Blessed are the bones of the elbow,
    they are a jolt and crazy surprise.

For even when the muscles let go,
    they conduct the live wire.

Blessed are the wristbones,
    they pull strings.

Flower and lever, doorbell and window and phone,
    they say hello, so long, good-bye.

Blessed are the bones of the knuckles,
    they open up.

For they are raised on raps and hard knocks,
    they are the teeth of the fist.

Blessed are the fingerbones,
    they make waves.

Harp and guitar, cymbal and trumpet and drum,
    they scale the rainbow, they scatter light.

Blessed are the bones of the neck,
    they form the corridors of silence and speech.

Tower and temple and tomb,
    they raise the gates, they lay the cornerstone.

Blessed are the jawbones,
   they break the ice.

For their words sprout like new grass
   from a spring without end.

Blessed are the bones inside the ear,
   they hear the truth.

They never stop listening,
   they are a bundle of nerves.

Blessed are the bones that shelter the eye,
   they are the quarry of sight.

Their veins are races of crystal,
   they are the light pipes of the mind.

Blessed are the skullbones,
   they are the mask, they are the theater of the soul.

For the stars walk in their sleep,
   and the flames radiate.

*Paul Jones*

## Morning Song

Even at dawn I imagine the chances
a life must take: each leaf offers
an enemy when dinner means eaten as well
as fed, the path's dark turns take us far
from our learning, and new choice fathers
greater fear—the rabbit seeing the black
earth coming red asks grass fire or blood-
edge of hawk's shadow? Across the field
the housewife, safe from nature,
authors romance against the insidious
coil of routine; the dishes dirtied then
cleaned. Her husband, the engineer, turns
from his terminal to carve primitive
figures, his brow folded into the problem.
Even as my hand trails over the covers
to meet yours, I distrust the dependable
morning trill breaking from the quince
and the trite concert of crickets
completing another night. These days
before us are well-worn and treacherous
steps. At every predictable descent,
at each precious peril, we stoop
to meet the cost; we bow in hope to rise.

*Debra Kaufman*

## Dialogue Concerning a Blue Convertible

What night?
  *The night the moon fell*
I don't know what
  *Blue convertible*
You must have dreamt it
  *You wore a white scarf*
Well I might have
  *It trailed behind you*
Years ago that
  *Whose voice was it*
You would have been just
  *Who was that man Ma*
I wasn't even
  *Peepers singing a cold pond*
My early twenties
  *Something sank there*
But you were sleeping
  *Air so sullen*
Do you remember
  *A field of larkspur*
You couldn't have been more
  *Where was Daddy*
than three years old then
  *Who was that man*
He was somebody
  *Pulled dimes from my hair*
I met him somewhere
  *I wasn't laughing*
A smooth dancer
  *He undid your*
It must have been when
  *He ignored me*
The man could whistle
  *He undid your*
Like Mel Torme any tune
  *I wasn't sleeping*
That was so long
  *Why did you bring me*
I repented

*You looked so different*
I smoked Camels
　*Deep red lipstick*
Mack the Knife kept
　*The scarf fluttered*
Repented all that
　*around your shoulders*
Why stir up old
　*Did you tell Daddy*
What good does it do
　*You forgot me*
You want to punish
　*You repented*
Yes yes long ago
　*You turned into*
I couldn't help it
　*The clouds thinned and*
Some things are better
　*floated up like*
left alone
　*scarves let loose*
So why mention
　*in high wind*
So why ask me
　*I had to remember*
You're not going
　*I can't help it*
to write about me
　*Yes I'm going to*
Well try to show some
　*The whippoorwill kept*
There are the fine points
　*Don't give me whitened*
All I mean is
　*I see it all now*
a good writer
　*I could forgive you*
always shows her
　*You were gorgeous*
characters
　*and I thought then*
a bit of sympathy
　*almost free*

*Mark Smith-Soto*

## Lying Out

The sky is pure, only one cloud appears
to be headed this way, and the new sun
licks the body gently, as if to prove
dermatologists liars, and all our fears
of wrinkles, moles and cancer overdone.
The breeze does bring some cold, but still we love
to stretch out full in Spring, and to forget
the shrubs we lost, the pipes January cracked
between its teeth, the hundred dollar debt
to Piedmont Gas. And so flat on our backs
we sip our icy beer, enjoy our hiccup,
and talk of it all as over and done.
We lie happy, even should the wind pick up,
the single cloud fit right over the sun.

## Bubble

The heat hunkers trenchant, loud.
Lilies are budding on the lake.
Calf-high grass quivers.

He has wanted this moment to exist:
the insect flares blue on a sticky branch,
opening and closing, the size of his hands.

His heart pumps a bubble over the world;
it holds.

*Michael Chitwood*

## Weave Room

Because the room roared,
two hundred Draper looms
throttled to make the most
of extra-yard bonus,
and because they made
the machines sing until
they carried deafness
home like an empty
lunch box,
they mastered a speech
held in hands.
I've seen fights begin
from the way one
took hold of another
to move him away
from a breakdown.
Gossip traveled
on fingertips.
But best of all
was the semaphore
they invented
with the flashlights
they used to understand
the greased hearts of looms.
Hanging in thongs,
voices potent as the rock
in David's sling.
They spoke across
the scream of the room,
shot the air
with syllables of light.

## Big House

Leaves hurry in the yard.
The Johnson grass sways, the sumac and thistle,
the stem in the seed still on the stem.

Wind is the road out of here.
Wind is the color of what it goes around.
It repeats itself.

What bothers you, bothers you.
The thing you don't see
puts the tear in your eye.

The wind is a big house.
You can lean on it.
It's where you hang your hat.

Wind says what there is to say.
Curtains worry at the window.
The wind thumbs a page.

It will slam your doors
and rattle the what-nots.
The heavy-headed grass nods.

You can believe in the wind.
It tastes like praying,
like paper, like a moth wing, like breathing.


## I'll Fly Away

There's a snag in the oak.
A dust of snow reveals the harvest stubble
as lines on a page
and they are only rows of harvest stubble.
There's the red fruit of the holly
and the cedar's blue.
There's the glitter of the moon on ice
and it's only glitter.
There's a snag in the oak
I can't get by.

*

Rodney said he wouldn't go.
I said I wouldn't.
Wendell said he would and was gone
from the back pew
to where the reformed Hindu, now evangelist, wept
because his mother and father died
Hindu and he would never see them
on the Shores of Glory.
I went.

*

Can God make a door so small
he can't get through it?
Can he do anything?
There was only the moon
in its cold path, straight and narrow.

*

Beggar's lice on my knees keep asking for the field.
I believe what they believe.
I believe in the thistle at the right hand,
the moral rip,
the salt of the body.

*Keith Flynn*

## The James River Express

It was something he said to her
when they stepped off the platform
and into the James River bus,
something sharp, but stated
in a low voice, something
only a stranger would understand.

The cities retreated on both sides.
The wine swam round in their bottle
as her fingers crawled up his leg,
through his hair, on his chin.

The windows looked down
and held them swimming,
their fierce instincts strutting
like weasels, but their faces
and skin were silent,
their bodies barely moved.

Patience hung between them
like a wreath,
like an early morning wind
that blows its soft tempo
from room to room.

Her mother told her,
all men are dogs, watch them
and she did, she watched him sleeping,
watched one hair curl like a comma
on his cheek.

Then she knew her mother's horror
and felt fear enough to kiss him,
to whisper softly in his mouth,
Giselle, Giselle, her name.

*Al Maginnes*

### Father-Son Basketball, 1970

This year the fathers had practiced,
rising early to shoot fouls and lay out plays
while we stuffed ourselves under winter blankets
for an extra hour's rest.
Now they owned the empty gym,
running our skinny butts till breath
twisted a harsh rag in our chests.

Point by point our fathers left us behind.
My own father was everywhere, rising
in his red sweatshirt for every rebound, elbowing
for every loose ball. Bad wind
and the sweat that rained in his eyes
and blotted his chest would not slow him.

It was the last simple competition we had.
Ahead of us, years of pointless drill
over responsibility and hair, behind us
the years I patterned all my moves after his.
Just before the last buzzer, he met me at mid-court,
snaked the ball out of my lazy dribble.
No one came near him.

Here is the memory I keep:
my father alone under the basket,
the shot falling while I run toward him,
still foolish enough to try and save
a basket worth more every year
than the two points the board shows.

*Deborah Pope*

## Another Valentine

I have come to expect
forsythia stunning
the ragged twigs with random yellow,
the hard spears forking
from the rat's nest of February.
I have come to expect
the south wind treading the lawn
while snow still heaps
like egg shells
in the shade.

Moving up stairs all afternoon
the four o'clock light
holes up in our room,
fingers the careless sheets.
The closets are holding their breath.
In the kitchen stiff cuttings
clatter in a glass jar,
pink clots of quince.
I have had the clippers waiting.

And you, you
sweat easily all morning
raking the winter away,
come in with cool edges,
the smell of raw sun
in your palms,
swing open my heart like a hinge.
I have come to expect it.

## The Secret

Two years, and our son half seems
a preposterous ruse whose mastermind
has dropped from sight, some stranger's heir
we've been given the secret care of,

thrust through the window, slipped
in the hasty bed with barely time
to get our stories straight.
We have played along, try not to call
attention to ourselves, blend
into the scenery as *mother, father.*

But when, his bright hair flying,
he runs without looking back
into the tangible rain of willows,
where sunlight spills like wet paint
in the leaves, and shouts of others
leap the ravine, we know there is
someplace else he belongs,
like the plane he watches
drone high and small
through the August afternoon.

So far, no one has come
to take him back.
He breathes in the air of the place,
the neighbors have been paid off.
At night his head bobs absently in sleep.
It is only we who remember it
otherwise, lying in the fitful dark,
listening as the skeptical wind
still sighs, *whose boy,*
*whose boy?*

*Becke Roughton*

## Passage

Morning, the magic owl has disappeared
into night's black hat. Pines whisper secrets.
She is lost, my grandmother who taught me
to read tree leaves and sing to birds,
lost between night and morning
without a door, a star.

She wanders, touches the cool walls
of her room, her white hair the moon's halo.

I close my eyes and the owl flies back to his tree.
Grandmother rises from the table, tells me
to come in before dark, wipes flour from her hands.
It sifts like a dream of once-a-year snow.

Her flashlight swings through the cricket calls
and wet grass. Her apron is fragrant
with honey bread.

Now it is later than belief.
She stands in the doorway like a lost child,
holds out her hands to be filled
with anything real. I hug her
and we hold on.

*Michael White*

## Postcard

All the west
Lay clear and luminous, blue

And purple and pure dark crimson,
And then it rained like a soft shadow

Into the trees. If I could tell you
Anything, it would be how the rivers

Of aspen lining the northern ravines
Of Grandeur Peak, just turning then,

And far more gold than their riffling leaves
Could hold, were spilling them upwards, into

The air, like bright arpeggios;
How the switchbacks coiled down through

Those caverns of flames of the incandescent
Maples and oaks that live up there;

And how—if I had looked—the city
Beneath, beyond the canyon mouth,

Shook out its tentacles of lights.
If you see this, love, imagine my descent

Through waves of enormous color, the ache
In my legs which vanished with the hour

In a dreamlike glaze of orange light,
And picture me floating down through the fires

Of this day and the next.

*Grey Brown*

## Bear

We were attracted most by the smell,
the black musky odor that caught us by the gate.
Still, we waited, saving him for last.
We'd kill time, throwing Cracker Jacks at the monkeys
taking careful aim at the baboons who displayed,
watching the alligators that never moved,
though I remember one afternoon
we saw the big one crack a turtle in its jaw.
Finally, the trail led up the hill
past the goats and by the pony
who never came when we called.
And then nothing stood between us.
His cage was dark
and farthest from the orange railing
where we rested our chins.
Through the gray bars
it was hard to tell true bear from shadow
as the two paced and turned to pace again.
We were silent for the clanking chain.
He never gave one snarl or growl
in the hours that we waited,
just an occasional umph,
a small passing of gas,
and the deep, slow sigh
that freed us to go.

*Lenard Duane Moore*

## The Song Poem

I will sing in the rising
of wind, the warming
of sun, and peeling
of skin—will sing
of pain, the wailing,
the swelling, the blood
strumming sun-colored notes.

I am song, to the woman,
when the river floods
in my manhood.
I am black song,
blasting stern language
from a deep heart
in the morning light.

I hear the currents surge
and rhythm, pitch by pitch,
in the flow of my blood.
I am the song's note of wind,
the pain oozing from the throat,
a chord tuning its scale:
harmony itself, itself.

## Pathway: From Son to Father

Father, how sharp you stand
in the mirror.
I see myself.
Your praise and love—
something any son weeps for—
overtake me.

I remember you young, teaching me
to set out tomato slips,
the earth already scooped

in the morning light,
thin roots and
water from the dripping bucket.

You taught me, hungry,
a finger pointing into the void
and you were Moses
leaning against the backyard fence.

You picked roses for mother to
put on the table with dinner.
A woman of grandeur
who'd go beyond ordinary cause for family.
Her dreams were large.

I am a man, your oldest son,
praying depths of silence,
for a son to show the pathway,
a daughter to pick the whitest rose.

## Raleigh Jazz Festival, 1986

On the Fayetteville Street Mall
a lean man bobs his head.
His sax shines like copper in a sunbeam,
a splendid rising rhythm....
The swingman inches
across the homemade platform...
his angled jaws shaping and reshaping
while pigeons go on answering
pigeon secrets. Jazz notes blend
with the singing silence.
People dance on red-bricked walkways,
their fingerpoppings
echo off tall marble buildings.
And now the saxophonist bows.
The silence resumes.
The pigeons improvise;
wings (never so numerous as now)
darken the town clock's face.

In thick bus fumes
the crowd scatters,
their spirits rising
insolent against the sun's setting.
The hobos linger for leftovers,
in a sacred space of dogwoods.

## From *Desert Storm: A Brief History*

shadowy moonlight
a bullet-hit canteen
leaking in the sand

   . . .

warm burst of rain—
a woman marine at daybreak
drawing in the sand

   . . .

a dead soldier
staring from the ground
the shifting light

   . . .

alone in his tent
black GI's clasped hands
in a shaft of moon

   . . .

bulldozers pushing
corpses into the deep hole
another dawn

   . . .

back home
soldier listens to birdcalls
marking sunrise

*Stuart Dischell*

## Magic Fathers

One appears in a snowstorm just as you're worrying
how you will get home.

Another in costume puts you on his knee.

Another buys a new car so you'll pass your driver's test.

And one crawls out from under the bed, having chased
the goblins away.

Oh, magic fathers, I summon you in the bleak time
when the rum has given out and the glass has left circles
on the table.

Oh, magic fathers, you will buff them out, you will carry
us upstairs, you will watch us sleep.

For you are the dollar under the pillow.

You are the blanket, the wall, the window.

You in your anger the wrecker's ball.

*Gail Peck*

## Heaven

Ye shall be made whole, the Bible says,
so I picture Uncle John in need
of two shoes with both pants legs cuffed
instead of one pinned at the knee.

Terry, the foster child my grandparents
kept for a year, no longer on the floor
tugging braces up to his thighs,
pushing with his hands to stand.

My brother who was never able
to speak — words spewing
like water through a stone figure's mouth.

They're all there, I tell myself,
even the nonbelievers and suicides,
God realizing at that point
there are no more lessons to learn.

I'm not sure about the angels
shuffling between worlds,
with smooth faces, never aging.
I'd rather be like the Navajo woman
I once saw in Santa Fe, the wrinkles
creased like a fan along her face,

a face always open, watchful
except when she lay down
and the earth slept, having turned
on its side from the sun.

*Cathy Smith Bowers*

## Learning How to Pray

When I heard my brother
was dying    youngest
of the six of us    our
lovely boy    I who in matters
of the spirit
had been always suspect
who even as a child
snubbed Mama's
mealtime ritual
began finally to
pray    and fearing
I would offend
or miss completely
the rightful target of my pleas
went knocking everywhere
the Buddha's huge
and starry churning    Shiva
Vishnu    Isis    the worn
and ragged god of Ishmael
I bowed to the Druid reverence
of trees    to water    fire
and wind    prayed to weather
to carbon    that sole link
to all things
this and other worldly
*our carbon who art in heaven*
prayed to rake and plow
the sweet acid stench of dung
to fly    to the fly's soiled
wing    and to the soil

I could not stop
myself    I like a nymphomaniac
the dark promiscuity
of my spirit    there
for the taking    whore
of my breaking heart    willing
to lie down    with anything.

*David Hopes*

## Driving Home

Out of the night's crush and solitude, out of rage and
time and the dark and walled city, accelerating
up Pisgah Highway, a tic in the torment of days,
flame-eyes of my Ford juggernauting dim townlands down,
I find, unaccountable, at bend of the mountain,
calm animal eyes: farm cat
stalking topaz; heron;
opossums foraging in gleam
and shuttering of jewels;
marsh compassionate with lights,
void but for black and fire.
I see my road is the highway of the wayfare moon,
that beasts, moon-praising, night-studding, link their steps to some
majestic partner buck-dancing on the floor of lights.
Deers' ruby low on the slopes.
Opal of hunting owl.
Fillet on Pisgah of the
nighthawk's flying, hem of
the she-bear circling lonely
all the velvet ramparts.
Beast glance lanterns from the dark. Catamount aflame. Sky
mirrored in the spider's multiplicity of gaze.
Dance of the mountain Ladies in their glow-worm baubles.
It is the hour I transfigure from my fury to
be one of them. My lights give them light. My car becomes
moon's dragon blazing the road
benediction torch-eyed
in the abysses, splendor blasting into
splendor all that watches, hungers, moves, that scatters to
join by morning behind Pisgah in a sphere of praise.

*Richard Chess*

## Two and One

Two roses I gave the therapist,
One for my thorny soul, one for hers.
Two answers to a step-daughter,
One in the hollow voice of her father.
Two days with an old friend,
One to recover the past,
One to recover from the past.
But I turn to one God only
When I lie down and rise up,
One God at the end of a day
When I empty the pockets,
And at dawn when I fill them again.

A proverb I recalled for my father
The day he confessed he was broke:
*Rich man and poor man meet;*
*The Lord made them both.*
He listened patiently.
Two gifts for the bride,
One of this world, one of the world to come.
But I labor to repair one world only
When I walk by the way.

Two coins for the beggar,
Two loaves for the Sabbath
Which ends when three stars open
In the Saturday night sky.
Two parents, neither one on this earth.
Two hands, one with which to give,
One with which to take away.
Two ears with which to hear, O Israel,
The Lord our God, the Lord is One.

*Barbara Presnell*

### Clarissa and the Second Coming

An ordinary woman, why her?
she wonders. A sinner, even, not
musically inclined, just one half-tuned
ear and a taste for rock and roll.
But there he is, night black
hair that wind and rhythm wave,
lip snarling when he smiles, eyes pure
and blue as the sky over Graceland.
She watches him, eight-year-old
body tight as an E string,
riding his bike like any other boy.
He doesn't know who he is,
how he'll change the world,
how already he's changed her,
how at night while he sleeps,
she kneels by his bed
cradling his immaculate hand,
whispering thank-yous for miracles
to the moon and stars
that stud the blue suede sky.

*MariJo Moore*

### Solidarity in the Night

This was the night
all the people sang together.

This was the night
all the people dreamed together.

This was the night
all the people danced together.

This was the night
all the people prayed together.

This was the night
all the people began to heal.

### Ahlawe Usv' Tsigesvgi
(*Eastern Cherokee translation
"Solidarity in the Night."*)

Usv'tsigesvgi
nigata yvwi duninogisv.

Usv' tsigesvgi
nigata yvwi anasgitskvgi.

Usv' tsigesvgi
nigata yvwi analskvgi.

Usv' tsigesvgi
nigata yvwi anadadolistihvgi.

Usv' tsigesvgi
nigata yvwi anadaleni unidiwisga.

## Invisible Tongues

If you desire to communicate
    with the *Nunnehi*
go and touch the branches of willows
swaying in whispering winds.

    Go and sit on sanctioned rocks
boldly stationed along talking rivers.
Go and sleep on breathing mountains
    looking over murmuring valleys.

    The Spirits are there
ever listening, ever hearing
    and ever speaking
        to you.

*Dannye Romine Powell*

## Let's Say We Haven't Seen Each Other since Ninth Grade and We Meet as Adults at a Welcome Center in Southside, Virginia

And we begin to kiss
the way we used to kiss
before you moved
with your parents
to Michigan: after school
out by the chain link fence
near the basketball court
on the sea well
by the bay
in the church parking lot
after choir practice
flat on our backs
in the grass
at slumber parties
before the boys had to leave
or on the beach at Matheson Hammock
when your sister
would drive us there
then go off somewhere else
to work on her tan.

It takes us a few seconds
to adjust our arms
because you are taller now
but it all comes back
how we used to take turns
catching our breath,
where your right ear lobe
is fleshy, how your collar smells
of heather, which tooth protrudes,
the scar on your chin
that used to be higher.

I can smell the cream
of gardenias in the purple bowl

on our homeroom teacher's desk,
I can even remember her name—
Mrs. Bleier—and I can see the dance
of mimosas in the patio after lunch,
the hair on my arms standing up
when the sun slid behind clouds
and how you kept them up
until the sun eased out again,
the choir singing deep
and wide, deep and wide,
there is a fountain flowing
deep and wide
and how I always thought of you
instead of Jesus when we sang
I've got joy joy joy joy
down in my heart, down in my heart,
the way I do now, kissing you
at a Welcome Center
just over the state line
in Southside, Virginia.

*John York*

## Eleventh Grade: 1971
*— for Hayes & Gail NcNeill*

All morning low clouds rain on black-gray hills,
  on flat buildings, while we sit
in fluorescent light, or while we nudge to fit
under walkways' covers.
        Mini-skirted girls
watch each other flirt with the quarterback,
  while uncrossing legs spark
daydreams, while Mr. Green chats with Miss Clark,
while I sit invisible in the back
 of the room, where I imagine rock tunes
   and write "Richard Nixon
lies/The eagle skeleton cries": and on

and on the verses flow: while Mr. Jones
discusses the wrestling team's current season,
  while Miss Clark reviews the days
of the week (*loondi, merdi, macradi*...),
while equations loom up behind Miss Gleeson.

 But Mr. McNeill walks in as the bell
rings and proclaims *There was a child went forth
every day.* After class, I show him my song,
  and he says *This image is strong,
this one flies*: and I sing as I trot to sixth
period gym, though my songs will never sell,
though, instead of baskets, I zap teammates' heads,

   though "my mind has been cornered, a rusting gun,"
though "in freezing rain my soul has bowed like grass,"
  though "my faraway drummer has
   been thumping a practice pad":
I've been alerted, thawed,
  charged, aimed, fired, called
   to march at last.

*Maureen Douglass Sutton*

## High Noon at the Matinee

If you ask me, I'm a feminist.
Why then, again, thirty years later
with children in my lap and Tex Ritter
modulating my heart beat, do I sit through "High Noon"
like a parched twelve-year-old, lapping Gary Cooper's eyes
like deep-well water?

When Grace Kelly pleads, "Why must you go back to town
and face Frank Miller's gang?" my stoic Cooper
straight-lips it, "If you don't know, I can't explain it"—
the very thing you don't say to a feminist—and
I just love it and think, how perfect.

I've injected Steinem and Jong, Friedan and Beauvoir.
Still no immunity against a man's gotta do what a man's gotta do
and when Cooper drills Miller, me and the kids
whoop like Comanches, and he could track Hadleyville dust
through my bedroom anytime.

Am I stuck still in the Great Dismal Swamp of the '50s?
Or is it that Lady Grace, the Coop's Quaker bride, finally
backshoots the bad guy.

*Diana Pinckney*

## Lot's Wife Looks Back

Can't you see her, turned forever
toward home, that lush valley where her girls
grew into women in a city that had grown
like a party out of control,
spilling people into streets
from houses and tents where no one slept.
One last look before leaving
everything, including her name.
Was Lot's wife allowed to carry a favorite bowl
or the shawl woven by her mother?
No time for turtledoves puttering in the grooves
of her roof or the lamb she hand fed,
its mother killed by jackals running wild
down the alleys of Sodom.
The two men hurrying them said hide
in the high country, but what did she know of hills
or caves damp and dark enough for a man
to warm himself with wine and daughters?
Rushed by angels pulling her hand
and air hot enough to dry the sweat on her skin,
of course she turned to look. The way we are drawn
to check the stove again or the coffee pot,
running our fingers over the door lock,
backing down the drive,
the house and yard shrinking
the way the shore does when we leave
the land, the way boat people surely start out,
staring back across the waves,
trees and sand swaying
until the black line on the horizon is nothing
but the sea stinging their eyes.

*Annette Allen*

## This River

Just as sun shivers on the silver
skin of rivers, the course of our love
lights my hand and thigh. I want

to float on the whitest of bone
down the channels of breath.
This river swings east, snapping

past loss and fissured land;
it carries us beyond flesh
and life's fractured surfaces.

Love, let us swim to the ocean
where no difference between
drowning and dreaming exists,

where our fatelines connect
mind to heart and nothing
separates the giver from the gift.

*Carole Boston Weatherford*

## Yeast Rolls & Water Biscuits

The kitchen was her sanctuary;
she hummed hymns to keep it holy,
baked sweet inspiration, dished up redemption
and held us in her hands down home, down home.

Hovering over cast iron and steam, she lost
herself in aromas of rhubarb. Daydreams
descended into the root cellar; she eventually
forgot them. She stored tomorrow in the pie safe

alongside her treasures, drank
pot likker to stay strong, sifted truth twice
for good measure and kept a hanky in her apron
pocket to wipe the worry from her brow.

She bided time like the God-fearing,
floorwalking sisters who came before her,
women who gazed into kerosene lamps and kept
vigils at midnight for children gone astray.

She kneaded dough with a passion that only pain
could summon and translate into prayer;
Her recipes gave rise to yeast rolls and water biscuits,
gave wings to angel's food.

*Marty Silverthorne*

## Barrel of Prayer

Grandmother, if I could fold
myself into hallelujah folds,
I would press my palms into steeples,
unfold arthritic fingers and knuckles
cursed by whiskey's time and tap
in the rhythm of God if I could
fold myself in prayer.

Grandmother, if I could bend
myself into your beliefs,
I would bow into blessings, deliver us
from the cross you are convicted to.
If I could help you by knuckling
in prayer, I would press my elbows
into the pew, and give grace in hallelujahs
if I could bend myself to believe.

But, Grandmother, all I have are humble
whispers that echo from my chest
and bound to this cripple's chair
it is hard to put to sound
your bucket of blessings,
your pail of promises and
sweet prayer. I shall sing
as long as *hallowed be thy name,*
as long as *hallowed be thy name.*

*Debra Kang Dean*

## Immigrants

To be always carrying
this stone whose own inertia
keeps doubling its weight even

as I hold it in my hand—
in truth I would cast it off
if I could

      though it cool the
sweat of my palm, suffer it-
self to be touched. Know I would

heft it at water or glass
simply to hear one thing
deafen another awake

to hear fragments falling like
stars to wound or baptize
everything

      compassed inside
the arc of its wake—but for
one thing: my grandmother gave

this stone to my mother, and
she to me, saying each hand
need have something hard to fill

its grasping, something only
time and touch can transmute in-
to an object,

      beautiful,
this stone from Okinawa
where the grains of sand are stars.

*Sarah Lindsay*

## U S

This is not a country that needs me to speak for it

This is not a country with one great wound
    at which I can cry out
    and be heard

This is no place small enough for a cradle,
    no green palm of a hand, embraceable chain of red mountains

It will not condense, it will not yield to a single music,
    no two of its horizons take the same line

This is not a country that counts me
    when it goes to its storehouse to count,
    when it dials up majority wedges of pie,
    when it tunes in its screens with their Nielsen boxes

Not my mother, not my father,
    scatterer of sisters and brothers
    among the prairie-dog holes, the skyscraper ant farms

It's too big, too built to bury love in

The love spilled on it, viscous white, sticky red,
    won't soak in — scours the mere ground
    and bears it downhill

Dry rock lies by swollen rivers
    and the dry rocks groan
    and the rivers shout
    and sometimes they're on TV

This is not a country that asks me to speak

*Susan Meyers*

## My Father Never Talked of Love

*The ear possesses the very odd*
*characteristic of imagining*
*the existence of the fundamental*
*even when it is not present,*
*if the harmonics are strong.*
                    *—Oliver Read*

For years no one in the family would dive
into the water to drag up the song.
                        Did we think
we would drown under the weight
of its words, kick bottom yet never rise,
catch glints of light but never
break through to the unsentimental air?
Over time we quit swimming
in the weedy water, needing less
to look for words when we could hum the tune.

Now in the fundamental chill
of a March morning
a breath of air hangs visible
above the pond. One harmonic note
lingers, waits for the rising sun
to forgive the moon its weight
and silvered pull no sun can ever know.
Nothing clears the air like forgiveness,
above all in the morning,

and I think how perhaps one time,
when I was almost three,
                        and sinking into sleep,
my father said the words.

*Debora Kinsland*

## Ahaluna

A thirsty Spring this year, behind
the Easter Squall, a careless spark ignites
the mountainside. The flames begin to wind
around the fighters at the ancient sites
of dance and feast. A Bureau worker seeks
to find a break to slip from death.
*Da ga li wo tsi.* On Coopers Creek
amidst the ring of fire, his eyes are met
with yesterday. *Aganunitsi stands*
*inside a pine cone ring of fire.*
*This great Shawano medicine man*
*has killed Uktena near the mire*
*on Mount Gahuti chanting song of death.*
He chants the song of death.

---

* *Ahaluna* in Cherokee means *ambush* and also refers to Soco Gap, which marks the Qualla Boundary line (Cherokee Reservation.) *Da ga li wo tsi* means *he will die.* Uktena, according to James Mooney (*Myths of the Cherokee*) is the "keen-eyed…mythic great-horned serpent with a talismanic diadem." According to one of Mooney's collected stories, Aganunitsi, a Cherokee captive and a Shawano medicine man, killed the Uktena.

*Denise Blue*

# Apocalypse

Time is drawing near
say all the old folks.
Everybody should live in fear.

Look at the signs. They're right here.
Chickens are laying eggs with no yolks.
Time is drawing near.

The new preacher drinks beer
and his wife tokes.
Everybody should live in fear.

The cow's milk is clear.
And listen to the way that frog croaks.
Time is drawing near.

Look at the cloven feet of the deer.
They're shaped all wrong, say the old folks.
Everybody should live in fear.

Pack all your spiritual gear.
God don't like no slow pokes.
Time is drawing near.
Everybody should live in fear.

*L. Teresa Church*

## Tending and Turning

Big Popper Thornton
Once a man
a child again
bones bent
by hospital sheets.
I lay on hands
to hush the hurt
wind the moans into music
of your 'bacco-field fingers
picking blues
outa guitar strings
stretched 'tween polebeans
and collard greens.
I tend to the pain
turn your body
lift you up from bedsores
to the God of good men.
I speak your name
on the spread of angel wings
pray that the train run easy
while Jesus making up
your dying bed.

## Cafe Au Lait

Cafe au lait
like your sugar
refined and light
you'll taste
what you missing
if Molasses Brown
sweeten your cup
some night.

*Margaret Rabb*

## Dogwood Alarm

By pairs and threes they crash
and spin to the shoulder, drivers
stunned, unable to keep their eyes,
wheels, the tingle in their fingertips
from bark and open drifts of silk,
the looseblown momentary bloom.

April. They pass, retreat sideways,
floating away from the little accident.

A specimen tree in a suburban yard
is one thing, fertilized, gravid, buds
popped out all over, azaleas snapping
at its knees. But the woods at the edge
of plowed fields are another story, a waltz
at the dogwood diner, the dance that slays us:

Four or five flowers hover over a branch,
crossed, notched, whiter than this world allows.

*Keith S. Petersen*

## How Long Did It Take?

I wrote a poem once
about something I'd just read
and I recited it to a guy
who liked it a lot but asked me,
How long did it take? And I shrugged:
Coupl' hours, I said.

I didn't tell him, Yeah,
two hours of standing there
freezing in my pyjamas,
leaning over the chest of drawers
in a small circle of lamplight
scribbling almost faster than I could think
before the tremor faded, only 4.8
on the Richter Scale, but strong enough
to drive me out of my house of bedclothes
into the streets to run till it stopped
which it started to do
when the first draft shaped itself,

no, it took the whole night
that began with the reading,
the pages that turned inward,
into the heat of the cauldron,
the pressure of plates on each other,
the deliberate counting of sheep,
one hundred and twelve, one hundred
and thirteen, the two bright blanks
of the backs of my eyelids,
the wreck of the covers,
the roar of the clock
racing toward daylight and,

no, it took forty years.
What the poem was about
were earlier dawns and midnights
the reading had rediscovered,

the rocks it turned over: a job,
a joke, a burial, tears of laughter
at a kitchen table, tears of relief
in a hospital bedroom, a football game
in a downpour, one telephone call
that ate fatigue, the sweet silence
of a sunrise once in the mountains,

like the first morning. No,
it took forever.

*Fred Chappell*

# Afterword

If someone asked me to name a distinguishing characteristic of North Carolina poetry, I might say, "Quantity." This term would be especially accurate, as Sally Buckner notes, of the periods from 1955 to the present time. Some of the reasons for the state's startling efflorescence after midcentury are obvious; increased financial prosperity and an increasingly widespread literacy might be chief among them. I have conjectured that this latter factor gives rise to a certain cultural ebullience: people begin to write poetry because they know what it is and find that they can learn how to do it. I have also conjectured that the first human being who learned how to speak immediately burst into song and shortly thereafter set out in search of a voice coach. Not every cultural anthropologist has concurred with my speculations.

The overbalance here toward newer work must be attributed to the fact that so many more poets are writing than formerly. Even so, the poetry in the older idiom seems a little faded in comparison with those in the contemporary. Newer work has the older work behind it to build upon and is for that reason more complex, more sophisticated, than some of the earlier poetry; it has the advantage of a running start, so to speak. It is not so much that Robert Morgan's poetry is better than that of James McGirt or John Charles McNeill, but that there is a sense in which his rural meditations include and subsume that earlier tradition. Without the earlier and more native poetry to react against and build upon, Morgan's poetry would be very different from what he gives us now. The same can be said for A. R. Ammons, James Applewhite, Michael McFee, R. T. Smith, Eleanor Ross Taylor, and many others.

This is not to say that the poets included here set out consciously to create a North Carolina tradition of poetry, a "Tar Heel School." Perhaps if our state were a separate nation rather than part of the union, the attempt might have been made. It is amusing to think of Sam Ragan marshalling such poets as Stephen Smith, Shelby Stephenson, Paul Green, and Grace Gibson in an effort to define and then create a specifically Carolinian brand of verse. It has been done in other places, most successfully in Ireland and Norway perhaps. But it is impossible to imagine poets like William Harmon, Ron Bayes, Ann Deagon, Heather Ross Miller, Gerald Barrax, or Norman Macleod joining up; their aims are more general and some of them despise the notion that their poems might be primarily of regional appeal. Amon Liner used to rail against "the dear old red clay verities" as a matter of habit.

Yet "regional" does not mean "provincial," and this exhausted dichotomy has been pretty well discarded. No one is more determinedly cosmopolitan in tone than Jonathan Williams, but few have so carefully examined and recorded local speech and custom. The interests of Charles Edward Eaton and Randall Jarrell, Chuck Sullivan and Steven Lautermilch, Reynolds Price and Carole Boston Weatherford, Sarah Lindsay and A. R. Ammons are broadly aesthetic, religious, historical, and scientific in nature, but these poets do not disdain local reference or material; they employ it eagerly as ballast for their more abstruse ambitions. By the same token, the regionally focused lines of Jim Wayne Miller, Mary Kratt, Hilda Downer, and John York can hardly to be said to lack philosophical implication or wide significance. Contemporary poetry, like a rifle barrel, seems to have two gunsights, one near the eye to define the larger field and a farther one to pinpoint locality and specificity. The job of the poet is to line up the sights, to aim true in every poem.

But large quantity has its drawbacks, especially in an undertaking like this anthology. The fact that so many strong Tar Heel poets are writing means that many strong ones have had to be omitted because of considerations of physical feasibility. A book can contain only so many pages, and it is easy, though painful, for me to list a good two dozen names that ought to have been included but could not be. Regret is inherent in the selection process.

On the other hand, enough poets are represented to produce a certain salubrious leveling effect. Publication and critical reception are chancy propositions, more often a matter of luck than editors and critics and some poets like to admit. Those who are lucky are too often considered the superior writers while poets of sterling and indisputable worth get less attention. But in a selection such as this one, equality stands a better chance. Faithful admirers of Randall Jarrell and Charles Olsen, Maya Angelou and Alan Shapiro have opportunity to become acquainted with figures less well known than they. I would hope that Ruth Moose and Emily Wilson, Gladys Hughes and Margaret Baddour—and all the others!—begin to acquire the readership they deserve.

And the sheer quantity of poetry North Carolinians produce has another advantage; perhaps its (sometimes forbidding) bulk might help to defeat that bedraggled old canard about poetry dying out in our time. As Kathryn Stripling Byer reports in "Mountain Time," even one of our national Poets Laureate has remarked to a news reporter that by the year 2000 no one will read poetry. "Thus she / prophesied. End of that / interview! End of the world / as we know it." [For the entire poem, see page 195.]

Byer responds to this prediction with a parable about a North Carolina mountain woman named Delphia whose patient labor with children and as a quilter emblemizes the quietly industrious, lovely artisan whose rarely regarded labor is one of the things that helps to hold our society together. "Mountain Time" compares the quilter to the poet, finding in the intensely local a powerful broadest significance:

> This labor to make our words matter
> is what any good quilter teaches.
> A stitch in time, let's say.
> A blind stitch
> that clings to the edges
> of what's left, the ripped
> scraps and remnants, whatever
> won't stop taking shape even though the whole
> crazy quilt's falling to pieces.

# Major North Carolina
# Literary Awards

*A number of annual awards honor poets and writers in this state. Some are given for single books, others for lifelong contributions to literature and/or the fine arts. Below are the major annual awards and the poets who have been so honored.*

## Brockman-Campbell Book Award

The Brockman-Campbell Book Award was initiated in 1976 as the Zoe Kincaid Brockman Award in honor of one of the founders of the North Carolina Poetry Society. In 1997, the name of the award was changed to also honor Mary Belle "Peg" Campbell, poet and founder of Persephone Press. The competition is endowed by Campbell and by the late Christine Rose Sloan, a North Carolina journalist and poet and the first NCPS president. Judged by a nationally recognized poet, the competition is open to native North Carolinians or current residents who have lived in this state for three years at the time of the book's publication.

1977: John Moses Pipkin, *Half-After Love*
1978: Paul Baker Newman, *House on the Saco*
1979: Ann Deagon, *There Is No Balm in Birmingham*
1980: Kathryn Bright Gurkin, *Terra Amata*
   Shelby Stephenson, *Middle Creek Poems*
1981: Fred Chappell, *Earthsleep*
1982: A. R. Ammons, *A Coast of Trees*
1983: Stephen Knauth, *Night Fishing on Irish Buffalo Creek*
1984: Charles Edward Eaton, *The Thing King*
1985: Elizabeth Sewell, *Acquist*
1986: Charles Edward Eaton, *The Work of the Wrench*
1987: R. T. Smith, *Birch-Light*
1988: Peter Makuck, *Pilgrims*
1989: Betty Adcock, *The Case for Gravity*
   Jim Wayne Miller, *First Light*

1990: James Applewhite, *Lessons in Soaring*
1991: James Seay, *The Light as They Found It*
1992: Stephen Smith, *The Complete Bushnell Hamp Poems*
1993: Michael Chitwood, *Salt Works*
1994: Judy Goldman, *Wanting to Know the End*
1995: Barbara Presnell, *Snake Dreams*
1996: Deborah Pope, *Mortal World*
1997: Kathryn Kirkpatrick, *The Body's Horizon*
1998: James Applewhite, *Daytime and Starlight*

## Oscar Young Award

Sponsored by the Poetry Council of North Carolina, this award has been presented annually at the Council's fall meeting since 1959. Eligible books must contain at least twenty poems and must be written by a North Carolina poet.

1959: Olive Tilford Dargan, *The Spotted Hawk*
1960: Charlotte Young, *Speak to Us of Love*
1961: Walter Blackstock, (record of title not available)
1962: Lena Marie Shull, *Red Leaf Carols*
1963: Thad Stem, Jr., *Penny Whistles and Wild Plums*
1964: Victor R. Small, *The Feel of Earth*
1965: Sam Ragan, *The Tree in the Far Pasture*
1966: Edward R. Garner, *For All the Lost and Lonely*
1967: Walter Blackstock, *Leaves Before the Wind*
1968: Heather Ross Miller, *The Wind Southerly*
1969: A. R. Ammons, *Selected Poems*
1970: Guy Owen, *The White Stallion*
1971: Charles Edward Eaton, *On the Edge of the Knife*
1972: Sam Ragan, *To the Water's Edge*
1973: William Harrold, *Beyond the Dream*
1974: Dorothy McCartney, *Lemmus Lemmus*
1975: Susan Bartels [now Susan Ludvigson], *Step Carefully in Night Grass*
1976: Francis Hulme, *Mountain Measure*
1977: Ellen Johnston-Hale, *We Don't Do Nothin' in Here*
1978: Charlotte Young, *Thunder in Winter*
1979: Ann Deagon, *There Is No Balm in Birmingham*
1980: Fred Chappell, *Wind Mountain*
1981: Phyllis Stump, *The Heart Knows*
1982: Grace DiSanto, *The Eye Is Single*
1983: Mary Kratt, *There Are Mountains*

1984: Leroy Sossamon, *These My Mountains, This My Land*
1985: William Paulk, *The Beholden Hills*
1986: Robert L. Madison, *To the Children of Oxford Orphanage*
1987: Efraim Rosenzweig, *The Singer*
1988: Virginia L. Long, *Squaw Winter*
1989: Ann T. Jester, *Where Violets Grow*
1990: Christine Sloan, *In Reserve*
1991: Sam Ragan, *The Collected Poems of Sam Ragan*
1992: Carolyn Kyles, *Lines to Someone*
1993: Chuck Sullivan, *Longing for the Harmonies*
1994: Judy Goldman, *Wanting to Know the End*
1995: Mary Snotherly, *Directions*
1996: Ruth Moose, *Making the Bed*
1997: Joseph Bathanti, *This Metal*
1998: Al Maginnes, *Taking Up Our Daily Tools*
1999: Barbara Presnell, *Unravelings*

## Roanoke-Chowan Award

Sponsored by the Roanoke-Chowan Group of Writers and Allied Artists, this award has been presented annually since 1953 to an original volume published during the past year by an author who has maintained legal or physical residence, or both, in North Carolina for the three preceding years. The competition is presented annually by the North Carolina Literary and Historical Association.

1953: Frank Borden Hanes, *Abel Anders*
1954: Thad Stem, Jr., *The Jackknife Horse*
1955: No award
1956: Helen Bevington, *A Change of Sky*
1957: Dorothy Edwards Summerrow, *Ten Angels Swearing*
1958: Paul Bartlett, *Moods and Memories*
1959: Olive Tilford Dargan, *The Spotted Hawk*
1960: Carl Sandburg (Body of his work)
1961: Carl Sandburg, *Wind Song*
1962: Helen Bevington, *When Found, Make a Verse Of*
1963: Herman Salingar, *A Sigh Is the Sword*
1964: E. S. Gregg, *Reap Silence*
1965: Randall Jarrell, *The Lost World*
1966: Thad Stem, Jr., *Spur Line*
1967: Walter Blackstock, *Leaves Before the Wind*
1968: Paul Baker Newman, *The Cheetah and the Fountain*
1969: Guy Owen, *The White Stallion and Other Poems*
1970: Charles Edward Eaton: *On the Edge of the Knife*

1971: Paul Baker Newman, *The Ladder of Love*
1972: Fred Chappell, *The World Between the Eyes*
1973: Ronald H. Bayes, *The Casketmaker*
1974: Campbell Reeves, *Coming Out Even*
1975: Marian Cannon, *Another Light*
1976: Fred Chappell, *River: A Poem*
1977: Norman W. Macleod, *The Distance*
1978: Mary Louise Medley, *Seasons and Days*
1979: Fred Chappell, *Bloodfire: A Poem*
1980: Fred Chappell, *Wind Mountain, a Poem*
1981: James Applewhite, *Following Gravity*
1982: Thomas Heffernan, *The Liam Poems*
1983: Reynolds Price, *Vital Provisions*
1984: Betty Adcock, *Nettles*
1985: Fred Chappell, *Castle Tzingal*
1986: James Applewhite, *Ode to the Chinaberry Tree and Other Poems*
1987: Charles Edward Eaton, *New and Selected Poems, 1942–1987*
1988: Lochlin Walker, *Musings While Adrift*
1989: Fred Chappell, *First and Last Words*
1990: Sam Ragan, *Collected Poems of Sam Ragan*
1991: Charles Edward Eaton, *A Guest on Mild Evenings*
1992: Julie Suk, *The Angel of Obsession*
1993: James Applewhite, *A History of the River*
1994: Judy Goldman, *Wanting to Know the End*
1995: Robert Watson, *The Pendulum*
1996: Fred Chappell, *Spring Garden: New and Selected Poems*
1997: James L. Seay, *Open Field, Understory: New and Selected Poems*
1998: Kathryn Stripling Byer, *Black Shawl*

## Ethel Fortner Writer and Community Award

Presented by St. Andrews Presbyterian College, this award is named for Ethel Nestell Fortner, teacher, editor, and benefactor of literary arts. Instituted in 1986, the award is presented to individuals whose distinguished contributions to their community have furthered writing. The following North Carolina poets have received this award.

1986: Charleen Whisnant Swansea
1987: Martha Gibson
1989: Mary Belle Campbell
      Grace L. Gibson

1992:  Ann Deagon
       Charles Joyner
1993:  Charles Edward Eaton
       Gladys Owings Hughes
1994   Margaret Boothe Baddour
       Mary Kratt
1995:  Evalyn Pierpoint Gill
       Frank Borden Hanes
1996:  Emily Herring Wilson
1997:  John Foster West
1998:  Charles Fort
       Judy Goldman

## Sam Ragan Fine Arts Award

Created in 1981 to honor Samuel Talmadge Ragan, this award is presented by St. Andrews Presbyterian College to honor persons for outstanding contributions to the Fine Arts of North Carolina over an extended period—including, but above and beyond—the recipient's own primary commitment. The following North Carolina poets have received this award.

1982:  Harriet Doar
1983:  Mae Woods Bell
       Frank Borden Hanes
1985:  Charleen Swansea
1986:  Sallie Nixon
1989:  Shelby Stephenson
       Stephen Smith
1990:  Kate Blackburn
1991:  Gerald Barrax
       Marsha Warren
1993:  Marty Silverthorne
       Sally Buckner
1994:  Marie Gilbert
       Kathryn B. Gurkin
1995:  Joseph Bathanti
       Nancy Bradberry
1996:  Anthony Abbott
       Ruth Moose
1997:  Ellen Johnston-Hale
       Susan Rose
1998:  Betty Adcock
1999:  Georgann Eubanks

## The North Carolina Awards

Each year the state presents its highest honors, the North Carolina Awards, in four categories: Fine Arts, Literature, Public Service, and Science. The following poets have received the North Carolina Award in either Fine Arts or Literature:

1965: Paul Green
1971: Guy Owen
1973: Helen Bevington
1974: Thad Stem, Jr.
1977   Reynolds Price
        Jonathan Williams
1979: Sam Ragan
1980: Fred Chappell
1983: Heather Ross Miller
1986: A. R. Ammons
1987: Maya Angelou
1988: Charles Edward Eaton
1989: Ronald Bayes
1991: Robert Morgan
1995: James Applewhite
1996: Betty Adcock

## The North Carolina Literary Hall of Fame

Authorized by the General Assembly in 1993, the North Carolina Literary Hall of Fame was established to honor and celebrate the state's rich literary heritage. It held its first induction on the grounds of its site, the Weymouth Center for the Arts & Humanities in Southern Pines, in 1996. Members are chosen by a committee of writers, and the North Carolina Writers' Network oversees the entire program. The following poets have thus far been inducted:

1996: James Boyd
        Paul Green
        George Moses Horton
        Randall Jarrell
        Guy Owen
        Thad Stem, Jr.
1997: Samuel Talmadge Ragan
1998: John Charles McNeill
        Pauli Murray
        Jonathan Williams

# Biographical Notes

*Notes:*
- Rather than cite in these brief biographical sketches each of the *state* awards won by North Carolina poets, a listing of those awards is provided beginning on page 267.
- Certain colleges and universities have undergone name changes during the century. In the sketches below we have used the name of the institution at the time the poet worked there.

Born in California, **Anthony Abbott** grew up in New England and received degrees at Princeton and Harvard universities before coming to North Carolina. Since 1964 he has served as chair of English at Davidson College. An active member of the state's literary community, he has published two collections and served as president of both the Charlotte Writers' Club and the North Carolina Writers' Network. His service, his teaching, and his poetry have won him a number of honors, including the Thomas Jefferson Award and Hunter-Hamilton Love of Teaching Award.

A Texas native, **Betty Adcock** came to North Carolina with her husband, musician Don Adcock. Soon after enrolling in a creative writing class under Guy Owen, she began publishing poetry in national journals. Each of her four collections has won awards and she has received both an National Endowment for the Arts Fellowship and a North Carolina Individual Artist Fellowship. She has conducted workshops, served on panels, and read her work throughout the United States, including at the Library of Congress. A former advertising writer, she is currently Kenan Writer-in-Residence at Meredith College.

**Annette Allen** was born in Iowa and lived in New Jersey, Texas, and Ghana, West Africa before coming in 1990 to Salem College in Winston-Salem. Formerly Dean of the College, she currently serves as Director of the Center for Women Writers, which holds a yearly series of readings, workshops, and community courses. She has been awarded numerous grants and fellowships, including the New Jersey State Council on the Arts Poetry Fellowship Award.

After growing up on a tobacco farm near Whiteville, **A. R. Ammons** received a degree from Wake Forest College, and served as an elementary school principal in Hatteras, but he has lived most of his adult life outside his native state. His interest in writing developed during long hours aboard ship when he served a term of duty with the Navy. In 1964 he joined the faculty at Cornell University, where he is currently Goldwin Smith Professor of English. Among his many honors are the Bollingen Prize, the National Book Award (twice), the MacArthur Fellowship, and the 1998 Tanning Prize from the Academy of American Poets.

Born near Winston-Salem, **Shirley Anders** (1933–1994) began to write poetry seriously while working as a secretary at Wake Forest University. After earning an MFA at Bennington College she won both a North Carolina Arts Council Fellowship and the 1986 Devins Award for Poetry from the University Press for her collection *The Bus Home*. She taught at UNC-Greensboro, Guilford College, and, as writer-in-residence, at two universities in Wisconsin before her unexpected death in 1994.

Born Marguerite Johnson in St. Louis, Missouri, **Maya Angelou** has achieved international attention with plays, poems, stories, and a multi-volume autobiography. Also noted as a composer, actress, and public speaker, she was invited to write and present a poem for President Bill Clinton's first inauguration. She served on President Jimmy Carter's Commission of the International Women's Year and worked with Dr. Martin Luther King, Jr. in the Southern Christian Leadership Conference. In 1980 she was named Reynolds Professor at Wake Forest University.

After Stantonsburg native **James Applewhite** studied under noted writing teacher William Blackburn at Duke University, he taught at UNC-Greensboro, working, as Guy Owen notes, "under the informal guidance of Randall Jarrell and Allen Tate." Since 1972 he has taught at Duke University and authored eight collections of poetry. His work is deeply rooted in place, especially his native Wilson County. His many awards for both writing and teaching include the American Academy and Institute of Arts and Letters' Jean Stein Award in Poetry, grants from the National Endowment for the Arts, and election to the Fellowship of Southern Writers.

Although **Stewart Atkins** (1913–1961) was born into a prominent Gastonia family which owned and published the *Gastonia Gazette*, for which Atkins worked as advertising director and city editor, much of the poetry which he wrote during his relatively short life centers on the lives of sharecroppers and textile workers. When only nineteen, Atkins helped found the North Carolina Poetry Society and served as editor of *The North Carolina Poetry Review*. His poetry collection was published in 1952.

**Margaret Boothe Baddour**'s varied career has included serving as a journalist, director of the Goldsboro Community Arts Council, and instructor at Wayne Community College, Mount Olive College, and Barton College. A Greensboro native with two poetry collections, she is noted for her support of the arts; she as served as an officer of Arts Advocates of North Carolina, a founding member of the North Carolina Writers' Network, and president of the North Carolina Poetry Society. Honors include the 1996 North Carolina Poetry Council Award given for contributions to the arts in this state.

Born in Alabama, **Gerald Barrax** moved to Pittsburgh at the age of ten. After serving four years in the Air Force, he received degrees from Duquesne University and the University of Pittsburgh. In 1969 he came to Durham to teach at North Carolina Central University, then moved to North Carolina State University, where he taught until 1997. As well as publishing five poetry collections, he has served as poetry editor of *Callaloo* and as editor of *Obsidian II*. His many awards include the 1993 Raleigh Medal of Arts, a Woodrow Wilson Fellowship, and the Edward Stanley Award.

Pittsburgh native **Joseph Bathanti** came to North Carolina in 1976 as a VISTA volunteer and later taught at a number of North Carolina colleges, often serving as artist-in-residence. Now he is writer-in-residence and program coordinator of the humanities division at Mitchell Community College in Statesville. His one-act play that won the Playwright's Fund of North Carolina Prize was produced at the University of Knoxville in Tennessee. He has received a North Carolina Arts Council Fellowship and has been a Pushcart nominee for short fiction and essays.

**Ronald Bayes,** who began writing limericks when he was a seventh-grader in Oregon, has studied in Ireland and Canada, as well as this country. Repeated residencies in Japan whetted his appetite for Oriental poetry. Since 1968 he as taught at St. Andrews Presbyterian College, where he is now writer-in-residence and a distinguished Professor of Creative Writing and has won the Distinguished Faculty Award. The founder of both St. Andrews Review and St. Andrews Press, he is revered for his teaching and editing as well as numerous collections of award-winning poetry.

Born in Concord, **Jeffery Beam** has lived in Charlotte and Chapel Hill, where he currently works in the Biology Library. He has edited *Sanskrit* and *Oyster Boy Review* and published eight volumes of poetry, one of which was nominated for the Pushcart Prize in 1990. He is especially interested in integrating oral, visual, and written arts in varied presentations. In 1998–99, he was award a Mary Duke Biddle Foundation grant.

After growing up in upstate New York and receiving degrees at the University of Chicago and Columbia University, **Helen Bevington** came to Durham in 1943 with her husband Merle, a professor of English. She, too, joined the English faculty and began writing poetry, "some of it very light verse," she says, "probably because of the particular pleasure of living in the country in North Carolina." Her poems have frequently appeared in the *New Yorker*. Honors include the University of Chicago Award for Distinguished Achievement and the Mayflower Cup.

A lifelong resident of Robeson County, **Denise Blue** began writing poetry under the tutelage of Kathryn Stripling Byer while undertaking studies for an M. A. in English at Western Carolina University. Her thesis was a collection of poetry, *The Lumbee: Lies, Lives, and Legends.* Currently she teaches at Pembroke Middle School and Robeson Community College.

**John Henry Boner** (1845–1903) grew up in Winston-Salem, then worked at the *Salem Observer* as a printer's devil, typesetter, and proofreader. This experience led him to the District of Columbia, where he worked in the government printing office; while there, he wrote his first volume of poetry. Later he moved to New York and served as literary editor of *New York World*, then associate editor of *Literary Digest.* In 1901, he came home in poor health, and died of tuberculosis in 1903. His collection, *Poems*, was reprinted in 1943 by John Blair, Publishers.

Born in Lancaster, S.C., **Cathy Smith Bowers** came to North Carolina in 1993. Currently she serves as poet-in-residence at Queens College in Charlotte. Her work has appeared in two collections, as well as numerous periodicals, including *Atlantic Monthly*, *Georgia Review*, and *Poetry.* Before moving to this state, she was awarded a South Carolina Poetry Fellowship. She has also received the General Electric Award for Younger Writers.

After military service during World War I, **James Boyd** (1888–1944) moved from his native Pennsylvania to Moore County, in search of both a mild climate and a quiet place to work. There he wrote nationally acclaimed historical novels, edited and published the weekly *Pilot*, and became a leading citizen of the region and the state. During World War II, he and other American writers formed the Free Company of Players to produce original radio plays in response to antidemocratic attitudes caused by the war. His poems were written during his last years, and the collection was reissued on the fiftieth anniversary of his death.

In addition to being a poet, **Earl Braggs** is also a visual artist specializing in montage and collage; his work has been exhibited in several southern states. A native of Wilmington, Braggs was one of the winners in the 1989 North Carolina Writers' Network Black Writers' Competition. His poetry has been praised "for the range and depth of its subject matter alone—family history and its intersections with public history and pop culture and the intricacies of race and poverty." His awards include the Anhinga Prize for Poetry in 1992 and the Jack Kerouac Literary Prize in 1995.

At the age of sixteen, **Zoe Kincaid Brockman** (1893–1975) marked two major achievements: she married and she published her first poem. After growing up in Gastonia, she began writing for the *Gastonia Daily Gazette*, eventually becoming woman's editor. During the following years, she published short fiction and won awards for both poetry and reporting. She became the first president of the North Carolina Poetry Society, which she had helped organize, and was associate editor of *The North Carolina Poetry Review.*

Rocky Mount native **Grey Brown** began working with patients when she was a graduate student at New York University. This has led to a position which she has held twice (1986–1989, and 1994–present): Director of Literary Arts at the Duke University Medical Center. There she uses poetry as a healing art form with patients, both reading poetry to them and collecting poems written by patients and staff, and publishing them in chapbooks. She also handles details for the weekly Osler Literary Roundtable. In 1992, her own work won the Harperprints Chapbooks poetry competition.

After completing school in Akron, Ohio, **Linda Beatrice Brown** studied at Bennett College. Years later, after earning her doctoral degree and teaching at UNC-Greensboro and Guilford College, she returned to Bennett, where she now is a Distinguished Professor of Humanities. In 1984 her first novel, *Rainbow Roun Mah Shoulder,* won the North Carolina Coalition Prize. She was also awarded a North Carolina Arts Council Fellowship. Her poetry has been published in places as varied as scholarly journals and children's magazines.

Born in Statesville, **Sally Buckner** grew up in Albemarle. A former journalist, she has taught at every level from kindergarten through graduate school, and recently retired after twenty-eight years on the faculty at Peace College. She has published poetry, plays, non-fiction, and short fiction. In 1991 she edited *Our Words, Our Ways,* an anthology of North Carolina literature designed to accompany eighth-grade studies of state history. She is also the editor of this anthology. Honors include the Ragan-Rubin Award given to writers for their contribution to education.

Although **Kathryn Stripling Byer** grew up in Georgia, she has lived most of her adult life in Cullowhee near her grandmother's home territory in the Blue Ridge Mountains. She also received her M.F.A. at UNC-Greensboro, studying with James Applewhite, Fred Chappell, and Robert Watson. She has served as poet-in-residence at Western Carolina University and has held residencies at other colleges. Her work has won major awards, including the Anne Sexton Poetry Prize and the Lamont Poetry Selection, and she has received writing fellowships from the NEA and the North Carolina Arts Council.

Born in Illinois, **Mary Belle Campbell** worked as a freelance writer, journalist, and teacher before moving to Moore County in 1973. She has authored four books, including two of poetry, and has taught at Sandhills Community College. She also established Scots Plaid Press and Persephone Press, which holds an annual chapbook competition. In 1998 she retired, having developed a foundation to continue the two presses (Persephone under the direction of the North Carolina Writers' Network) and having endowed the

Brockman/ Campbell Book Award annually given by the North Carolina Poetry Society.

After studying at Barnard College, **Marion Cannon** (1906–1996) lived in Belgium until 1942, when she fled the turbulence to return to her native Charlotte. After her husband's death, she began writing poetry and eventually published three collections; her *Collected Poems* was reprinted six times. She devotedly supported the arts and civil rights causes with her money, her time, and her energy. In an obituary, Gerry Hostetler of the *Charlotte Observer* wrote, "Poetry was her life in her later years, and in a way, her life *was* her poetry."

**Fred Chappell** began his varied literary career by writing science fiction while an eighth-grader in Canton. He then turned to poetry, which he studied under William Blackburn at Duke University before joining the English faculty at UNC-Greensboro in 1964. To date he has published eight novels, two collections of short fiction, two of essays, and over a dozen of poetry. His writing has been recognized by many state, national, and international awards, including the Bollingen Prize and the T. S. Eliot Award. He was also presented the O. Max Gardner Award for his teaching. In 1997 he was named North Carolina Poet Laureate.

Born in Los Angeles, **Richard Chess** grew up in New Jersey. Formerly a communications associate with the Federation of Jewish Agencies in Philadelphia, since 1988 he has taught at UNC-Asheville, where he is director of the Center for Jewish Studies. His first collection, *Tekiah*, appeared in 1994. His work is also included in *Telling and Remembering: A Century of American Jewish Poetry* (Beacon, 1997). He has served on the Board of the North Carolina Writers' Network. In 1989 and 1990 he was a Writing Fellow at the Virginia Center for the Creative Arts.

Virginia native **Michael Chitwood** has worked as a science writer in Research Triangle Park, as free-lance journalist, as book editor for *The Independent*, and as lecturer in the creative writing program at UNC-Chapel Hill. A winner of a North Carolina Arts Council Fellowship, he has published five collections of poetry. His essays for North Carolina's largest National Public Radio affiliate were also published in 1998. Many of his poems deal with his growing up in Virginia and with the lives of textile mill workers of his region.

In addition to poetry, **L. Teresa Church** has authored articles and award-winning plays. Born in Virginia, in 1987 she came to this state, where she works as an archivist at UNC-Chapel Hill. A member of the Carolina African American Writers Collective, she participated in the tenth annual Blumenthal Writers and Readers Series. Her third play was awarded the 1989 North Carolina Arts Council Playwrights Fellowship, was included in an anthology of works by North Carolina playwrights, and was produced by the Carolina Playwrights Center in 1995.

Born in Kentucky just after the Civil War, **Olive Tilford Dargan** (1869–1968) lived and wrote in this state from 1906 until the late fifties. Publishing her first novel when she was only twenty, she authored plays, poetry, and novels — the latter under the pseudonym of Fielding Burke. *The Cycle's Rim*, a sequence of sonnets on her husband's death, won the 1917 William Houston Patterson Memorial Cup. *The Spotted Hawk*, her last collection, published when she was 90, won both the Roanoke-Chowan Award and the Thomas Wolfe Literary Award.

**Ann Deagon** has remarked that she didn't begin writing until she was forty, "when that three-headed dog love death and poetry took me in its teeth and shook me." The Alabama native, then a professor of classics at Guilford College, quickly made up for lost time, publishing six collections of poetry. She has also written fiction and worked in film and theatre. At Guilford College she founded Poetry Center Southeast, precursor to the North Carolina Writers' Network. Among her awards is a National Endowment for the Arts Literary Fellowship.

Born in Hawaii of Korean and Okinawan ancestry, **Debra Kang Dean** served in the United States Air Force before receiving three college degrees and moving with her husband to Greenville, where she served as contributing editor to *Tar River Poetry*. In 1997, her chapbook *Back to Back* was published as winner of the Harperprints competition sponsored by the North Carolina Writers' Network, and her full-length collection, *News of Home*, was published a year later.

In addition to being a poet, **Grace DiSanto** (1924–1993) worked as reporter and drama critic with several newspapers. A Connecticut native, she moved to this state in 1961 and lived in Morganton until her death. Almost two hundred of her poems appeared in literary magazines as well as in her 1982 collection, *The Eye Is Single*. She won eleven awards for poetry, including designation as Poet of the Month by the New York Poetry Forum. She was a member of the North Carolina Poetry Society, the Poetry Council of North Carolina, and Centro Studie Scamb Internationale in Rome, Italy.

A native of New Jersey, **Stuart Dischell** completed degrees at Antioch College and The Writer's Workshop at the University of Iowa. He came to North Carolina in 1992 and now is a member of the graduate faculty of the MFA program in creative writing at UNC-Greensboro. He has published two volumes of poetry, one of which, *Good Hope Road* (1993), was a selection of the National Poetry Series. He has been an Allen Collins Fellow at Breadloaf and has won a Pushcart Prize and, in 1996, an NEA Fellowship.

Charlotte native **Harriet Doar** (1912–1999) developed a literary career focusing on journalism and poetry. For many years she was a journalist for the *Charlotte Observer*, serving as reporter, columnist, editor of the book page, and women's editor. She was co-founder and president of North Carolina Press Women. Her poetry was collected in *The Restless Water* and was anthologized in *Eleven Charlotte Poets* and *North Carolina Poetry: The 70s*.

A native of Bandanna in Mitchell County, **Hilda Downer** received two degrees at Appalachian State University, where she studied with John Foster West, and an M.F.A. at Norwich Univeristy in Vermont, where she studied with Jack Myers. Her collection *Bandanna Creek* was accepted while she was still a college junior. She has been writer-in-residence with the Poetry-in-the-Schools program and a volunteer for local schools in both poetry-writing and art. As she continues her writing, she currently works as a nurse.

One of North Carolina's most prolific writers, **Charles Edward Eaton** has published a novel, four collections of short stories, a play, a critical biography, and fourteen volumes of poetry. A native of Winston-Salem, he served as Vice Consul at Rio de Janeiro during World War II, taught at the University of North Carolina in Chapel Hill, then moved to Woodbury, Connecticut to devote his entire time to writing. His work has won a number of state and national awards, including two from the Poetry Society of America and an honorary doctorate from St. Andrews College.

Born in Asheville, **Keith Flynn** studied at Mars Hill College and UNC-Asheville, where he founded the student newspaper and won the Sandburg Prize for Poetry. His rock band, The Crystal Zoo, has produced three albums. His poems have appeared in this country and in Europe, and as musician and poet he has performed in the United States and Canada. Awards include the Emerging Songwriter Prize from the American Society of Composers and Publishers and the Paumanok Poetry Prize. He is founder and managing editor of *Asheville Poetry Review*.

Before coming from his native Connecticut to North Carolina in 1982, **Charles Fort** taught in several northeastern colleges. At UNC-Wilmington, he founded and directed the creative writing program and advised and edited literary publications, including the *Wilmington Review*. In 1989, he was awarded literary fellowships from both the National Endowment of the Arts and the North Carolina Arts Council. He also received awards from the Poetry Society of America, as well as the Randall Jarrell Poetry Prize. He currently holds an endowed chair at the University of Nebraska at Kearney.

Born in Greenville, S.C., **Becky Gould Gibson** came to North Carolina in 1968. She has taught at the North Carolina School of the Arts and, currently, at Guilford College. In addition to teaching creative writing, she has led poetry workshops in schools and prisons. She has also participated in numerous readings, including the Blumenthal Series and the Emrys Foundation program in South Carolina. She is the recipient of the North Carolina Writers' Network Chapbook Competition, 1989, and the White Eagle Coffee Store Press Chapbook Competition, 1995.

When she was still a child, Virginia native **Grace Gibson** began writing for a children's page in the Richmond *Times-Dispatch*. After completing university studies she was a reporter on the *Times-Dispatch*, then the Durham *Sun*. For years she has lived in Laurinburg, teaching writing at St. Andrews College and UNC-Pembroke, where she also served as associate editor of *Pembroke Magazine*. When she retired from UNC-Pembroke, she was honored by establishment of the Grace E. Gibson Scholarship Fund for creative writers.

Two states can make a strong claim on **Marie Gilbert**. She was born in South Carolina, won major poetry prizes there, and still maintains a home in Georgetown. But she and her husband also live in Greensboro, and she has been an active member of this state's literary community, serving as president of the North Carolina Poetry Society from 1990–92. Many of her poems, published in four collections, deal with places in both states.

Born in Boulder, Colorado, **Evalyn Gill** has called North Carolina home since 1972. She has taught English at Saginaw Valley University and UNC-Greensboro and has also published four poetry collections. The founding editor of *International Poetry Review,* she has served as editor or member of the editorial board of several anthologies, including *O. Henry Festival Stories* (1985 and 1987), *More Than Magnolias, Women of the Piedmont Triad,* and, most recently, *A Turn in Time: Piedmont Writers at the Millennium.*

Born just across the state line in Rock Hill, S.C., **Judy Goldman** moved with her family to Charlotte in 1967. There she has not only written her own poetry, but taught poetry workshops at Queens College and in the Poetry-in-the-Schools program. Her essays have appeared on local National Public Radio stations. She has also read her poetry and directed workshops all over the Southeast. Her second volume, *Wanting to Know the End*, was winner of the 1992 Gerald Cable Poetry chapbook Competition. Recently she published her first novel, *The Slow Way Back.*

**Jaki Shelton Green** has spent her entire life in her native town, Efland, where she has worked in community economic development and served as director of YouthBuild. Combining professional experience with her poetry, she has directed "Creating Community Through Poetry" workshops. The author of two collections, Green has served on the boards of the North Carolina Writers' Network and the North Carolina Humanities Council. She has performed and taught poetry in the United States, the Caribbean, Europe, and Brazil.

Born near Lillington, **Paul Green** (1894–1981) interrupted his education at UNC-Chapel Hill in order to serve with the Army in World War I. Back at the University, he began writing plays with Professor Frederick Koch, director of the Playmakers. He wrote poetry, nonfiction and screenplays, but his national reputation is based on his plays: *In Abraham's Bosom* won the Pulitzer Prize, and *The Lost Colony* began a whole new tradition of historical outdoor dramas. He also exerted major influence for cultural and social causes throughout the state. Among his many honors are the Albert Schweitzer Medal for Artistry and the Frank Porter Graham ACLU Award.

A native of Mississippi, **Lucinda Grey** grew up in various Southern states and studied at Lake Erie College, Vanderbilt University, and the University of Valencia in Spain before coming to Charlotte in 1969. She has taught at Winthrop College and is currently senior lecturer in English and creative writing at UNC-Charlotte. She has also served as associate editor of *Southern Poetry Review*. She has received significant awards, including the La Napoule Writer's Residency in France, the Quentin R. Howard Poetry Prize, and the Andrew Mountain Poetry Prize.

Since 1969, **Robert Waters Grey**, a native of Maryland, has taught at UNC-Charlotte, where he is associate professor of English. For several years he also served as editor of *Southern Poetry Review*. His poetry has appeared in a number of national journals and in two collections. In addition, he has co-edited two anthologies: *11 Charlotte Poets*, with Charleen Whisnant (Swansea), and *White Trash: An Anthology of Contemporary Southern Poets*, with Nancy Stone.

Born in Whiteville, **Kathryn Bright Gurkin** has spent much of her adult life in Clinton, where she has written her own poetry and served the cultural community as a founder of the Sampson County Arts Council. She has worked as Executive Director of the Council and served on the board of directors of the North Carolina Poetry Society. Her humorous essays have appeared in periodicals in this country and Spain. Her poetry collections have won a number of honors, including the Sidney Lanier Award.

Born in Leaksville (now Eden), **R. S. Gwynn** received degrees at Davidson College and the University of Arkansas. Since 1973 he has lived in Texas, where he is professor of English at Lamar University. The author of five collections of poetry, he has edited reference books, anthologies, and textbooks. His collection *The Drive-In* was winner of the Breakthrough Award given by the University of Missouri Press.

**Frank Borden Hanes** began writing poems while serving as an ensign in the United States Navy during World War II. When he returned to his native Winston-Salem, he joined the staff of the *Twin City Sentinel*. His novel in verse, *Abel Anders*, was the first winner of the Roanoke-Chowan Award in 1951; ten years later, a prose novel, *The Fleet Rabble*, won the Sir Walter Award for fiction. He has also received numerous awards for his participation in cultural affairs, especially those dealing with education and the arts.

Born in Concord, **William Harmon** served for seven years in the U.S. Navy, then received a Ph.D. at the University of Cincinnati. He returned to his native state to teach at UNC-Chapel Hill, where he is currently James Gordon Hanes

Professor of English. He has published critical studies as well as five volumes of poetry. Honors include a Lamont Poetry Selection and the William Carlos Award. A specialist in light verse, he has also edited three major anthologies of poetry, including *The Oxford Book of American Light Verse*.

After serving in the Navy during the Vietnam War, Illnois native **Thomas Hawkins** came to this state to study creative writing at UNC-Greensboro. There he studied with Fred Chappell and Robert Watson and met his future wife, fellow poet Anna Wooten-Hawkins. A public affairs writer and editor for the National Institute of Environmental Health Sciences in Research Triangle Park, he has served on the board of the North Carolina Writers' Network. In addition to *Paper Crown*, a collection of short-short stories, he has published poetry and fiction in varied journals.

Born in Akron, Ohio, **David Hopes** came to North Carolina in 1983. A professor of literature and humanities at UNC-Asheville, he is deeply involved in the arts. He has published several volumes of poetry, one of which—*The Glacier's Daughters*—won the Juniper Prize, and a collection of nature essays. He has also published several plays and seen them produced. In addition to his work on the editorial staff of the *Asheville Poetry Review*, he serves as director of the Pisgah Players Theater Company, the Urthona Press, and the Urthona Art Gallery in Asheville.

For thirty-five years South Carolina native **Gladys Owings Hughes** taught in Alamance County elementary classrooms. Although she had written verse and children's plays since childhood, only after retiring did she begin to write poetry for publication. She has held office in both the North Carolina Poetry Society and the North Carolina Poetry Council, both of which have recognized her contributions by dedicating publications to her.

**Randall Jarrell** (1914–1965) spent his childhood in his birthplace—Nashville, Tennessee—and California. From his Army Air Corps experience in World War II, he wrote the poetry which first brought him national attention. In 1947, Jarrell began teaching at the Woman's College of the University of North Carolina, where he remained until 1965. From 1956–58 he served as Consultant in Poetry at the Library of Congress. In addition to poetry, he wrote criticism, four children's books, and a novel. In addition to literary honors, including being named to the National Institute of Arts and Letters, in 1962 he received the O. Max Gardner Award for his "contribution to the welfare of the human race."

Born in Fremont, Nebraska, **Lance Jeffers** (1919–1985) received degrees from Columbia University, then taught at several major universities, including Talladega College, for which he won the Distinguished Scholar Award, and North Carolina State University, where he taught English from 1974–1985. He published four collections of poetry, and his work has been included in over 39 anthologies and periodicals. He was awarded the Francis T. Baker Citation from Columbia University. In 1948, his fiction was included in *Best American Short Stories.*

The writing of **Paul Jones** spans both the technological and the artistic worlds, as does his education: a B.S. in computer science and an M.F.A. in poetry. A native of Hickory, he has spent most of his professional life in Chapel Hill, where he serves on the faculty and as director of Metalab. He has edited *Internet Poetry Archive*, served as vice-president of the North Carolina Writers' Network, and directed the ArtsCenter's Poets' Exchange. His poetry has been recognized by a North Carolina Arts Council Writers Fellowship and the Harperprints Chapbook Award.

Mebane resident **Debra Kaufman** grew up in Illinois and Iowa and worked as waitress, reporter, and editor in Portland, Maine, before coming to North Carolina. In addition to working at the Duke Law Library, she has served as president of the North Carolina Writers' Network. Currently a managing editor, she divides her writing attention between poetry and drama, and has had plays produced both in this state and in California. *Still Life Burning* won the Kinloch Rivers Memorial Chapbook Award.

A lifelong resident of the Qualla Boundary, home of the Eastern Band of Cherokee, **Deborah Kinsland** received her M.A. from Western Carolina University, studying poetry under Kathryn Stripling Byer. Currently she is writer/consultant for the Cherokee Ministry Association and continues work on *Do You Just Say My Words?* a collection of contemporary oral literature intertwined with narrative that introduces the tellers and elaborates on Cherokee heritage and culture.

Born in Milwaukee, **Stephen Knauth** grew up in Pittsburgh. He began writing poetry after college, and has won two fellowships each from the North Carolina Arts Council and the National Endowment for the Arts. For some years he lived in Cold Water (Cabarrus County), then moved to Charlotte. He has worked as writer and producer of educational media and as a free-lance writer. Currently a senior writer with Healthcare Software, he has published four poetry collections.

**Mary Kratt's** writing career encompasses poetry, biography, and history—and sometimes she combines the three. A native of West Virginia, she has taught English and American Studies at UNC-Charlotte, and has written histories and biographies centered in her adopted city, Charlotte. She has published eleven books, including four collections of poetry. She has received the MacDowell Fellowship in poetry, an North Carolina Arts Council grant, and two prizes for her history writing. She also won the Icarus chapbook competition.

Ohio native **Steven Lautermilch** moved to Greensboro in 1973. The author of six poetry collections, he has won numerous honors, including awards from *The Centennial Review, The Devil's Millhopper,* and *International Po-*

*etry Review.* As a Fulbright Travel Fellow he lectured at Johannes Gutenberg Universitat, Mainz, Germany. Now retired as associate professor emeritus from UNC-Greensboro, he lives in Kill Devil Hills, where he works full time at writing and photography. He also offers workshops and seminars in dream study, meditation, and writing.

After coming to North Carolina from her native Iowa in 1982, **Sarah Lindsay** earned her M.F.A. at UNC-Greensboro, studying with Fred Chappell. The former managing editor for Unicorn Press, she now works as a copy editor for *Sky* magazine, as senior editor for *Voyageur* at Pace Communications, Inc., and as a professional cellist. Her collection *Primate Behavior* was a one of five finalists for the 1997 National Book Award in poetry. Her varied subject matter often focuses on natural and mythological worlds.

Because of a congenital heart defect, the life of **Amon Liner** (1940–1976) was short and his physical action limited, but he not only outlived the predictions of physicians but filled his years with notable activity in the arts. Born in Charlotte, he studied at several colleges and earned his M.F.A. at UNC-Greensboro. As well as reviewing books for the *Charlotte Observer* and editing poetry for *Red Clay Reader*, he composed enough poetry for five collections, three of which were published posthumously.

For thirty years Brooklyn native **Lou Lipsitz** taught political science at UNC-Chapel Hill, publishing a widely-used text on politics as well as scholarly articles. More recently he has established a second career as a psychotherapist in Raleigh and Chapel Hill. During all these years he was writing and publishing poetry, including three collections. He also published a textbook, *American Democracy*. In 1968–69 he was awarded a writer's grant from the National Endowment for the Arts. He has been deeply involved in the men's movement for the past decade.

**Robert Hill Long** has published two collections of poetry, one of which, *The Work of the Bow,* won the 1995 Cleveland State University Center Poetry Prize. A native of Wilmington, he was founding director of the North Carolina Writers' Network in 1985. Currently he teaches at the University of Oregon. The recipient of fellowships from both the North Carolina Arts Council and the National Endowment for the Arts, he is involved in publication on the World Wide Web and helps produce a monthly program of multi-generational poetry and prose for National Public Radio affiliate KLCC in Eugene, Oregon.

**Susan Ludvigson** moved from her native Wisconsin to Charlotte in the 1970s. A professor of English and poet-in-residence at Winthrop College in Rock Hill, S.C. (just over the state line from Charlotte), she has won ten grants, including Fulbright and Rockefeller fellowships, and has read her work not only throughout this country—including the Library of Congress—but in France, Yugoslavia and Crete. She has published twelve collections of poetry and has served on advisory boards of both North Carolina and South Carolina writers' networks.

Born in Salem, Oregon, 1906, **Norman Macleod** was a prolific poet and novelist who founded and/or edited some of the leading little magazines in American and Europe. He was also the founder of the New York City Poetry Center. He has been credited as one of the first editors of this century to recognize the historical and cultural contributions of Native and Spanish Americans. After coming to Pembroke State University, he founded *Pembroke Magazine* in 1969 and edited it for 10 years. He was presented the Horace Gregory Award in 1973.

Although he was born in Massachusetts, **Al Maginnes** grew up in the southeast and received degrees from East Carolina University and the University of Arkansas, where he studied with Heather Ross Miller, among others. His work has won two Lily Peter Foundation Fellowships, two McKean Awards for literary merit, and the John Ciardi Award given by the University of Arkansas. He has taught at Louisburg College and, currently, at Wake Technical Community College. His work has appeared in many national journals as well as two collections.

Among previous occupations, **Peter Makuck** lists, "truck driver, painter, mechanic," but he is best known as writer and as Distinguished Professor of Arts and Sciences at East Carolina University. He has published a collection of short stories and five collections of poetry as well as numerous essays, and received the International Poetry Forum's Charity Randall Citation. A Connecticut native, he has been a Fulbright Lecturer at the Universite de Savoie, Chambery, France. He is founder and editor of *Tar River Poetry*.

In 1976 Indiana native **Rebecca McClanahan** came to Charlotte where, for a number of years as Coordinator of the Poets-in-the-Schools program for Charlotte/Mecklenburg Schools she taught poetry to students of all ages. She has studied with A. R. Ammons, Audre Lorde, and George Garrett, and been both a MacDowell Fellow and a Bread Loaf Scholar. Her honors, include a Pushcart Prize for fiction and the Wood Prize from *Poetry*. She has published collections of poetry and nonfiction, and a poem was included in *Best American Poems, 1997*.

Salisbury native **Harold G. McCurdy** devoted his professional career to teaching biology, psychology, and philosophy, eventually becoming Kenan Professor of Psychology at UNC-Chapel Hill. During those years his poems appeared in *The New Yorker* and *Prairie Schooner* as well as regional magazines and anthology. In addition to poetry collections, he published four other books on psychological subjects. A former recipient of the Tanner Teaching Award at the University, he is now retired.

**Agnes McDonald** has taught English at Barton College and UNC-Wilmington and directed workshops across the state. A native of Durham, she was selected for the Blumenthal Writer & Readers Series. Her poetry has been published in literary periodicals, her own collection, and *Four North Carolina Women Poets*. She also edited *Journey Proud*, an anthology of writings from contemporary Southern women's journals. In 1985 she was awarded the first writer-in-residence in poetry at the Atlantic Center for the Arts, where she studied with James Dickey.

Born in Arden, **Michael McFee** grew up in Asheville. He has served as editor, librarian, reviewer, and teacher at a number of universities and workshops. Currently he teaches in the creative writing program at UNC-Chapel Hill. He has received grants from the National Endowment for the Arts, Ingram Merrill Foundation, and the North Carolina Arts Council and has won awards for both poetry and teaching. In addition to publishing five poetry collections, he compiled and edited *The Language They Speak Is Things to Eat: Poems by Fifteen Contemporary North Carolina Poets*.

Born near Lumberton, **James McGirt** (1874–1930) graduated from Bennett College in 1895. His first book was *Avenging the Main*, a lyric poem on the love of land and rural life. In 1903 he moved to Philadelphia, where he was editor and publisher of *McGirt's Magazine*, an illustrated monthly devoted to art, science, literary, and general interest. He published a collection of poetry and some short fiction, then came back to Greensboro, where he and his sister established several successful businesses.

Riverton native **John Charles McNeill** (1874–1907) was often referred to as "poet laureate," although there was no such official designation during his lifetime. After studying under Benjamin Sledd at Wake Forest College, McNeill taught school, practiced law, and served in the state legislature until 1904, when the Charlotte *Observer* invited him to join the staff. For the next three years until his untimely death he wrote hundreds of poems, and his first collection, *Songs Merry and Sad* was awarded the brand new Patterson Cup. Within weeks after his death, his second collection was published, and in 1977 a third collection was edited by Richard Walser.

Born in Albemarle, **Susan Meyers** grew up in Greenville, N.C., but now lives in Georgetown, S.C. She has worked as copy editor and book editor in Minnesota and has taught writing courses in community programs and at colleges in South Carolina and Minnesota. In 1996 she received the South Carolina Academy of Authors' Poetry Fellowship, but she has retained her North Carolina ties, serving as board member and as president of the North Carolina Poetry Society. *Lessons in Leaving* was the winner of the 1998 Persephone Press publication award.

**Heather Ross Miller** is a member of the Ross "writing family" of Stanly County, which includes her father, Fred; her uncle, James; and her aunt,

Eleanor Ross Taylor. After studying under Randall Jarrell at the Woman's College of UNC, she lived with her family for several years at Singletary Lake State Park. She has taught at several universities—currently at Washington & Lee University in Virginia—and has published fourteen books of poetry and fiction Among her awards are the Sir Walter Raleigh prize for fiction and three creative writing fellowships from the National Endowment for the Arts.

Born in Leiceister, near Asheville, **Jim Wayne Miller** (1936–1996) established a triple career: as professor at Western Kentucky University, as writer, and as scholar of Appalachian life. He published nine collections of poetry, two of translations, and a novel; he also edited an anthology of Appalachian literature. Among his many awards, given both for literary work and for public service, are the Thomas Wolfe Award and the Appalachian Writers Association Book of the Year Award. In 1988 Emory & Henry College held a Jim Wayne Miller Literary Festival in his honor.

**Shirley Moody** began writing stories and keeping journals while growing up in Raleigh. She graduated from Peace College and studied at North Carolina State University with Thomas Walters. While serving as a legal secretary, she began publishing poetry in literary journals, in *Four North Carolina Woman Poets*, and in her own collection. For twenty-one years she has participated in the Writer-in-Residence programs throughout the state, serving over 200 schools. Her poetry often deals with daily moments and close relationships.

After serving in the U.S. Army, Jacksonville native **Lenard Duane Moore** moved to Raleigh where he worked with the North Carolina Department of Public Instruction and served as writer-in-residence in public schools. Currently he teaches at North Carolina State University and writes poetry, reviews, and essays. He is founder and executive director of the Carolina African American Writers' Collective, whose members have published and read their works widely. Moore, whose work has been translated into six languages, received the 1997 Margaret Walker Creative Writing Award and two Haiku Museum of Tokyo Awards.

Dreams of her Cherokee grandfather led Tennessee native **MariJo Moore** back from England to study and write about her Native American heritage. She has published two poetry collections reflecting that heritage and current Native American life. A resident of Asheville, she manages a publishing company and teaches workshops. Currently she is researching myths and gathering material for a non-fiction book on Cherokee women. She received the 1998 North Carolina Distinguished Woman of the Year Award in Arts.

Ever since **Ruth Moose** completed high school in Albemarle, she has published work in a variety of genres: essays, newspaper columns, reviews, short stories, and poetry. Her work has won honors such as the 1994

Robert Ruark Foundation Award, a North Carolina Writers' Fellowship, the Carl Sandburg Award, and a MacDowell Fellowship. The author of four collections of poetry and two of short fiction, she has been a librarian at Pfeiffer College and has taught in the Poetry-in-the-Schools program. Currently she teaches creative writing at UNC-Chapel Hill.

After growing up on the family farm in Zirconia—near Hendersonville—**Robert Morgan** began college at North Carolina State University, intending to study math. A creative course under Guy Owen turned him instead to poetry. Since 1971 he has taught at Cornell University, where he is now Kappa Alpha Professor of English. He has published ten collections of poetry and six works of fiction. In 1986 he was a Hawthornden Fellow in Poetry in Scotland. His writing has been recognized with many honors, including four National Endowment for the Arts grants, a Guggenheim Fellowship, and the Hanes Poetry Prize from the Fellowship of Southern Writers.

Born in Baltimore, **Pauli Murray** (1910–1985) came to live with her grandparents in Durham when she was only four. After completing high school there and receiving professional degrees, she became a lawyer, professor, college administrator, deputy attorney general of California, and—in her sixties—the first black woman Episcopalian priest in this country. Before turning to a legal career, she was guided in her writing by Stephen Vincent Benet. Throughout her varied career she maintained her interest in writing and produced a biography of her grandfather, her own autobiography, and a volume of poetry.

Born in Chicago, **Paul Baker Newman** received degrees at the University of Iowa and the University of Chicago. After serving in the army for five years during World War II and teaching in Kansas, in 1963 he came to Charlotte, where for almost thirty years he taught English at Queens College and wrote poetry, collected in seven volumes. Among his honors is the William Billings Fiske Award for poetry at the University of Chicago. He has made two films integrating his poetry with filmmaking.

Although Henderson native **Sallie Nixon** did not begin to write seriously until she was in her fifties, she has published three volumes of poetry and contributed vigorously to the the state's cultural life. She participated in Poetry-in-the-Schools programs and served as president of the North Carolina Poetry Society, secretary of the North Carolina Poetry Council and board member of the North Carolina Arts Council. Her writing has been recognized by awards from the Poetry Society of America and the 1970 American Academy of Poets Award from the University of Nebraska.

Massachusetts native **Charles Olson** (1910–1970) had taught at Harvard, worked in Franklin Roosevelt's administration, and published two books when he first came to this state to teach writing at Black Mountain College in fall, 1948. He was considered an inspiring teacher and served as rector from 1953–1956. Olson founded *Black Mountain Review*, which helped launch the careers of Allen Ginsberg, Jack Kerouac, and others. After leaving Black Mountain, he taught at SUNY-Buffalo and the University of Connecticut.

After growing up on a Bladen County farm, serving in the army during World War II, and receiving degrees from UNC-Chapel Hill, **Guy Owen** (1925–1981) established a multi-faceted career as poet, novelist, editor, essayist, and teacher of writing. He is probably best known for his novel *The Ballad of the Flim-Flam Man*, which was made into an award-winning movie, but readers also admire his poetry, and many poets owe him gratitude for his encouragement as founder and editor of *Southern Poetry Review* and as a distinguished professor at North Carolina State University from 1962 until his death. He received major awards for both his writing and his teaching.

Our second state poet laureate, **James Larkin Pearson** (1879–1981) was mainly self-educated, but he began composing poems very early in his childhood and throughout his extraordinarily long life dedicated himself to poetry. At age twenty-one the Wilkes County native learned the printer's trade. He then edited a monthly newspaper, *The Fool Killer*, which at one time had 50,000 readers. Upon recommendation of the North Carolina Literary and Historical Association, Governor William B. Umstead appointed him poet laureate in 1953, a position he held until his death at 101 in 1981.

Born in Virginia, **Gail Peck** came to North Carolina in 1982. She has taught creative writing for the adult education degree program at Queens College in Charlotte. Her first poetry collection, *New River*, won the Harperprints Award in 1994. She has frequently lectured on poetry for libraries and poetry organizations. She won a 1998 grant for study at Vermont Studio Center and won first place in poetry in the Deep South Writers Competition.

**Keith Petersen** was born in Massachusetts and taught in Arkansas before coming to this state in 1966 to teach political science at North Carolina State University. He began publishing poems in 1973, and since has published widely in journals and little magazines. He has won a number of honors, including the Virginia Prize awarded by *The Lyric* in 1988. His first collection, *The Grandfather Poems*, was published in 1998. Now retired, he lives and writes in Raleigh.

Greensboro, where he was born and educated, has always been home base for **Bruce Piephoff**, but his career as poet/songwriter/performer has taken him throughout this country, Canada, and Holland. Piephoff learned to play guitar from his father and honed his writing skills under Fred Chappell and Robert Watson at UNC-Greensboro. He has worked as visiting artist at a number of community colleges and public schools and has published a collection of poetry and eight albums of original folk/blues/ country songs on the Flyin' Cloud label.

**Diana Pinckney** grew in up Columbia, S.C., but has lived many years in Charlotte, where she is an active member of the literary community. She teaches poetry writing in the Queens College continuing education program and has conducted a number of workshops in the state. She has also served on the boards of the Charlotte Writers' Club and the North Carolina Poetry Society. Her work has won a number of state awards and her two chapbooks were both winners of publication competitions sponsored by Persephone Press and Nightshade Press.

A native of Cincinnati, **Deborah Pope** has lived in North Carolina since 1980. A professor of English at Duke University, she has published three collections, two of which were nominated for the Pulitzer Prize. Her work has also appeared in major anthologies. Her teaching of poetry, creative writing, women's literature, and women's studies has won her a Distinguished Teaching Award at Duke.

Florida native **Dannye Romine Powell** began writing in Phillips Russell's creative writing course at UNC-Chapel Hill. Since 1963 she has lived in North Carolina, serving as a teacher, writer, editor, and translator. For seventeen years she was book editor and feature writer for the *Charlotte Observer*, which she now serves as columnist. In 1993 she was awarded an National Endowment for the Arts grant for her poetry. In addition to writing and publishing poetry, she has authored short fiction and a book on Southern authors: *Parting the Curtains: Interviews with Southern Writers*.

After growing up in Randolph County, **Barbara Presnell** received degrees at UNC-Greensboro and the University of Kentucky. For several years she lived and taught (in both colleges and the Poetry-in-the-Schools program) in Kentucky. Currently she teaches English at Catawba College. She has received a number of grants to pursue her work, including awards from the Kentucky Foundation for Women, the Kentucky Arts Council, and the North Carolina Arts Council. She has published two collections.

In 1962 **Reynolds Price** burst upon the literary scene with *A Long and Happy Life*, a novel which won him the William Faulkner Award for fiction at the age of 29. Since then he has produced more than thirty volumes, including fiction, poetry, translations, plays, and memoirs. Born in Macon, Price grew up in eastern North Carolina and studied under William Blackburn at Duke University. A Rhodes Scholar, he is now James B. Duke Professor of English. Among his many honors are the National Book Critics Circle Award and and the Levinson, Blumenthal, and Tietjens awards for poetry.

Granville County native **Sam Ragan** (1915–1996) began a journalistic career by working on weekly and daily papers before serving in military intelligence during World War II. Afterward, he became executive editor of the Raleigh *News and Observer*, then editor/publisher of the *Pilot* in Southern Pines. He also served as North Carolina's first secretary of what is now the Department of Cultural Resources. Ragan wrote six collections of poetry and four works of nonfiction. He held many state and national offices, including director of the American Society of Newspaper Editors, and won numerous honors for his contributions to the cultural and artistic life of this state.

Born in Minnesota, **Margaret Rabb** came to North Carolina in 1970 to attend the University of North Carolina at Chapel Hill, where she concentrated on creative writing. She has occasionally taught at the University, and since 1977 has been director of design services at Southern Media Design & Production Inc. All along she has written and published poetry, winning such awards as the 1998 Harperprints Chapbook Award, the 1997 Louisiana Literature Prize for Poetry, and the Lullwater Prize for Poetry from Emory University.

**Becke Roughton** is a lifelong resident of North Carolina, but she has held residencies in such noted settings as the Yaddo Colony, the McDowell Colony, and the Millay Colony. Currently an instructor of fine arts at James Sprunt Community College, she was formerly an editor for Red Clay Books and now serves as co-editor of the arts and literary magazine *Wellspring*. She has also held residencies in the Poets-in-the-Schools program. Her poetry has been recognized by a fellowship from the North Carolina Arts Council and the Denny Award.

Born in Raleigh, **Gibbons Ruark** grew up in eastern North Carolina and taught at UNC-Greensboro before going to the University of Delaware, where he has served on the faculty since 1968. His poetry has appeared in a wide variety of periodicals and in various anthologies and texts. They have won him three National Endowment for the Arts fellowships and a Pushcart Prize. Seventy poems chosen from his six previous selections appear in his new collection, *Passing Through Customs: New and Selected Poems*.

The poetry of **Rebecca Ball Rust** is firmly rooted in North Carolina, but it has earned her awards in Hawaii, Japan, New Zealand, and the People's Republic of China. A native of Raleigh, she was working as exhibits curator for the North Carolina Department of Archives and History when she became fascinated by haiku. A former president of the North Carolina Poetry Society, she founded the North Carolina Haiku Society, which has attracted members from many states and Canada, and wrote a book describing the techniques for writing haiku, *The Outside of a Haiku*.

**Carl Sandburg** (1878–1967) is closely identified with his native state, Illinois, where he established a firm reputation with poetry which exalted the prairie, his native Chicago, and, above all, the common people. But in 1945 he and his family moved to Connemara Farm near Flat Rock and lived there until his death twenty-two years later. A major volume of poems, *Honey and Salt*, was published during his sojourn there, and twice our state honored him for his poetry. Other honors include the Presidential Medal of Freedom and a decoration by the King of Sweden. His estate is now a National Park.

A native of Georgia, **Roger Sauls** came to North Carolina in 1968, where he worked for many years as a publisher's representative. His poetry has appeared in numerous journals as well as in several collections, the most recent of which is *The Hierarchies of Rue*. Currently he lives in Richmond, Virginia.

Mississippean by birth, **James Seay** has taught at Chapel Hill since 1974, for some years directing the creative writing program there and currently serving as Bowman and Gordon Gray Professor. He has published several collections of poetry as well as articles and essays. In 1988 he received an award given by the American Academy and Institute of Letters "to honor and encourage writers in their creative work." He went to Russia as member of a delegation focused on "The American South in Books," and his work was included in poetry exhibition at the Centre Culturel Americain in Paris.

**Mab Segrest** grew up in Alabama, but moved to North Carolina in 1971. She has taught at Campbell University and currently serves as coordinator of the Urban-Rural Mission, U.S.A., sponsored by the World Council of Churches. In addition to poetry, she has published memoirs, articles, and essays. In 1994, *Memoir of a Race Traitor* was cited by the Myers Center for the Study of Human Rights as a notable book on human rights in North America; it also won the Editor's Choice Lambda Book Award.

**Elizabeth Sewell** was born in Coonoor, India, and lived in numerous places in the United States and England before establishing permanent residence in North Carolina in 1974. For a number of years she was Rosenthal Professor of Humanities at UNC-Greensboro. In addition to poetry, she has published criticism, fiction, essays, and memoirs. Major honors include a national award for fiction, poetry, and non-fiction presented by the American Academy and Institute of Arts and Letters in 1981.

The author of five collections of poetry, Massachusetts native **Alan Shapiro** taught for a number of years at Northwestern University, then came to North Carolina in 1986 to join the faculty at UNC-Greensboro. Currently he now teaches in the creative writing program at Chapel Hill. In addition to poetry, he has published two memoirs. He is the recipient of National Endowment for the Arts and Guggenheim fellowships. Among his honors is the 1987 William Carlos Williams Award, presented by the Poetry Society of America and a Lila Wallace-*Reader's Digest* Writers' Award.

For many years, **Marty Silverthorne** has lived in Greenville, where he serves as a clinical substance abuse counselor for Pitt County Mental

Health. A graduate of St. Andrews Presbyterian College, he has published in numerous periodicals and published two chapbooks, one of which, *Pot Liquor Promises*, won the 1997 Persephone Press Book Award. He has been active in the North Carolina Writers' Network, the North Carolina Poetry Society, and the Disability Awareness Network. His honors include an award for Pitt County Citizen of the Year.

Born in Miami, Florida, **Nancy Simpson** came to live in west-ern North Carolina in 1969. "I did not write before I came to live in the mountains," she says. "The mountains of North Carolina have profoundly changed me and changed my life." For twenty-four years she has been a teacher of exceptional children. Currently she is also creative writing instructor at TriCounty Community College and Resident Writer at John C. Campbell Folk School. She was awarded a North Carolina Arts Council Writing Fellowship, and her poems have been published in two collections.

A native of Virginia, **Benjamin Sledd** (1846–1940) taught at Wake Forest College for over fifty years. He was greatly beloved by his students; among them were the poet John Charles McNeill and the journalist and fiction writer Gerald Johnson. He published two collections of his own poetry during his lifetime; fifteen years after his death, a third collection, *A Young Man's Visions, An Old Man's Dreams*, was published.

**Mark Smith-Soto** was born in Washington, D.C., and spent most of his childhood in his mother's country, Costa Rica. After receiving his Ph.D. at the University of California at Berkeley, he came in 1975 to UNC-Greensboro, where he is professor of Spanish and has served as head of the Department of Romance Languages. Since 1992, he has also served as editor of *International Poetry Review*. In addition to scholarly publications, he has published poetry in numerous periodicals and was a finalist for the Pablo Neruda Award presented by *Nimrod*.

Born in Washington, D.C., **R. T. Smith** moved with his family to North Carolina when he was six years old. During his adult life, he has taught and/or served as writer-in-residence at a number of universities, including Auburn in Alabama and, currently, Washington and Lee in Virginia. The former editor of *Southern Humanities Review*, he is currently editor of *Shenandoah*. His poems have appeared in a variety of periodicals and four collections, and he has received an National Endowment for the Arts Fellowship in poetry.

Born in Maryland, **Stephen Smith** came to this state to attend college and stayed to teach at Sandhills Community College, where he directs the honors program and edits *The Sandhills Review*. He has won the *Poetry Northwest* Young Poet's Prize and received a writing fellowship from the North Carolina Arts Council. In addition to three collections of poetry, he has published a book of stories and a novella, edited an anthology (*New*

*North Carolina Poetry: The Eighties*), and written lyrics for a number of award-winning songs. He also writes a weekly column on the literary scene for the Southern Pines *Pilot.*

Growing up in Raleigh, **Mary Snotherly** studied under renowned English teacher Phyllis Peacock at Broughton High School before receiving a degree from Meredith College. For seventeen years she worked for Eastern Airlines. After turning to writing, in recent years she has taught as writer-in-residence with Wake County Schools. She also has served on the board of directors for the North Carolina Writers' Network as well as chair of the North Carolina Writers Conference. Her poetry appears in three collections, one of which, *Direction*, won the Persephone Press Award.

Poet and essayist **Thad Stem, Jr.** (1916–1980) left his beloved Oxford only long enough to earn a degree at Duke University, write for newspapers in western North Carolina and Florida, and serve in the U.S. Army during World War II. During the remainder of his life he resided on the same street on which he was born, earned his living as a veterans' service officer, and wrote fiction, essays, editorials, history, biography, and poetry, publishing a total of sixteen books. He also served on the state Library Board and for his efforts to expand library services earned a national award for his service to libraries.

As a Johnston County schoolboy **Shelby Stephenson** wrote country songs; as a man, he has published six collections of poetry and dozens of reviews and essays. He has been chair of English at Campbell University and, since 1979, professor of English at Pembroke State University, where he edits *Pembroke Magazine.* Stephenson, who lives on the farm where he was born near Benson, has also served numerous state and local organizations dealing with the arts. He and his wife, who often sing at literary events, have produced a CD, *Hank Williams Tribute.* In recognition of his contributions, in 1996 UNC-Pembroke held Shelby Stephenson Day.

**Henry Jerome Stockard** (1858–1914) grew up on a farm in Chatham County. He served as county superintendent of Alamance County schools and on the faculties of several colleges before becoming president of Peace College in 1907, a position he held until 1912. Even as he pursued his academic career, he was writing and publishing poems in such national magazines as *Atlantic Monthly.* His own collection was first published in 1897, and a second volume, *Poems*, was published posthumously in 1939. He also edited *A Study in Southern Poetry,* published in 1911.

A native of Alabama, **Julie Suk** has lived for many years in Charlotte, where she worked in a nature museum. In addition to authoring three volumes of her own poetry, she has co-edited (with Anne Newman) *Bear Crossings: An Anthology of North American Poets.* Her collection *The Angel of Obsession* won the 1991 University of Arkansas national poetry competition, and in

1993 she won the Bess Hokin Prize given by *Poetry* magazine. She serves as Associate Editor of *Southern Poetry Review.*

**Chuck Sullivan** came from his native New York City to North Carolina on a basketball scholarship to Belmont Abbey and began writing while a VISTA worker with migrant workers. He has been basketball coach and chair of humanities at Bishop McGuinness High School in Winston-Salem, National Endowment for the Arts poet-in-residence at Butler University, and writer-in-residence for community colleges and public schools. The author of six poetry collections, Sullivan was chosen by a readers' and critics' poll as Charlotte's Best Poet in 1996 and 1997.

In 1966 **Maureen Sutton** moved from her native Texas to North Carolina. A former airline hostess, she now teaches Spanish at the Episcopal Day School in Southern Pines. She credits encouragement from Sam Ragan, Stephen Smith, and Mary Belle Campbell with furthering her writing of poetry. In addition to publishing in numerous journals and anthologies, she has published a chapbook, *To Encourage the Dawn,* winner of the 1995 Persephone Press Book Award.

For **Eleanor Ross Taylor**, writing is a family affair. The Stanly County native is sister of three writers—brothers James and Fred Ross and sister, Jean—aunt of poet and fiction writer Heather Ross Miller, and widow of distinguished fiction writer Peter Taylor. While her husband taught at varied universities and wrote fiction, she wrote poetry, publishing her first collection in 1960 and her most recent in 1999. Honors include an award from the American Academy of Arts and Letters, and the Shelley Memorial Award from the Poetry Society of America in 1998.

Award-winning playwright **Rudy Wallace** came to North Carolina in 1984 to teach English at Shaw University. A native of St. Thomas in the Virgin Islands, he has also conducted poetry and playwriting workshops at the North Carolina Correctional Institution for Women. His plays have been produced by two Raleigh community theaters and North Carolina Central University; two were produced off-Broadway by the Negro Ensemble Players. The author of a chapbook, he has also won awards for his poetry and received the City of Raleigh Arts Commission Emerging Artists grant in 1990.

The sadly short life of **Thomas Walters** (1935–1983) was filled with teaching and the arts. After receiving his education and serving in the Marine Corps, the Edgecombe County native taught at North Carolina State University. He published two poetry collections, taught in the Poetry-in-the-Schools program, wrote a novel for young readers, painted, sculpted, and worked with film. Highly regarded both as a teacher and as a teacher of teachers, he was elected to membership in NCSU's Academy of Outstanding teachers in 1977.

While in high school in New Jersey, **Robert Watson** began writing poems, and he continued his interest during university studies. In 1953 he joined the English faculty at the Woman's College of the University of North Carolina. His first collection, *The Paper Horse,* published in 1953, has been followed by four other volumes, the most recent in 1995. He is also the author of two novels. He has received an *American Scholar* Poetry Prize and awards from the National Endowment of the Arts and the American Academy and Institute of Arts and Letters.

Born in Baltimore, Maryland, **Carole Boston Weatherford** came to North Carolina in 1985. Here she has worked as a director of communications and as an adjunct instructor at Guilford Technical Community College and High Point University. She divides her writing activity between poetry and children's books. Her poetry collection, *The Tan Chanteuse,* won the 1995 Harperprints Chapbook Competition. She also received a North Carolina Arts Council Writer's Fellowship.

The son of a Wilkes County sharecropper, **John Foster West** helped found the *Carolina Quarterly* during his years at UNC-Chapel Hill. After World War II service in the Army Air Corps, he taught at Elon College, Old Dominion University, and Appalachian State University from which he recently retired as professor emeritus. In addition to a collection of poetry, he has published nonfiction, science fiction, and two novels, one of which, *The Summer People,* won the Appalachian Press Consortium Award. He has served as president of the North Carolina Folklore Society.

After growing up in Missouri, **Michael White** lived in California and Utah before coming to North Carolina in 1994. He now teaches at the University of North Carolina in Wilmington. His work has appeared in numerous periodicals and *Best American Poetry*. His second poetry collection, *Palma Cathedral,* won the 1998 Colorado Prize from the Center for Literary Publishing/University Press of Colorado. He has also won fellowships from the National Endowment for the Arts and the North Carolina Arts Council.

According to her own testimony, **Carolyn Beard Whitlow** "walked away from [her] Adult Education dissertation at Cornell to write poetry." The Detroit native worked in administration at Brown and Cornell universities and taught at a number of colleges and universities before coming to Guilford College, where she currently teaches English and serves as chair of African-American Studies. She has published and read her work widely and has won awards for both teaching and poetry, including the Rose Low Rome Memorial Poetry Prize.

After studying at Princeton University and the Institute of Design in Chicago, **Jonathan Williams** returned to his native Asheville region, where he became part of the unique educational experience known as Black Mountain College. Since then he has established a wide reputation not only for his own experimental poetry, but for founding and managing Jargon Society, which published some of Black Mountain's most noted poets. He has served in poet-in-residence in this country and abroad and given over 1200 readings, lectures, and seminars. In 1980 he was one of 21 poets invited by Rosalynn Carter to read at the White House.

College drew **Emily Wilson** from her native Georgia to North Carolina. She has worked as an instructor at Reynolda House, a faculty member at Salem College, and a writer-in-residence in Poetry-in-the-Schools programs. Meanwhile, she has published four poetry collections and four volumes of non-fiction, including *North Carolina Women: Making History* (with Margaret Supplee Smith). In 1992 she was project director for a remarkably successful conference of North Carolina Women Writers. She has received grants from the National Endowment for the Humanities and the North Carolina Arts Council.

After growing up in Kinston and receiving degrees at Hollins College and UNC-Greensboro, **Anna Wooten-Hawkins** has taught English at Campbell University, where she was faculty editor of *The Lyricist*; at St. Mary's College, where she coordinated the annual Muse literary festival; and at Meredith College. In 1986 her collection *Satan Speaks of Eve in 7 Voices, After the Fall* won the 1986 North Carolina Writers' Network chapbook competition. In 1985 she received the City of Raleigh Arts Commission Award for excellence in writing and service to the arts.

Born in Winston-Salem, **John York** grew up on a farm in Yadkin County, and for twenty years has taught English in North Carolina public schools; currently he is a member of the faculty of Southeast Guilford High School. Meanwhile he has acquired an M.F.A. in creative writing from UNC-Greensboro and published two poetry collections. He was named a Mellon Fellow at UNC-Chapel Hill in 1987 and a National Endowment for the Humanities Teacher-Scholar in 1993. In 1985, he received the *Greensboro Review* Literary Award for Poetry.

Boone native **Isabel Zuber** has published two collections of poetry and served as an editor for both the *Arts Journal* and the *Crescent Review*. She was also a founding editor of Jackpine Press. Her fiction and poetry have appeared in numerous periodicals, and she has published two chapbooks, one of which, *Oriflamb*, won the North Carolina Writers' Network Chapbook Competition. Now a resident of Winston-Salem, where she works as circulation librarian at Wake Forest University, she won the Appalachian Writers' Association Lee Smith Award for fiction.

# Selected Bibliography

*Note: Many of our poets have published in other genres and their work has been widely anthologized. Only their collections of poetry are listed below.*

Abbott, Anthony. *The Girl in the Yellow Raincoat.* Laurinburg, NC: St. Andrews Press, 1984.
———. *A Small Thing Like a Breath.* Laurinburg, NC: St. Andrews Press, 1993.
Adcock, Betty. *Nettles.* Baton Rouge, LA: Louisiana State University Press, 1983.
———. *Beholdings.* Baton Rouge, LA: Louisiana State University Press, 1988.
———. *The Difficult Wheel.* Baton Rouge, LA: Louisiana State University Press, 1995.
Allen, Annette. *Country of Light.* Mount Olive, NC: Mount Olive College Press, 1996.
Ammons, A. R. *The Selected Poems.* New York: W. W. Norton, 1986.
———. *Garbage.* New York: W. W. Norton, 1993.
———. *The North Carolina Poems,* ed. Alex Albright. Rocky Mount, NC: North Carolina Wesleyan Press, 1994.
Anders, Shirley Bowers. *The Bus Home.* Columbia, MO: University of Missouri Press, 1986.
Angelou, Maya. *Shaker, Why Don't You Sing?* New York: Random House, 1983.
———. *The Complete Collected Poems of Maya Angelou,* New York: Random House, 1994.
Applewhite, James. *Statues of the Grass.* Athens, GA: University of Georgia Press, 1975.
———. *A History of the River.* Baton Rouge, LA: Louisiana State University Press, 1993.
———. *Daytime and Starlight.* Baton Rouge, LA: Louisiana State University Press, 1997.
Atkins, Stewart. *The Halting Gods.* Atlanta, GA: Banner Press, 1952.
Baddour, Margaret. *Easy Magic.* Laurinburg, NC: St. Andrews Press, 1991.
Gerald Barrax. *Leaning Against the Sun.* Fayetteville, AR.: University of Arkansas Press, 1992.
———. *A Person Sitting in Darkness:* New and Selected Poems. Baton Rouge, LA: Louisiana State University Press, 1999.
Bathanti, Joseph. *Anson County.* Greenville, NC: Williams and Simpson, Inc., 1989.
———. *The Feast of All Saints.* Troy, ME: Nightshade Press, 1994.

Bayes, Ronald. *The Casketmaker*. Winston-Salem, NC: John F. Blair, Publisher, 1972.

———. *A Beast in View: Selected Shorter Poems, 1970–1980*. Laurinburg, NC: St. Andrews Press, 1985.

Beam, Jeffery. *The Fountain*. Rocky Mount, NC: North Carolina Wesleyan Press, 1992.

———. *An Elizabethan Bestiary: Retold*. Raleigh, NC: Horse & Buggy Press, 1999.

Bevington, Helen. *When Found, Make a Verse Of*. New York: Simon and Schuster, 1961.

———. *Dr. Johnson's Waterfall and Other Poems*. Boston, MA: Houghton Mifflin Co., 1946.

Boner, John Henry. *Poems*. New York and Washington, DC: Neale Publishing Company, 1903.

Bowers, Cathy Smith. *The Love That Ended Yesterday*. Lubbock, TX: Texas Tech Press, 1992; Oak Ridge, TN: Iris Press, 1997.

———. *Traveling in Time of Danger*. Oak Ridge, TN: Iris Press, 1999.

Boyd, James. *Eighteen Poems*. New York: Charles Scribner's Sons, 1944. Wilmington, NC: The Friends of Weymouth and Bookmaker Press, 1994.

Braggs, Earl S. *Hat Dancer Blue*. Tallahassee, FL: Anhinga Press, 1993.

———. *Walking Back from Woodstock*. Tallahassee, FL: Anhinga Press, 1997.

Brockman, Zoe Kincaid. *Heart on My Sleeve*. Atlanta, GA: Banner Press (Emory University), 1951.

Brown, Grey. *Staying In*. Chapel Hill, NC: Harper Chapbooks, 1992.

Brown, Linda Beatrice. *Love Song to a Black Man*. Detroit, MI: Broadside Press, 1974.

Byer, Kathryn Stripling. *The Girl in the Midst of the Harvest*. Lubbock, TX: Texas Tech Press, 1986.

———. *Wildwood Flower*. Baton Rouge, LA: Louisiana State University Press, 1992.

———. *Black Shawl*. Baton Rouge, LA: Louisiana State University Press, 1998.

Buckner, Sally. *Strawberry Harvest*. Laurinburg, NC: St. Andrews Press, 1986. Raleigh, NC: Bookwrights Press, 1991.

Campbell, Mary Belle. *On the Summit: A Poetic Quest*. Whispering Pines, NC: Scots Plaid Press, 1988.

Cannon, Marion. *Another Light*. Charlotte, NC: Red Clay Books, 1974.

———. *Collected Poems*: Charlotte, NC: Red Clay Books, 1980.

Chappell, Fred. *Midquest*. Baton Rouge, LA: Louisiana State University Press, 1981.

———. *C*. Baton Rouge, LA: Louisiana State University Press, 1993.

———. *Spring Garden: New and Selected Poems*. Baton Rouge, LA: Louisiana State University Press, 1995.

Chess, Richard. *Tekiah*. Athens, GA: University of Georgia Press, 1994.

Chitwood, Michael. *Salt Works*. Athens, OH: Ohio Review Books, 1992.

———. *The Weave Room*. Chicago, IL: University of Chicago Press, 1998.

Church, L. Teresa. *Hand-Me-Down Calicos*. Raleigh, NC, 1998.

Dargan, Olive Tilford. *The Cycle's Rim*. New York: Charles Scribners Sons, 1916.

———. *The Spotted Hawk*. Winston-Salem, NC: John F. Blair, Publisher, 1958.

Deagon, Ann. *Poetics South*. Winston-Salem, NC: John F. Blair, Publisher, 1974.

———. *There Is No Balm in Birmingham*. Boston, MA: Godine Press, 1977.

Dean, Debra Kang. *News from Home*. Rochester, NY: BOA Editions, Ltd., 1998.

DiSanto, Grace. *The Eye Is Single*. Davidson, NC: Briarpatch Press, 1981.

Dischell, Stuart. *Good Hope Road*. New York: Viking Press, 1993.

Doar, Harriet. *The Restless Water*. Laurinburg, NC: St. Andrews Press, 1983.

Downer, Hilda. *Bandanna Creek*. Charlotte, NC: Red Clay Press, 1979.

Eaton, Charles Edward. *New and Selected Poems*. New York: Cornwall Books, 1987, © 1987 by Associated University Presses, Inc.

———. *The Fox and I*. New York: Cornwall Books, 1996, © 1996 by Associated University Presses, Inc.

Flynn, Keith. *The Talking Drum*. Asheville, NC: Animal Sounds, 1991.

———. *The Book of Monsters: Poems*. Asheville, NC: Urthona Press, 1994.

Fort, Charles. *Town Clock Burning*. Laurinburg, NC: St. Andrews Press, 1985; Carnegie Mellon, Classic Contemporary Edition, 1991.

———. *Darvil*. Laurinburg, NC: St. Andrews Press, 1993.

Gibson, Becky Gould. *Off-Road Meditations*. Chapel Hill, NC: North Carolina Writers' Network, 1989.

———. *First Life*. Greenville, SC: Emrys Press, 1997.

Gibson, Grace. *Drakes Branch*. Laurinburg, NC: St. Andrews Press, 1982.

———. *Frayed Edges: Poems, 1982–1994*. Laurinburg, NC: St. Andrews Press, 1994.

Gilbert, Marie. *Myrtle Beach When*. Laurinburg, NC: St. Andrews Press, 1989.

———. *Connexions*. Laurinburg, NC: St. Andrews Press, 1994.

Gill, Evalyn Pierpoint.: *Southeast of Here: Northwest of Now*. University Center, MI: Green River Press, 1986.

———. *Entrances*. Whispering Pines, NC: Persephone Press, 1996.

Goldman, Judy. *Holding Back Winter*. Laurinburg, NC: St. Andrews Press, 1987.

———. *Wanting to Know the End*. Eugene, OR: Silverfish Review Press, 1993.

Green, Jaki Shelton. *Conjure Blues*. Durham, NC: Carolina Wren Press, 1996.

Green, Paul. *Paul Green's War Poems*, ed. John Herbert Roper. Rocky Mount, NC: North Carolina Wesleyan College Press, 1993.

Grey, Lucinda. *Letter to No Address*. Hartford, CT: Andrew Mountain Press, 1987.

———. *Ribbon Around a Bomb*. Lexington, KY: Wind Publications, 1994.

Grey, Robert Waters. *Saving the Dead*. Charlotte, NC: Briarpatch Press, 1992.

Gurkin, Kathryn Bright. *Terra Amata*. Laurinburg, NC: St. Andrews Press, 1980.

———. *The Stainless Steel Soprano*. Laurinburg, NC: St. Andrews Press, 1990.

Gwynn, R. S. *The Drive-In*. Columbia, MO: University of Missouri Press, 1986.

———. *No Word of Farewell*. Pikeman Press, 1996.

Hanes, Frank Borden. *Abel Anders*. New York: Farrar, Straus & Cudahy, 1951.

———. *The Seeds of Ares*. Davidson, NC: Briarpatch Press, 1977.

Harmon, William. *One Long Poem*. Baton Rouge, LA: Louisiana State University Press, 1982.

———. *Mutatis Mutandis: 27 Invoices*. Middletown, CT: Wesleyan University Press, 1985.

Hopes, David Brendan. *The Glacier's Daughters*. Boston, MA: University of Massachusetts Press, 1981.

Hughes, Gladys. *A Cell, A Door*. Whispering Pines, NC: Persephone Press, 1989.

———. *Response*. Laurinburg, NC: St. Andrews Press, 1995.

Jarrell, Randall. *The Lost World*. New York:MacMillan, 1965.

———. *The Complete Poems*. New York: Farrar, Straus and Giroux, 1969.

Jeffers, Lance. *When I Know the Power of My Black Hand.* Detroit, MI: Broadside Press, 1974.

Jones, Paul. *What the Welsh and Chinese Have in Common.* Chapel Hill, NC: North Carolina Writers' Network, 1990.

Kaufman, Debra. *Family of Strangers.* Troy, ME: Nightshade Press, 1990.

———. *Still Life Burning.* SC: Kinloch Rivers Chapbook Competition, 1997.

Knauth, Stephen. *Night-Fishing on Irish Buffalo Creek.* Ithaca, NY: Ithaca House, 1982.

———. *The River I Know You By.* New York: Four Way Books, 1999.

Kratt, Mary. *On the Steep Side.* Charlotte, NC: Briarpatch Press, 1993.

———. *Small Potatoes.* Laurinburg, NC: St. Andrews Press, 1999.

Lautermilch, Steven. *The Meaning of No.* Whispering Pines, NC: Persephone Press, 1993.

———. *Circle, Triangle, Square.* Kill Devil Hills, NC: Hour Press, 1998.

Lindsey, Sarah. *Primate Behavior.* New York: Grove Press, 1997.

Liner, Amon. *Marstower.* Charlotte, NC: Red Clay Press, 1972.

———. *Rose, a Color of Darkness.* Durham, NC: Carolina Wren Press, 1981.

Lipsitz, Lou. *Cold Water.* Hanover and London: Wesleyan University Press, 1967.

———. *Seeking the Hook: New and Selected Poems.* Chapel Hill, NC: Signal Books, 1998.

Long, Robert Hill. *The Power to Die.* Cleveland, OH: Cleveland State University Poetry Center, 1987.

———. *The Work of the Bow.* Cleveland, OH: Cleveland State University Poetry Center, 1997.

Ludvigson, Susan. *The Swimmer.* Baton Rouge, LA: Louisiana State University Press, 1984.

———. *New and Selected Poems* (Scheduled). Baton Rouge, LA: Louisiana State University Press, 2000.

Macleod, Norman. *The Distance: New and Selected Poems, 1928–1977,* supplementary issue of *Pembroke Magazine,* © 1977 by *Pembroke Magazine.*

———. *The Selected Poems of Norman Macleod.* Boise, ID: Ahsata Press, 1975.

Maginnes, Al. *Outside a Tattoo Booth.* Troy, ME: Nightshade Press, 1991.

———. *Taking Up Our Daily Tools.* Laurinburg, NC: St. Andrews Press, 1997.

Makuck, Peter. *The Sunken Lightship.* Rochester, NY: BOA Editions, Ltd., 1991.

———. *Against Distance.* Rochester, NY: BOA Editions, Ltd., 1997.

McClanahan, Rebecca. *Mother Tongue.* Orlando, FL: University Press of Florida, 1987.

———. *The Intersection of X and Y.* Providence, RI: Copper Beech Press, 1996.

McCurdy, Harold G. *The Chastening of Narcissus.* Winston-Salem, NC: John F. Blair Publisher, 1970.

———. *And Then the Sky Turned Blue.* Davidson, NC: Briarpatch, 1982.

McDonald, Agnes. *Quickest Door, Smallest Room.* Laurinburg, NC: St. Andrews Press, 1992.

McFee, Michael. *Vanishing Acts.* Frankfort, KY: Gnomon Press, 1989.

———. *Colander.* Pittsburgh, PA: Carnegie Mellon University Press, 1996.

McGirt, James E. *For Your Sweet Sake.* Philadelphia, PA: John C. Winston Company, 1906.

McNeill, John Charles. *Songs Merry and Sad*. Charlotte, NC: Stone and Barringer, 1906.

———. *Possums and Persimmons*, ed. Richard Walser: Wendell, NC: Broadfoot Bookmark, 1977.

———. *The Pocket John Charles McNeill*, ed. Grace Gibson. Laurinburg, NC: St. Andrews Press, 1990.

Meyers, Susan. *Lessons in Leaving*. Whispering Pines, NC: Persephone Press, 1998.

Miller, Heather Ross. *Hard Evidence*. Columbia, MO: University of Missouri Press, 1990.

———. *Days of Love and Murder*. Maryville, MO: Green Tower Press, Northwest Missouri State University Press, 1999.

Jim Wayne Miller. *The Mountains Have Come Closer*. Boone, NC: Appalachian Consortium Press, 1980.

———. *The Brier Poems*. Frankfort, KY: Gnomon Press, 1997.

Shirley Moody. *Charmers*. Laurinburg, NC: St. Andrews Press, 1990.

Lenard Moore. *Forever Home*. Laurinburg, NC: St. Andrews Press, 1992.

———. *Desert Storm: A Brief History*. San Diego, CA: Los Hombres Press, 1993.

Moore, MariJo. *Returning to the Homeland*. Asheville and Alexander, NC: World-Comm Press, 1994.

———. *Spirit Voices of Bones*. Asheville, NC: rENEGADE pLANETS pUBLISHING, 1997.

Moose, Ruth. *Making the Bed*. Charlotte, NC: Sandstone Publishing, 1995.

———. *Smith Grove Poems*. Abingdon, VA: Sow's Ear Press, 1998.

Morgan, Robert. *Groundwork*. Frankfort, KY: Gnomon Press, 1979.

———. *Sigodlin*. Middletown, CT: Wesleyan University Press, 1990.

———. *Topsail Road* (Scheduled). Baton Rouge, LA: Louisiana State University Press, 2000.

Murray, Pauli. *Dark Testament and Other Poems*. Norwalk, CT: Silvermine Press, 1970.

Newman, Paul Baker. *The Ladder of Love*. New York, Horizon Press, 1970.

———. *The Light of the Red Horse*. Durham, NC: Carolina Wren Press, 1981.

Nixon, Sallie. *Spiraling*. Whispering Pines, NC: Persephone Press, 1990.

Olson, Charles. *The Maximus Poems*. Asheville, NC: Jargon/Corinth Books, 1966.

Owen, Guy. *The White Stallion and Other Poems*. Winston-Salem, NC: John F. Blair, Publisher, 1969.

Pearson, James Larkin. *Fifty Acres*. Wilkesboro, NC: Pearson Publishing Company, 1933.

Peck, Gail. *New River*. Chapel Hill, NC: North Carolina Writers' Network, 1993.

———. *Drop Zone*. Huntsville, TX: Texas Review Press, 1994.

Petersen, Keith. *The Grandfather Poems*. Raleigh, NC: 1998.

Piephoff, Bruce. *Honky Tonk Stradivarius: Poems and Songs by Bruce Piephoff*. Williamston, NC: Yonno Press, 1995.

Pinckney, Diana. *Fishing with Tall Women*. Whispering Pines, NC: Persephone Press, 1996.

———. *White Linen*. Troy, ME: Nightshade Press, 1998.

Pope, Deborah. *Fanatic Heart*. Baton Rouge, LA: Louisiana State University Press, 1992.

———. *Falling Out of the Sky*. Baton Rouge, LA: Louisiana State University Press, 1999.

Powell, Dannye Romine. *At Every Wedding Someone Stays Home*. Fayetteville, AR: University of Arkansas Press, 1994.

Presnell, Barbara. *Snake Dreams*. Troy, ME: Nightshade Press, 1994.

———. *Unravelings*. Fayetteville, NC: Longleaf Press, 1998.

Price, Reynolds. *The Collected Poems*. New York: Scribners, 1997.

Rabb, Margaret. *Figments of the Firmament*. Chapel Hill, NC: North Carolina Writers' Network, 1998.

Ragan, Sam. *The Collected Poems of Sam Ragan*. Laurinburg, NC: St. Andrews Press, 1990.

Ruark, Gibbons. *Reeds*. Lubbock, TX: Texas Tech University Press, 1978.

———. *Passing Through Customs: New and Selected Poems*. Baton Rouge, LA: Louisiana State University Press, 1999.

Rust, Rebecca. *The Outside of a Haiku*. Raleigh, NC: North Carolina Haiku Society Press, 1984.

Sandburg, Carl. *Honey and Salt*. New York: Harcourt Brace Jovanovich, 1978.

Sauls, Roger. *Hard Weather*. Columbia, SC: The Bench Press, 1987.

———. *The Hierarchies of Rue*. Pittsburgh, PA: Carnegie Mellon Press, 1999.

Seay, James. *The Light As They Found It*. New York: William Morrow, 1990.

———. *Open Field, Understory: New and Selected Poems*. Baton Rouge, LA: University of Louisiana Press, 1997.

Segrest, Mab. *Living in a House I Do Not Own*. Durham, NC: Night Heron Press, 1982.

Sewell, Elizabeth. *Poems, 1947–1961*. Chapel Hill, NC: University of North Carolina Press, 1962.

———. *Acquist*. Durham, NC: The Acorn Press, 1984.

Shapiro, Alan. *Covenant*. Chicago, IL: University of Chicago Press, 1991.

———. *Mixed Company*. Chicago, IL: University of Chicago Press, 1996.

Silverthorne, Marty. *Pot Liquor Promises*. Whispering Pines, NC: Persephone Press, 1997.

Simpson, Nancy. *Night Student*. Pittsford, NY: State Street Press, 1985.

———. *Across Water*. Pittsford, NY: State Street Press, 1983.

Sledd, Benjamin. *The Watchers of the Hearth*. Boston, MA: The Gorham Press, 1901.

———. *A Young Man's Visions, An Old Man's Dreams*. Riverdale, CA: Holt Publishing Company, 1957.

Smith, R. T. *The Names of Trees*. Troy, ME: Nightshade Press, 1991.

———. *Split the Lock*. Salmon, 1999.

Smith, Stephen. *Most of What We Take Is Given*. Canton, CT: Singular Speech Press, 1991.

———. *The Complete Bushnell Hamp Poems*. Charlotte, NC: Briarpatch Press, 1991.

Snotherly, Mary. *Direction*. Whispering Pines, NC: Persephone Press, 1994.

———. *Stars to Steer By*. Whispering Pines, NC: Persephone Press, 1994.

Stem, Thad, Jr., *The Jackknife Horse*. Raleigh, NC: Wolfshead Press, 1954.

———. *Journey Proud*. Charlotte, NC: McNally and Loftin, 1970.

Stephenson, Shelby. *Middle Creek Poems*. Laurinburg, NC: blue coot press, 1979.

———. *Finch's Mash*. Troy, ME: Nightshade Press, 1990.

———. *Poor People*. Troy, ME: Nightshade Press, 1998.

Stockard, Henry Jerome. *Fugitive Lines*. New York: G. T. Putnam's, 1897.

———. *Poems*. Raleigh, NC: Bynum Printing, 1939.

Suk, Julie. *The Angel of Obsession*. Fayetteville, AR: University of Arkansas Press, 1992.

———. *Heartwood*. Davidson, NC: Briarpatch Press, 1991.

Sullivan, Chuck. *The Juggler on the Radio*. Davidson, NC: Briarpatch Press, 1987.

———. *Alphabet of Grace: New and Selected Poems, 1969–1994*. Charlotte, NC: Sandstone Publishing, 1994.

Sutton, Maureen. *To Encourage the Dawn*. Whispering Pines, NC: Persephone Press, 1995.

Taylor, Eleanor Ross. *New and Selected Poems*. Winston-Salem, NC: Stuart Wright, 1983.

———. *Late Leisure*. Baton Rouge, LA: Louisiana State University Press, 1999.

Wallace, Rudy. *Sea Change*. Killeen, TX: Hackett Publishing Co., 1984.

Walters, Thomas. *The Loblolly Excalibur and a Crown of Shagbark*. Raleigh, NC: North Carolina Review Press, 1976.

Watson, Robert. *Selected Poems*. New York: Athenium, 1974.

———. *The Pendulum: New and Selected Poems*. Baton Rouge, LA: University of Louisiana Press, 1995.

Weatherford, Carole Boston. *The Tan Chanteuse*. Chapel Hill, NC: North Carolina Writers' Network, 1995.

West, John Foster. *Wry Wine*. Winston-Salem, NC: John F. Blair, Publisher, 1977.

White, Michael. *The Island*. Port Townsend, WA: Copper Canyon Press, 1992.

———. *Palma Cathedral*. Fort Collins, CO: University Press of Colorado, 1998.

Whitlow, Carolyn. *Wild Meat*. Providence, RI: Lost Roads Publishers, 1986.

Williams, Jonathan. *Get Hot or Get Out: A Selection of Poems, 1957–1981*. Metuchen, NJ: Scarecrow Press, 1982.

———. *Blues & Roots/Rue & Bluets: A Garland for the Southern Appalachians*. New York: Grossman Publishers, 1979.

Wilson, Emily. *Balancing on Stones*. Winston-Salem, NC: Jackpine Press, 1975.

———. *Arise Up and Call Her Blessed*. Emory, VA: Iron Mt. Press, 1982.

Wooten-Hawkins, Anna. *Satan Speaks of Eve in Seven Voices, After the Fall*. Chapel Hill, NC: North Carolina Writers' Network, 1986.

York, John. *Johnny's Cosmology*. Winston-Salem, NC: Hummingbird Press, 1995.

Zuber, Isabel. *Oriflamb*. Chapel Hill, NC: North Carolina Writers' Network, 1987.

———. *Winter's Exile*. Whispering Pines, NC: Scots Plaid Press, 1997.